More Praise for Jeroboam's Wife

Robin Gallaher Branch has taken a series of humble Scripture passages, generally overlooked and passed by, and revealed the wisdom and insight waiting for one who will simply give herself to them. Her careful scholarship, combined with a child-like joy in discovery, makes these women, many of whom Jesus would consider among "the least of these," come alive.

—Rev. Mike Gatliff, Pastor, Second
Presbyterian Church, Memphis, TN

Dr. Robin Gallaher Branch joyfully draws forth portraits of women and girls who find the middle road between being timidly inarticulate and stridently verbose. In separate chapters, Dr. Branch reveals the paths the seven least-known women and girls in the Hebrew Bible took to meet different life-challenges. She shows how each grew emotionally and spiritually to reach hope and finally to achieve surprising courage.

—Dr. Mary V. Battle, Associate Professor of
English, University of Memphis

Robin Gallaher Branch's penetrating probe into the stories of some of the forgotten—and even silent—women of the Old Testament is a tour de force, combining feminist hermeneutic with careful narrative and character analysis. There is a lot more here than most readers will expect. Branch's careful and illuminating interpretation of these texts is a necessary resource for all future attempts to understand them.

—Patrick D. Miller, Charles T. Haley Professor of Old
Testament Theology, Princeton Theological Seminary

D0619828

Robin Gallaher Branch has been writing extensively on the women of the Bible, especially those mentioned in the Old Testament/Hebrew Bible. This book is the fruit of many endeavors in this regard. It is well-written and brings some of the most obscure women of the Hebrew Bible to light. This major contribution should be read by everybody interested in the role of women in the Bible and in society.

—Herrie van Rooy, Professor of Old Testament,
North-West University, Potchefstroom, South Africa

Robin Gallaher Branch deftly walks the reader through a historically-informed, imaginative characterization of these relatively unknown women, thus introducing us to them. The cadre of women are silent no more! Their places within the story of God are overlooked no longer! Branch's love of stories is readily observable in her sensitivity to detail in the biblical accounts, as well as in her care and creativity as a (re-) teller of these stories.

—Troy A. Miller, Associate Professor of Bible
and Theology, Crichton College

Jeroboam's
WIFE

Jeroboam's WIFE

*The Enduring
Contributions of
the Old Testament's
Least-Known Women*

Robin Gallaher Branch

HENDRICKSON PUBLISHERS

Jeroboam's Wife: The Enduring Contributions of the Old Testament's Least-Known Women
© 2009 by Hendrickson Publishers, Inc.
P. O. Box 3473
Peabody, Massachusetts 01961-3473

ISBN 978-1-56563-745-0

All rights reserved. No part of this book may be reproduced or transmitted in any form or by any means, electronic or mechanical, including photocopying, recording, or by any information storage and retrieval system, without permission in writing from the publisher.

Biblical quotations, unless otherwise noted, are taken from the HOLY BIBLE, NEW INTERNATIONAL VERSION. Copyright © 1973, 1978, 1984 by International Bible Society. Used by permission of Zondervan Bible Publishers. All rights reserved.

Scripture quotations marked NRSV are from the New Revised Standard Version Bible, copyright © 1989 by the Division of Christian Education of the National Council of the Churches of Christ in the United States of America. Used by permission. All rights reserved.

Printed in the United States of America

First Printing — June 2009

Cover Art: "Study for Rizpah," © 1893. Leighton, Frederic (1830–1896). British Museum, London, Great Britain.

Photo Credit: HIP / Art Resource, N.Y.

Hendrickson Publishers pursues environmentally responsible printing practices. The pages of this book were printed using only soy or vegetable content inks.

Library of Congress Cataloging-in-Publication Data

Branch, Robin Gallaher, 1948–
    Jeroboam's wife : the enduring contributions of the Old Testament's least-known women / Robin Gallaher Branch.
        p. cm.
    Includes bibliographical references and indexes.
    ISBN 978-1-56563-745-0 (alk. paper)
    1. Women in the Bible. 2. Bible. O.T.—Criticism, interpretation, etc. I. Title.
    BS575.B648 2009
    221.9′22082—dc22
                                                    2009007120

This book is dedicated to my parents
Bob and Gwen Gallaher
and to my brothers
Harry and John Gallaher
with love and thanksgiving

TABLE OF CONTENTS

Permissions

PORTIONS OF SOME OF the chapters in this book have been drawn from the author's previously published journal articles. We thank the following journals for their permission to reprint portions of the listed articles:

"Athaliah, a Treacherous Queen: A Careful Analysis of Her Story in 2 Kings 11 and 2 Chronicles 22:10–23:21," *In die Skriflig* 38 no 4 (2004): 537–59. [chapter 9]

"David and Joab: United by Ambition" *BR* (Washington, D.C.) 19 no 4 (Aug., 2003): 14–23, 62–63. [chapter 5]

"Evangelism via Power and Lifestyle: Elijah's Method in 1 Ki 17," *Missionalia* 31 no 2 (Aug 2003): 293–304. [chapter 7]

"Rizpah: Activist in Nation-Building. An Analysis of 2 Samuel 21:1–14," *Journal for Semitics* 14/1, 74–94. [chapter 4]

"Rizpah: Catalyst in Kingmaking. An Analysis of 2 Samuel 3:6–11," *Journal for Semitics* 14/1:1–16. [chapter 3]

"The Wife of Jeroboam, 1 Kings 14:1–18: The Incredible, Riveting, History-Changing Significance of an Unnamed, Overlooked, Ignored, Obedient, Obscure Woman," *Old Testament Essays* 17:2 (2004): 157–67. [chapter 6]

"Women Who Win with Words," *In die Skriflig*, 37 no 2 (June 2003): 289–318. [chapter 4]

"'Your humble servant.' Well, Maybe. Overlooked Onlookers in Deuteronomistic History," *Old Testament Essays* 17:2 (2004), 168–89. [chapter 8]

Abbreviations

General

B.C.E.	before the Common Era
c.	century
C.E.	Common Era
cf.	*confer,* compare
ch.	chapter
cm	centimeter(s)
ed(s).	editor(s), edition(s)
Eng.	English
Heb.	Hebrew
ibid.	*ibidem,* in the same place
i.e.	*id est,* that is
lit.	literally
NIV	New International Version
NRSV	New Revised Standard Version
p(p).	page(s)
repr.	reprinted
v(v).	verse(s)
vol(s).	volume(s)

Biblical and Pseudepigraphal Books

Gen	Genesis
Exod	Exodus
Lev	Leviticus
Num	Numbers
Deut	Deuteronomy
Josh	Joshua

Judg	Judges
1–2 Sam	1–2 Samuel
1–2 Kgs	1–2 Kings
1–2 Chr	1–2 Chronicles
Esth	Esther
Ps(s)	Psalm(s)
Prov	Proverbs
Isa	Isaiah
Jer	Jeremiah
Ezek	Ezekiel
Hos	Hosea
Jon	Jonah
Mic	Micah
Zech	Zechariah
Matt	Matthew
Rom	Romans
Jas	James
1–2 Pet	1–2 Peter
Rev	Revelation
Jub.	*Jubilees*

RABBINIC LITERATURE

b. Ber.	*Babylonian Talmud Berakhot*
b. Meg.	*Babylonian Talmud Megillah*
b. Sotah	*Babylonian Talmud Sotah*
Exod. Rab.	*Exodus Rabbah*
m. Ketub.	*Mishnah Ketubboth*
m. Pesah.	*Mishnah Pesahim*
Midr. Prov.	*Midrash on Proverbs*

SECONDARY SOURCES

ABD	*Anchor Bible Dictionary.* Edited by David Noel Freedman. 6 vols. New York: Doubleday, 1992
AUSS	*Andrews University Seminary Studies*
BAR	*Biblical Archaeology Review*

BDB	*A Hebrew-English Lexicon of the Old Testament* Edited by F. Brown, S. R. Driver, and C. A. Briggs. Oxford: Clarendon, 1951. Repr. Peabody, Mass.: Hendrickson, 1996
Bib	*Biblica*
BibInt	*Biblical Interpretation*
BRev	*Bible Review*
BS	*Biblische Zeitschrift*
BT	*The Bible Translator*
BZ	*Biblische Zeitschrift*
CBQ	*Catholic Biblical Quarterly*
EDB	*Eerdmans Dictionary of the Bible.* Edited by David Noel Freedman. Grand Rapids: Eerdmans, 2000
EncBib	*Encyclopaedia Biblica*
EncJud	*Encyclopedia Judaica.* Edited by Cecil Roth. 16 vols. Jerusalem: Keter, 1972
ErIsr	*Eretz-Israel*
IB	*Interpreter's Bible.* Edited by G. A. Buttrick et al. 12 vols. New York, 1951–1957
IDS	*In Die Skriflig*
IEJ	*Israel Exploration Journal*
JAAR	*Journal of the American Academy of Religion*
JBL	*Journal of Biblical Literature*
JJS	*Journal of Jewish Studies*
JSOTSup	Journal for the Study of the Old Testament: Supplement Series
JSS	*Journal of Semitic Studies*
LJ	*Legends of the Jews*
NAC	New American Commentary
NIB	*New Interpreter's Bible.* Edited by L. E. Keck. 12 vols. Nashville: Abingdon, 1994–2004
NIBCOT	New International Biblical Commentary on the Old Testament
NIDOTTE	*New International Dictionary of Old Testament Theology and Exegesis.* Edited by W. A. VanGemeren. 5 vols. Grand Rapids: Zondervan, 1997
OTE	*Old Testament Essays*
PEQ	*Palestine Exploration Quarterly*

PSB	*Princeton Seminary Bulletin*
TWOT	*Theological Wordbook of the Old Testament.* Edited by R. Laird Harris et al. 2 vols. Chicago: Moody Bible Institute, 1980
USQR	*Union Seminary Quarterly Review*
VT	*Vetus Testamentum*
VTSup	Vetus Testamentum Supplements
WBC	Word Biblical Commentary
ZAW	*Zeitschrift für die alttestamentliche Wissenschaft*

Preface

I LOVE STORIES, ALL FORMS, all kinds. That's one reason I love the Bible. My love of stories combined with my love for the Bible and propelled me to change my course in midlife and to enter graduate school. I wanted to learn more about the Bible.

In graduate school, I discovered that biblical narration is the wide, scholarly term covering my love of biblical stories. I specialized in the Old Testament because the Old Testament contains more stories than does the New Testament. Furthermore, sometimes multiple stories highlight intriguing events in a character's life and allow the reader to see a more fully developed personality portrait. For example, the biblical text takes Moses from birth to death and Miriam (by tradition the older sister of the baby Moses in Exod 2:1–10) from childhood to death. This book began because of my ongoing interest in biblical characterization and in women in the Bible in particular.

This book traveled with me through graduate school at the University of Texas at Austin; through my two years serving as a replacement for a professor on sabbatical at the School of Theology and Mission at Oral Roberts University in Tulsa, Oklahoma; through my year as a Fulbright scholar on the faculty of theology at Potchefstroom University for Christian Higher Education in Potchefstroom, South Africa; and through my additional nineteen months in that same faculty at North-West University in Potchefstroom, as the university was renamed.

This book, based on my love of biblical stories and interest in women in the biblical text, builds on my dissertation and includes additional material. The chapters in this book grew out of material presented in some form at various academic conferences in the United

States and internationally or in peer-reviewed journal and magazine articles. Insights from colleagues have been included and criticisms considered in the chapters. The final form of this book, however, remains my own.

ACKNOWLEDGMENTS

As I near the completion of this book after years of work and study and think about those to thank, the names and faces of many people come to mind. Over the years a book in a sense becomes like a baby, and a baby growing up needs a family. A village of friends has nurtured this new family member! My thanks tumble forth from a grateful heart to those who have nurtured both me and this book during the writing and publication processes.

My thanks go first to Prof. Dr. Fika J. van Rensburg, Director of the School of Biblical Studies and Bible Languages, North-West University, Potchefstroom, South Africa, who invited me to spend a Fulbright year with the school, encouraged me to write, and expected me to publish constantly. His gift of administration has changed and enriched many lives, including mine. And to Prof. Dr. Herrie van Rooy, Director of Research at North-West University, for letting me drop by his office anytime and bounce ideas off him. What a wonderful scholar and great Old Testament friend!

I also wish to thank Dr. J. Andrew Dearman, professor of Old Testament, Austin Presbyterian Theological Seminary in Austin, Texas, for serving on my dissertation committee. From our first meeting in the fall of 1992, Andy always graciously treated me as a colleague and accepted me as a latecomer to a field he has known and loved since a teenager. Thanks as well to the other members of my dissertation committee: Drs. Harold Liebowitz, Avraham Zilkha, Esther Raizen, and Evan Carton. Each of these scholars provided outstanding teaching and guidance to me while I attended the University of Texas at Austin. The Office of the Vice President for Graduate Affairs said I had one of the best committees on campus, and I agree. These scholars held me to a high standard, and I grew because of their friendship, kindness, and rigorous academic demands. Thank you.

My thanks as well to Shirley Decker-Lucke, my editor at Hendrickson, for encouraging me to write the book and liking the way I handled the texts about these women and girls. Special thanks go to the Hendrickson editor assigned for this book, Dr. Mark House. Over three years and many emails we became friends. Mark helped me grow professionally as a writer and offered valuable insights about how to make this book better and how to broaden its practical use to a wider audience. I would also like to thank Nathan Brasfield for his fine indexing work.

I am indebted as well to friends who encouraged me throughout the writing, revising, and editing of this book. Hearty thanks go to the following dear friends: Sue Kinney, former assistant vice president, Graduate School, the University of Texas at Austin, graciously cheered me on. Lisa and Keith Thompson fed me many meals. Julia and David Thompson and Dr. Howard Moon, my dear friends in Washington, D.C., provided much-needed vacations. Evelyn Lupardus listened and listened and listened. Julie Butler, Kourtney Street, and Norma Sarvis knew the value of academics and the obedience and discipline required to do this kind of work. I am grateful to Melba Robbins, Julie Allison, and Karl Houk, fellow teachers at Austin Community College, with whom I shared many walks, talks, meals, and grading sessions. Linda Fryer, Kathleen Taylor, Gail McQuade, and Kathryn Miller, executives at Dell, GE, Nestle, and a nursing agency respectively, dressed me stylishly in their power suits. Bob Ascott kept my feet to the fire by asking each Sunday, "How's it going?" Walter Brewer, editor of special sections at the *Austin (Texas) American-Statesman*, had me write hundreds and hundreds of stories and thereby helped me finance graduate school. The Rev. Dr. Robert (Chip) Nix, rector of St. Matthews Episcopal Church, Austin, Texas, kept hugging me and saying, "You gotta get it done! You will get it done!" Dr. Cheryl Iverson, associate dean of the School of Theology and Missions, Oral Roberts University, remembered the dissertation process and how valuable friends are during its final stages. Dr. Robert Wharton, former chair of the department of business at Crichton College, has been so excited about the dissertation-that-became-a-book that he promised to give copies to his family. Elizabeth Dickinson, a lawyer, book lover, book reviewer, and one kind of reader this book hopes to engage, read the penultimate proofs and said, "It's great." She and these others will never know how their kind words and multiple kindnesses have extended *hesed*, the lovingkindness of the Lord himself, to me. Thanks—humble yet with the big shout you know me for!—to one and all.

Throughout the process, my family surrounded me love, counsel, food, vacations, advice, and laughter. They know me and continue loving me even amid the mood swings inherent in a writer's "wiring."

So to family, scholars, and friends, I exclaim, Blessings on you! I will return your many gracious gifts to me by cheerfully assisting other scholars who embark on books and dissertations.

Robin Gallaher Branch
Crichton College
Memphis, Tennessee
Thanksgiving 2008

Introduction
EMERGING FROM OBSCURITY—THE PATH SET

THIS BOOK RESPONDS TO a concern often expressed among
women who love and study the Bible. Many times over the years
while participating in group discussions about passages in the Bible, I
have seen women look downcast because of the apparent lack of importance the text as a whole seems to attribute to their historical sisters.
Some modern women interpret the relative lack of biblical space given
to women as meaning that women throughout the ages are of less importance to God and to society than are men. Yes, it is true that the biblical text allocates more space to men than it does to women. Yes, more
men than women in the Bible hold prominent positions in society. But
do these two facts mean that women are less important than men in
family, in society, and before God? I decided to probe more deeply this
question—and concern—by studying the women of the Bible.

I turned both to the Bible itself and to biblical scholarship for answers. I found that despite the markedly smaller space allocated to women
in biblical texts, they stand tall as important contributors to the story
of the Bible as a whole. Yet their contributions remain different from
and often seemingly less prominent than those of the men of Scripture.[1]
Historically, most biblical scholarship has been written by men, and,
proportionately speaking, only a few men have written about women.
But even as I—a middle-aged, white, American woman who grew up
in the Protestant Reformed tradition—write these words, I see changes
underway. Women faculty members and women authors occupy increasingly important positions in society and in the academy. Perhaps in the
near future the contributions of women scholars will come to be valued
equally with those of their male colleagues.

Meanwhile, as I studied the biblical text, I found that not only do
named, speaking men hold prominent roles as important characters, but

named, speaking women do as well. Men like Abraham, Isaac, and Jacob contribute much to the telling of the story of Israel's social, political, and theological development. But if we look closely, we find that the biblical text also presents Sarah, Rebekah, Rachel, and Leah as able, opinionated, and colorful consorts to these patriarchs.[2] Other women—such as Ruth, Esther, and Deborah—stand individually as important and decisive figures apart from the men in their lives.[3] These and other women hold their own as fully drawn, prominent characters in the Hebrew Bible.

But while the prominent men and women of Scripture often receive intense scholarly and lay interest and scrutiny, little scholarship has been devoted to less prominent figures who seem to play only minor roles in biblical history.[4] These characters play supporting roles such as servants, soldiers, spouses, and townspeople, yet they contribute a wealth of depth and color to the narrative. In the book of Ruth, for example, obscure figures grouped as "the whole town," "the elders," and "the women," though unnamed, are acknowledged for words and deeds that contribute significantly to the unfolding of that narrative.[5] In one instance the women of Bethlehem comment appreciatively on Ruth's love for her mother-in-law Naomi and her value by saying, "Your daughter-in-law . . . loves you and is more to you than seven sons" (Ruth 4:15).[6] The observation of these obscure women, not at all superfluous to the story's key events, adds depth and richness to the amazing narrative of Ruth.

Impressed by the oft-neglected contributions of such obscure biblical figures, I decided to focus my question—whether the biblical text presents women as less important than men—on a few women and girls who make only cameo appearances on the stage of biblical history.[7] Does the relative obscurity of these women and girls indicate that they are unimportant to the flow of the biblical narrative or to the purposes of God as reflected in biblical history?

This book, then, looks at five women and two girls in the Hebrew Bible who are all relatively obscure and investigates their importance in the biblical text. I consider and define these characters as obscure because they are silent, anonymous, marginalized in some way, and/or overlooked by other scholars. The five women and two girls as they appear are:

1. Miriam, the sister of Moses, a slave in Egypt (Exod 2:1–10);

2. Rizpah, daughter of Aiah and concubine of Saul, the first king of united Israel, who appears twice in the Hebrew Scriptures (2 Sam 3:6–11; 2 Sam 21:1–14);

3. The wise woman of Abel Beth Maacah, a city in northern Israel (2 Sam 20);

4. The wife of Jeroboam, the first king of divided Israel (1 Kgs 14:1–20);

5. A Gentile widow in Zarephath, a town just north of Tyre in Phoenicia (1 Kgs 17);

6. An Israelite slave girl, handmaiden to the wife of Naaman, commander of the army of the king of Aram (2 Kgs 5:1–5); and

7. Athaliah, queen of Judah (2 Kgs 11; 2 Chr 22:10–23:21).

These seven appear only briefly in the Bible. Scholarly material on them is piecemeal and sketchy. Assuming that their very presence in the text is an indication that they have some importance to the narrative, I studied their stories carefully, looking for textual clues as to how and why these women and girls were relevant. Why, I wondered, are they included and needed in the stories where more prominent named men and women appear? More importantly, since most women reading the Bible or this book are not likely to consider themselves prominent or powerful people, what lessons can contemporary women learn from the contributions made by these obscure women and girls?

Some readers may question my inclusion of Athaliah among these women and girls. After all, she is a named queen, receives a total of about fifty verses in 2 Kgs and 2 Chr, and says two words, "Treason! Treason!" (2 Kgs 11:14; 2 Chr 23:13). Yet there is relatively scant scholarly material about her. Moreover—and quite significantly, I think—the writer of the Gospel of Matthew either overlooks her or consciously chooses not to include her in the kingly genealogy of Jesus that cites Tamar, Rahab, Ruth, Uriah's wife, and Mary (Matt 1:3, 5, 6, 16).[8]

Athaliah and the other women and girls studied share a mixture of characteristics. The biblical text mentions each one tersely and with brevity.[9]

   🖉 Three women (the wise woman of Abel Beth Maacah, the wife of Jeroboam, and the widow living in Zarephath) and the two girls (Miriam, the sister of Moses, and the Israelite slave girl) remain anonymous.[10]

   🖉 Two women (Rizpah and the wife of Jeroboam) remain silent.

❧ Four women (Rizpah, the wife of Jeroboam, Athaliah, and the widow of Zarephath) face the death of members of their own households.

❧ One child (Miriam) faces the probable death of her baby brother by execution. The other child longs to see her beloved master relieved of the deteriorating condition of a dreaded skin disease.

❧ Three women (the wise woman of Abel Beth Maacah, the widow living in Zarephath, and Athaliah) engage in dialogue with named male characters. The two children engage in dialogue with older, unnamed women.

❧ One woman (the wife of Jeroboam) listens without comment to two men, Jeroboam I, king of Israel, and Ahijah, prophet of the Lord at Shiloh.

❧ One woman (the wise woman of Abel Beth Maacah) seeks to avert the destruction of her community; one (Athaliah) seeks the destruction of her family; and one (the wife of Jeroboam) learns of the upcoming destruction of her household and Israel.[11] The two children, operating from a foundation of love, seek to save the lives of a baby boy and a general, the commander of the army of the king of Aram.

❧ The two children deal positively with those the text usually considers the enemies of the covenant people (Pharaoh's daughter and Naaman the Syrian).

❧ The wise woman of Abel Beth Maacah orders the beheading of Sheba, an enemy within the covenant community; and the text sanctions the slaying of Athaliah and the annihilation of the house of Jeroboam—all renegade members of the covenant community.

The five named and unnamed adult women interact with named male characters in the stories where they appear.[12] Rizpah interacts with Abner, Saul's general, with Ish-Bosheth, Saul's son and the declared king of Israel, and indirectly with David, king of Israel. The wise woman of Abel Beth Maacah interacts with Joab, commander-in-chief of the army of Israel, and indirectly with David. The wife of Jeroboam interacts with her husband and with Ahijah, a prophet at Shiloh, and with her son, the boy Abijah. The widow of Zarephath interacts with Elijah, a prophet of Israel during the divided kingdom. Athaliah interacts with Jehoiada, priest of the Lord, and with Joash, her young grandson whom she tries to murder.

The two little girls interact primarily with unnamed older women. The sister of Moses confronts the daughter of Pharaoh, and in so doing she indirectly defies the greatest power in the biblical world at that time.[13] The Israelite slave girl speaks with her mistress about the skin condition of her master, Naaman, and thus sets in motion an international incident involving the heads of state of Israel and Aram.

My research methodology has to a large extent determined the book's structure and outcome. Throughout my study, I have endeavored to be in accordance with a long-standing first principle of biblical interpretation: *let the text interpret the text.*[14] In addition, I have followed Brevard S. Childs in taking a canonical approach to the biblical text. This approach, while it encourages critical and theological reflection on the text and its historical development, acknowledges that various parts of the text have become, as a completed canon, normative "scripture" within the community of faith.[15] Finally, I take J. P. Fokkelman's advice to approach biblical texts with confidence, expecting to find within the text itself keys to its understanding.[16] My confidence is bolstered by my respect, honor, and love for Scripture. Although acknowledging the mystery of the statement in 2 Tim 3:16, I believe it: "All Scripture is God-breathed and is useful for teaching, rebuking, correcting and training in righteousness."

Keeping these methodological principles in mind, I formulated six questions that grew out of my original question, six areas of study for examining the texts surrounding these obscure women and girls.

1. What personal characteristics do the passages, although brief, reveal about the woman or child in question? Are the characters able to emerge with *discernable personalities*?

2. What light does the interaction of these women with the named male characters shed on the *character development* of the other men and the women involved?

3. How do the biblical narrators then use this information in subsequent *plot development* in which the named men and older women figure?

4. In what ways do the stories of each of the five women and two children inform the *theological* and *political development* of Israel?

5. How do the stories about these five women and two girls embellish the biblical portrait of *the character and purposes of God*? In what ways do they reveal more of God's attributes and show God's actions as consistent with his self-descriptions such as that of Exod 34:6, where God describes himself as "the compassionate and gracious God, slow to anger, abounding in love and faithfulness, maintaining love to thousands, and forgiving wickedness, rebellion, and sin"?

6. What *spiritual benefit and practical lessons* can readers today derive from the examples of these obscure but very engaging women and girls? How do these women and girls comfort, warn, or encourage modern readers? Are they positive or negative role models?

The fact that the biblical text reveals little about these women and girls and records little or nothing they say may lead us to consider them as marginalized and unimportant figures. But despite the limitations the biblical text places on them—brevity, silence, namelessness, foreignness, low social standing, and even horror—these five women and two children not only provide important insights into the more prominent characters with whom they are associated,[17] but they also contribute to the social, political, and theological development of Israel and Judah.

Because I have studied these women and girls so carefully, I feel as if I have lived with them for years! They emerge in Scripture with distinct personalities. I believe it is possible to describe each character with terse adjectives and phrases. I found Rizpah tenacious and possessing the courage of a warrior; Athaliah isolated in her evil; the wife of Jeroboam flat, vapid, and overwhelmingly sad (probably because of domestic abuse); the sister of Moses winsomely audacious; the Israelite slave girl, a pint-sized heroine with a giant-sized faith; the widow of Zarephath feisty enough to make a prophet quail; and the wise woman of Abel Beth Maacah a straightforward manager for CEOs to emulate.

This book argues that these five women and two girls hold their own in the textual arena and contribute substantially to the biblical stories in which they appear.[18] Furthermore, although Rizpah and the wife of Jeroboam seem almost muzzled in the biblical narratives, their silent actions contribute significantly to the biblical text; these characters show that silence, like dialogue, is a powerful tool of narration.[19] So instead of overlooking, marginalizing, or ignoring these five women and two girls as many other scholars have done, this book investigates the stories in which they appear and assesses their contributions to the overall biblical text.[20]

A major theme that unites these characters is their undeniable influence on biblical history. Each changes the course of its flow. The steadfast testimony of an Israelite slave girl leads to the healing of Naaman. A Hebrew slave girl (traditionally thought to be Miriam) thinks on her feet and suggests a solution that delivers her baby brother from death. The wise woman of Abel Beth Maacah, through quick analysis and wise intervention, stills a rebellion and helps re-legitimize David's shaky throne. The wife of Jeroboam, truly living in an impossible situation, acts as the conduit that brings destruction on her house and nation. Athaliah, nefariously treacherous, dies in shame, mourned by none, her reign merely a hiccup in the Davidic line. Rizpah, perhaps the most intriguing character because of her double silence, grows from a pawn used at will by men of power to a regal heroine whose courage captures the imagination of a nation. The widow of Zarephath experiences the unimaginable: receiving her dead son back to life, the first such resuscitation in Scripture.

Another major theme that has emerged from the study of these obscure women and girls is that many of them are, in one form or another, political saviors. Miriam, a Hebrew slave child, for example, rescues her baby brother from death (Exod 2). The baby, Moses, grows up to become Israel's greatest deliverer and political savior.[21] Yet Miriam, her mother, and the princess of Egypt, all had critical roles in making that deliverance possible, and in this sense are political saviors as well. Actually, Moses was delivered by three deliverers. In the same way, Rizpah's beating off the scavengers from the dead bodies of the executed members of Saul's family propels her to national prominence. Her decisive action defies David, a passive king on this issue, and forces him to fulfill the demands of justice by conducting a proper burial.

The brief textual appearances of these seven women and girls raises questions about the place of women in the biblical text in general. In the biblical text are women generally of less importance to God and to society than men? My research points decisively to a negative answer to this central question! My research leads me to note that overwhelmingly when a woman (or girl) appears in the biblical text, this rarity *heralds* an upcoming event as important. Narrators may intentionally use a woman's or girl's entrance into the text to raise, as it were, a *red flag* that announces the significance of this part of the story.[22] Viewed in this way, women and girls, even the least likely ones, play a more prominent role in the biblical text as a whole than at first appears. Thus Rizpah, the wise woman of Abel Beth Maacah, the wife of Jeroboam, the widow of Zarephath, Athaliah, the sister of Moses, and the Israelite slave girl represent a host of anonymous, silent, or otherwise textually restricted characters in the Bible. These characters include other women as well as men and children. And these characters not only present new opportunities for continued investigation but also new avenues of appreciation for how God can use ordinary people in extraordinary ways.

1

HEARING THE STORY
APPRECIATING BIBLICAL NARRATIVES

THE STORIES STUDIED IN this book occur in a biblical genre
called narrative. One, the story of the interaction between the
older sister of Moses and Pharaoh's daughter (Exod 2:1–10), occurs
in the Pentateuch; the others in Samuel and Kings occur in the section biblical scholars call the Historical Books. The story of Athaliah
in 2 Kings is paralleled in 2 Chronicles.

NARRATIVE AS HISTORY AND STORYTELLING

Broadly speaking, biblical narrative is biblical history. Other biblical genres include law, prophecy, poetry, genealogies, wisdom literature, letters, apocalyptic literature, fables, and songs. Approximately
forty percent of the Hebrew Bible is narrative.[1] Although it is written as prose, narrative differs in a subtle way from prose. Prose states
things directly, while narration states things indirectly in the form of
a story. Narration relies on a selection of details, an arrangement of
events, and a bevy of rhetorical devices to convey its meaning.[2] In its
broadest sense, biblical narrative records specific events in space and
time that take place in the lives of specific people; the stories of these
events contain a beginning, middle, and end.[3]

The texts covered in this book are crucial parts of larger stories. Yet
even considered in themselves, they contain elements of a short story.
These elements include a central idea, characterization, conflict, point
of view, setting, and choice of language.[4] One could argue that one
of the stories, the one on Athaliah (2 Kgs 11), could be considered
a short story in itself. The plot, or central idea, takes place in scenes;
these scenes have a basic pattern of beginning, middle, and end.[5] In

the story about Athaliah, the beginning is Athaliah's murder of all her family members except Joash; the middle takes place six years later and involves a coup and Athaliah's execution; the end details the administrative moves Jehoiada the priest makes and the reaction of the populace. The epilogue, a single verse, says Joash began to reign when he was seven years old. This verse provides the transition to the next chapter or story, his repair of the temple (2 Kgs 12), and the larger story of the kings of Judah and Israel continues.

Hebrew Bible narrative is part of the great human tradition of storytelling. The story can be presented as a sequence of events or a journey, or it can employ a chiasm—a technique that brings a theme full circle. A chiasm seems to tie up the story with a bow because of a skillful choice of words.[6] Narrative sequence tells a story straightforwardly as the events take place. It can be read almost like a newspaper account. This technique occurs with the rise and fall of Athaliah (2 Kgs 11).

Several of the stories considered employ a journey. The baby later named Moses sets off among the reeds in a tiny ark down the Nile (Exod 2:3); Jeroboam orders his wife to go disguised to the prophet Ahijah in Shiloh (1 Kgs 14:2); Joab chases the troublemaker Sheba all over Israel and finally ends up in Abel Beth Maacah in Dan and there meets his match in one singularly described as a wise woman. A thematic chiasm occurs in 2 Sam 21. The *famine* in Israel is caused by the *blood*-stained house of Saul (verse 1) and the *famine* ends with the proper burial of the *bones* of Saul, Jonathan and the seven sacrificed Saulides (verse 14, italics added).

The narrative style in the Hebrew Bible is both subtle in providing a wealth of meaning in one word and emphatic in offering multiple words that emphasize a single point. Consider two examples of this from the stories studied in this book. First, the Hebrew word for good, *tov,* describes the child born to a Levite and his wife (Exod 2:2); that word can mean fair, pleasant, fine, and even merry.[7] A delightful picture emerges of a precious baby whom the text soon identifies as Moses (Exod 2:10). Second, Jehoiada the priest organizes and directs a palace coup with multiple commands to armed representatives (2 Kgs 11:5–8). The imperative instructions include things they must do like station themselves near the king and stay close beside the king.

Elements of Hebrew Bible narrative include description, direct speech, understatement, and repetition.[8] Description is rare, and when it comes, brief. Usually the biblical narrator uses one word or maybe two to describe a person.[9] The story of Sheba, a Benjamite, begins with the narrator describing him as a troublemaker (2 Sam 20:1). Consequently, when he loses his head, no one is surprised or even mourns. Readers and hearers expect a sad, violent end for this man because of the narrative clue provided by the introductory word *troublemaker.* My favorite example of biblical description is how the narrator describes Abigail, the woman who became David's third wife (1 Sam 25:42–43). By introducing her as both intelligent and beautiful (1 Sam 25:3),[10] the biblical narrator commits himself to validating both of these qualities in the subsequent narrative. Hardly an obscure woman,[11] Abigail has the longest recorded speech of any woman in the biblical text, one hundred and fifty-three words in Hebrew!

One way to read biblical narration is to be aware that narrative often leads up to and sets the stage for direct speech. Narration undergirds direct speech and showcases it. Robert Alter says everything in the narrative world gravitates toward the dialogue.[12] Consider two verses in the story of the wise woman of Abel Beth Maacah (2 Sam 20:18–19). The narrator sets the stage with three words (roughly translated, "And she spoke saying") whose structure emphasizes the importance of what is coming up. The next twenty-one words record the direct speech of the wise woman. As a result of her words, several things happen all at once: power in the siege suddenly shifts from those with battering rams to a lone, unarmed woman atop a city wall; Joab, put on the defensive, utters a mild oath twice; and the narrator's choice of adjective *wise* is suddenly verified. One can almost see the narrator bestow an approving nod on the wise woman.

Seldom does Hebrew Bible narrative employ a heavy hand. Instead, the light touch of the narrator prevails. The narrative is highly selective of the events it records, the people it selects, and the vignettes from the lives of the people it chronicles. Far from an arbitrary selection, the vignettes contribute to the broad themes of the larger book, and the larger book contributes to and complies with overall themes in the Bible. The richness shown in biblical narrative is in its conciseness, a brevity that reflects a profound and not a simplistic art. Taking a minimalist approach, biblical narrative is content with mystery (see Deut 29:29). Silence does not bother the narrator. With the exceptions of the older sister of Moses (by tradition Miriam) and Rizpah, the characters studied in this book make only cameo appearances in the biblical text. They enter the textual stage once and exit it a few verses later. However, their cameo appearances are all the narrator needs to make a point and carry on a book's larger themes. Their mystery, indeed the *understatement* of their personalities, engages the fascination of the readers and hearers, encouraging them to imagine the scenes themselves.[13]

Repetition is yet another narrative tool. Repeating a word or phrase emphasizes its importance. If repetition occurs in direct speech, it emphasizes the humanity of the speaker, for it is natural in speaking to repeat oneself. For example, Athaliah utters two words, "Treason! Treason!" (2 Kgs 11:14). These words show her perverted perspective. Her words also illustrate a narrative tool called irony. With gallows humor we laugh because Athaliah fails to see the irony in her words. The coup against her is anything but treasonous; it is justice meted out six years late. Consequently, her words are narrative irony and mean exactly the opposite of their face-value meaning.[14] Similarly, the garbled and jubilant speech of the widow of Zarephath upon receiving her dead son back alive (1 Kgs 17:24) emphasizes her humanity and serves to authenticate the story. The words of both women smack of real reactions.

THE NARRATOR AND NARRATIVE TOOLS

The stories throughout Hebrew Bible narrative are told from the perspective of someone scholars call the narrator, a single observer, a third person who watches the action from the corner of the stage or from a vantage point off stage.[15] The narrator leads readers and hearers through the stories. The narrator chooses the events told and orchestrates their telling. Often stories present some form of conflict and show some form of personal growth in the character. The narrator's choice of words may appeal to the imagination and evoke the senses.[16] Sometimes narrative approval or disapproval of an account is given. In 2 Sam 21, for example, the narrator presents Rizpah's defiant action favorably because of its results: the bodies of those exposed to the elements along with the bones of Saul and Jonathan receive a proper burial (2 Sam 21:11–14). Sometimes the narrator seems to be privately chuckling—as when the older sister of Moses arranges for the baby's mother to be paid as a wet nurse for her own son (Exod 2:7–9).

A look at the narrator entails a scrutiny of his methods, purposes, and tools. The biblical narrative in 1 Kgs 17 (which we now look at as an extended example) contains a well-edited story.[17] The Elijah cycle keeps silent on the details of Elijah's life like his call, his family history, his religious training, his journey to the Wadi Kerith, what he did and thought about while there, and what was happening meanwhile in Israel and Judah. It omits comment on the plight of the people because of the lack of rain and its resultant famine. The chapter introduces Elijah as a man of mystery and establishes his pattern of appearing and disappearing suddenly.[18] Elijah's hiding leads to a cat and mouse game with Ahab that spans several chapters. Yet the narrator well serves his hearers and readers by his choices, for he focuses on his thematic purposes. This chapter reveals God's miraculous power, how he reaches out evangelistically through Elijah to a woman outside the covenant, and how he verifies Elijah as a prophet.

The narrator also shows care to present events as they take place. From the way he constructs the narrative, he becomes a sidelines character who participates in the cycle, apparently allowing events as they unfold to convince him of Elijah's prophetic credentials. Narrators throughout the Hebrew Bible evaluate Elijah and major characters like him via the narrative tools of plot development and minor characters.

The narrator employs dialogue to describe the protagonists in the narrative. Their deeds likewise serve as a guide for evaluation.[19] Yet a major biblical character does not become major because of his or her rank; instead, the length of description about the character coupled with actions and words make a character significant or minor.[20] Following this rule, Elijah is a very large character and the widow is a significant one because of the amount of space the biblical narrator accords them in 1 Kgs 17. In this way, the widow clearly "outranks" Ahab in this chapter.

The use of minor characters like Ahab and the widow's son also helps move the plot forward.[21] The plot involves the real or alleged sins of Ahab and the boy's mother.[22] For example, Ahab's apostasy and foul deeds merit a drought. The widow's son dies, forcing the story to a crisis of faith and also to a showdown between the God of Israel and Baal, god of the region of Zarephath.[23]

Another narrative tool pits a positive character against a negative one. The Elijah/Ahab altercation illustrates this. Ahab hovers in the background of this segment of the Elijah cycle. Foreshadowing all their confrontations is the list of his spiritual offenses concluding 1 Kgs 16. Likewise, the text invites an examination of the widow versus Ahab; the text presents her positively and him negatively. A similar narrative tool displays a positive major character in an encounter with a positive minor character.[24] Following this model, the narrator offers the ravens and the widow's son (and even elements like rain, oil, and flour) as minor but positive characters that interact with Elijah.

Silence and motifs are yet other narrative tools. The lack of rain or dew and the resultant famine in Israel and throughout the known world interest the narrator only fleetingly; he, leaving much unsaid about the two conditions, spotlights other avenues instead as the main lines of plot development. The narrator's motifs in 1 Kgs 17 include comparing and contrasting word and mouth, food and drink, famine and drought, life and death, word and obedience, command and compliance, good and evil, unbelief and faith.

By 1 Kgs 17:16, a verse that states impersonally that the widow's flour and oil do not run out, the narrator recognizes Elijah's powers.[25] Up until this time, he seems to remain neutral—but willing to be persuaded—about Elijah's credentials and standing as the Lord's spokesman. The narrator then records the transformation of an all-too-common family tragedy and a prophet's desperation into an explosion of faith in Yahweh, thereby fulfilling the narrative's overall purpose: to show that Yahweh alone wins a great victory.

Through Elijah's words and Elijah's breath, life comes back into the boy! Then the narrator immediately resumes his impersonal tone, keeping again in the distance, with the declarative sentence that the child's life returns to him and he lives (1 Kgs 17:22). The narrator ends the section also without displaying any passion. He merely reports God's orders to Elijah to present himself before Ahab and (conditional upon that?) God's promise to send rain, and Elijah obeys (1 Kgs 18:2). The narrator indirectly raises this question: Will God send rain only if Elijah obeys? Truly, the narrator keeps the upper hand by remaining mysterious.

CHARACTERIZATION

A good story requires careful characterization. In general, in the biblical text, the words and actions of a character portray the kind of person that character is. Internal thoughts rarely receive textual space. An exception could be Isa 39:8, where the verb *said* is translated *thought* when speaking of Hezekiah: "For he *thought*, 'There will be peace and security in my lifetime'" (italics added). Indirect presentation, the kind common in the biblical text, lets a character's personality and motivation come through his or her actions and words.[26]

Characters can be flat or round, dynamic or static.[27] The wife of Jeroboam (1 Kgs 14) is both flat and static. She is a static character because she stays the same. She portrays no reaction to the triple-pronged news the prophet Ahijah gives her: the upcoming death of her son; the upcoming annihilation of her house; and the upcoming uprooting of her country. In contrast, the widow of Zarephath (1 Kgs 17) is a round character with a fully-developed personality. She may not have a name, but she has opinions and emotions—and plenty of each![28] She's scared, cranky, obedient, courageous, hospitable, feisty, generous, incredulous, thankful—and no matter what, she always gets the last word! The behavioral details the narrator supplies make her very human, very real.[29] She's a walking definition of *chutzpah!* In short, she is one of the most lovable women in the biblical text. She makes us grin.

SETTING

The setting is rarely arbitrary but instead is used by the narrator to enhance the meaning of a story.[30] For example, consider the importance of the temple in the story of Athaliah (2 Kgs 11). The baby Joash stays hidden from his murderous grandmother, Athaliah, in the *temple* for six years; Jehoiada's coup proclaiming Joash king takes place on the *temple* grounds; and Jehoiada proclaims that Athaliah must not be put to death in the *temple* of the Lord (2 Kgs 11:3, 12, 15). The setting also can reinforce the tone of the narrator.[31] The encounter between the older sister of Moses and Pharaoh's daughter sparkles because it takes place outside in the relaxed context of a bathing party to the Nile (Exod 2:1–10). A slave child would not have had a face-to-face meeting with the daughter of the world's most powerful ruler inside the princess's palace. But outside, on the banks of the life-sustaining Nile, such an encounter of social opposites is possible and believable.

CONFLICT

Conflict is the most essential element of any story. Throughout Hebrew Bible narrative, the focus of a story is on a sin, weakness, a problem, a hurt, or a need that forms the basis of the conflict. Often, the conflict is resolved because God intervenes. Consider this example.

Gen 11:27 begins the account of Terah. By verse 29, the account focuses on Abram and Sarai. By verse 30, a family problem is mentioned
and emphasized by its doubling: "Now Sarai was barren; she had no
children." From there on in Genesis, the story involves how Sarai's barrenness is solved and how God keeps his promise to Abram and subsequent generations. For a start, nine verses later God promises to give
the land of Canaan to Abram's *offspring* (Gen 12:7, italics added). A
son is finally born to Abraham and Sarah (Gen 21:2)—but Isaac comes
only after many crises, various journeys and adventures, and renewed
promises from God. He comes in a sense to parents made new because
God changed their names (Gen 17:5, 15). He comes to an established
family and has an older half brother, Ishmael, a son born by a union
between Abram and Hagar, Sarai's Egyptian maidservant (Gen 16).
Significantly, the text gives God the credit for solving Sarai's barrenness: "Now the Lord was gracious to Sarah as he had said, and the Lord
did for Sarah what he had promised" (Gen 21:1).

Conflict is apparent in the stories considered in this book. Indeed,
conflict is the force that drives a story.[32] In the story of Naaman, in
which the Israelite slave girl appears (2 Kgs 5:1–4), the general of Aram
faces the problem of an incurable skin disease. The driving force of the
story is the astounding statement of faith by the child: "If only my master would see the prophet who is in Samaria! He would cure him of his
leprosy." A helpful way to think of conflict is to see it as a cause-and-
effect relationship.[33] Consider the story of Jeroboam (1 Kgs 11:26–
14:20). It began with a glorious covenant relationship instigated by
God to make Jeroboam king over ten tribes of Israel (1 Kgs 11:31–39).
But Jeroboam brought in golden calves and proclaimed them the gods
who brought Israel out of Egypt (1 Kgs 12:28–29). This action forms
the basis of the clash between opposing forces, God and Jeroboam; the
clash leads to the prophetic word, a word of judgment, given by Ahijah
to the wife of Jeroboam (1 Kgs 14:1–20). The cause of the prophetic
word against the house of Jeroboam was Jeroboam's earlier apostasy.

POINT OF VIEW

Point of view is the position a writer takes in presenting the story.[34]
Thus, it is closely linked to other elements like characterization, language,
and conflict. The narrator in a story can tell the story in three ways. A
first person narration uses "I"; this is not the usual mode of the bibli-

cal text. Another point of view is omniscient narration. In this mode, the narrator gets inside a character's mind and shares the thoughts and feelings of one or more characters.[35] Omniscient narration occurs only rarely in the biblical text, and when it does, the narrator makes it plain. For example, a literal translation of 1 Kgs 12:26 is, "And Jeroboam said in his heart." This often is translated, "Jeroboam thought to himself." The most common form in which point of view in the biblical text is expressed is called dramatic or objective narration. Here, the narrator presents the words and actions of the characters and lets them stand alone on stage for judgment, so to speak. Dramatic or objective narration requires the most skill because the narrator must carefully construct the story so that possibilities for misinterpretation are minimal.[36]

BRINGING ALL THE ELEMENTS TOGETHER

All biblical narratives include elements of history, aesthetics, and theology.[37] Some stories emphasize one element over the other; some stories combine more than one element. For example, in the first story in which Rizpah appears (2 Sam 3), the kingdom changes hands at the mention of her name and during a dispute over sexual access to her. This short narrative contains a historical emphasis. By contrast, the story of the Israelite slave girl and Naaman (2 Kgs 5) combines all three elements: the disfiguring skin condition of Naaman (aesthetic); the conflict between Israel and Aram (historical); and the amazing statement that God not only heals but also will heal someone traditionally considered an enemy of Israel (theological).

Perhaps the most important element to remember in reading biblical narrative, however, is enjoyment. Biblical narrative invites the active participation of readers and hearers. Participation can mean imagining the scene with the characters as well as applying the message of the story to one's life. The best understanding of biblical narrative comes not from remaining on the sidelines or by maintaining a dry, analytic approach.[38] Instead, biblical narrative, a truly evangelical literary tool, makes joining in the stories easy, adventurous, and fun. The stories in biblical narrative mentor their readers and hearers by walking alongside them throughout their lives. Biblical stories told and read over and over again have a way of getting under one's skin and becoming part of who one is. In this way the great heritage of faith lives on from generation to generation.

2

MIRIAM, THE SISTER OF MOSES
OBSCURE YET AUDACIOUS

¹Now a man of the house of Levi married a Levite woman, ²and she became pregnant and gave birth to a son. When she saw that he was a fine child, she hid him for three months. ³But when she could hide him no longer, she got a papyrus basket for him and coated it with tar and pitch. Then she placed the child in it and put it among the reeds along the bank of the Nile. ⁴His sister stood at a distance to see what would happen to him.

⁵Then Pharaoh's daughter went down to the Nile to bathe, and her attendants were walking along the river bank. She saw the basket among the reeds and sent her slave girl to get it. ⁶She opened it and saw the baby. He was crying, and she felt sorry for him. "This is one of the Hebrew babies," she said.

⁷Then his sister asked Pharaoh's daughter, "Shall I go and get one of the Hebrew women to nurse the baby for you?"

⁸"Yes, go," she answered. And the girl went and got the baby's mother. ⁹Pharaoh's daughter said to her, "Take this baby and nurse him for me, and I will pay you." So the woman took the baby and nursed him. ¹⁰When the child grew older, she took him to Pharaoh's daughter and he became her son. She named him Moses, saying, "I drew him out of the water."

Exodus 2:1–10

Exodus 2:1–10 recounts the story of the birth and rescue of a Hebrew slave baby. The story of Moses, the name given the baby, is one of the Bible's most beloved narratives. Many years after his rescue as a baby, Moses, now a prince of Egypt, slays an Egyptian and flees into the wilderness to escape capital punishment (Exod 2:11–15). Many more years after that, the story picks up when Moses, now working as a shepherd for his father-in-law, emerges from obscurity and becomes God's chosen deliverer to lead his people out of Egyptian slavery.

At the beginning of the narrative however, Moses is a helpless baby, dependent upon three other people to deliver him from certain death through their clever actions, quick thinking, skillful use of words, and raw courage. As is so often true in biblical texts, the story twists; the tables turn. This makes for a delightful read. The three other deliverers are Moses' mother, who is a slave; his older sister, also a slave; and a princess of Egypt, who becomes his foster mother. The older sister is an amazing little girl. Probably no more than six or seven years old,[1] she slips past the Egyptian equivalent of security guards and addresses the daughter of the ruler of the mightiest country on earth. In doing so, she audaciously and single-handedly challenges the mightiest power in the known world. This child, hitherto obscure among the millions of her kin born into hereditary slavery, acts as the primary rescuer of the one who some eighty years later will deliver the Hebrew people out of slavery. Armed only with youth, winsomeness, vulnerability, and intelligence, she audaciously wiggles around a security contingent, defies a royal edict, and saves her baby brother's life! Her bold—seemingly spontaneous—actions constitute a prelude to a deliverance of her people so mighty that it continues to enthrall and inspire generations.

A Desperate Act of Faith

Exodus 2 opens with a common series of events: "Now a man of the house of Levi married a Levite woman, and she became pregnant and gave birth to a son" (vv. 1–2). The husband and wife are unnamed, although the Bible later identifies the couple and parents as Amram and Jochebed (Exod 6:20). The narrative gives the impression that this son was the couple's firstborn, but the text soon introduces an older sister, also initially nameless, whom Jewish and Christian traditions later identify as Miriam. To add to the complexity, an older brother, Aaron, is also introduced later (Exod 4:14; 7:7). The next time the Hebrew Scriptures mention Miriam, after a silence of a little more than eighty years, she is referred to as a prophetess (Exod 15:20), but none of her prophecies is recorded.[2]

The rabbis verify the legitimacy both of Miriam's prophetic gift and of the older siblings' births by explaining that Amram divorced Jochebed when the couple heard of Pharaoh's edict to the Hebrew midwives to kill the male Hebrew babies (Exod 1:15–19). Amram evidently thought it better to divorce his wife than to sire children by her and to see them exterminated. Other Hebrews in the community followed his lead. Miriam, the young daughter of Amram and Jochebed, rebukes her parents, and especially her father, for cowardice; she insists they marry each other again. She prophesies that the son born of their re-union will redeem Israel.[3]

In addition to opening with a common series of events, Exod 2 also opens on a deeper level: a family crisis and a national predicament.[4] Like all the Hebrew male babies, the son of Amram and Jochebed, whom the text describes as a fine child, is under Pharaoh's death sentence because he is a Hebrew (Exod 1:22). The baby's mother hides him for three months. She then makes a papyrus basket for him and coats it with tar and pitch. The Hebrew word translated "basket" is *tevah* ("ark"), a word that immediately recalls the other ark of deliverance that saved Noah and his family from the flood.[5] This textual hint heralds an upcoming, mighty deliverance. Mother and daughter determine when and where to launch the beloved baby,[6] and the ark, carrying its precious cargo, sets off down the Nile.[7]

Let us consider this launching in greater detail. On one hand, it is one of the most courageous acts of faith in the Bible. Will not the God who made a covenant with Abraham, Isaac, and Jacob intervene to save the life of this little boy? On the other hand, this act represents multiple levels of desperation. Will the ark-bassinette capsize? Will it be found by enemies and its infant cargo be put to the sword?[8] Notice, however, the three careful human calculations involved. First, the ark embarks from a relatively safe area, because it is the royal bathing area of the Egyptian princess, the daughter of Pharaoh. As such, it can be assumed to be a secure, secluded, and clean place, relatively free from reptiles and water mammals. We know it was not a stagnant pond, because the ark-bassinette floats with the current. Second, the baby's feeding schedule and the princess's bathing time coincide. The baby cries on cue![9] Third, the mother and sister gamble their lives and the life of this baby boy on the character of the princess. The mother and Miriam watch what will happen.[10]

A STRATEGIC CONVERSATION

Several possible interpretations arise from what happens next. The princess and her entourage come to bathe. The ark-bassinette floats among the reeds. The princess sees it and commands a slave to fetch it. The story's action carries with it the sense of an eyewitness account. The princess takes charge. Exodus 2:6 says, "She opened it and saw the baby. He was crying *and she felt sorry for him*. 'This is one of the *Hebrew* babies,' she said" (emphasis added).

Perhaps the watching, hiding, waiting mother and daughter had anticipated such an encounter. Perhaps they knew of the princess's compassion; potentially they knew or surmised that she longed for a child. The princess may have had a reputation for kindness and fair dealing.[11] Perhaps she was known for making independent decisions and sticking by them. The infant's mother and sister may have been aware that the princess disagreed with her father's edict of genocide. One thing seems certain: the mother and daughter set up an encounter with the princess that she could not avoid.

Scholars, however, differ as to whether or not Miriam's interaction with the princess of Egypt is planned or spontaneous.[12] An interpretation that allows for both elements seems best, mainly because the text gives ample evidence of two well-known facts. First, servants observe their masters, know how to please them, and manipulate situations to their own advantage.[13] Second, God's sovereignty recurs as a theme throughout biblical narratives. It seems plausible that the mother and young daughter knew the habits and character of the princess and planned their actions accordingly—while at the same time putting their trust in God.[14]

Presumptions of sympathy, however, do not diminish the fact that what happens next, the meeting between Miriam and the princess, exudes danger, sparkles with shrewdness, and changes history. A routine bathing excursion to the Nile suddenly becomes a national incident that tests Pharaoh's authority. The discovery of the ark and its cargo presents the princess with an immediate conflict. The princess faces the choice of obeying her father and ordering an attendant Egyptian guard to kill the Hebrew baby or publicly disobeying the royal decree and sparing the life of a child, whom the text endearingly describes in Hebrew as *tov,* a word meaning "good," "fine," and "beautiful" (Exod 2:2).[15]

Probably standing to the side, obscure and unnoticed, Miriam gives the princess a moment to express her surprise and to work through her initial emotions.[16] Then, audacious, prompt, and bold, she steps forward. She probably wiggles around and through any attendants who stand armed and ready to protect their princess. Remember, she is a slave, a child! Circumventing all the adults in the bathing party, she addresses the princess directly: "Shall I go and get one of the *Hebrew* women to nurse the baby for you?" (Exod 2:7, emphasis added).

In phrasing her question, Miriam immediately displays both her shrewdness and a healthy amount of intuition. Indeed, she knows how to persuade! A skillful persuader listens intently. Notice how Miriam repeats the same key word—*Hebrew*—that the princess used. Repetition shows someone tunes in when another person speaks. Repetition shows courtesy, for it utilizes language already on the table, so to speak. Repetition shows empathy, since one is using a word with which someone else is already comfortable.[17]

With her question, Miriam makes several amazing mental jumps. She assumes the princess wants the child, although the princess has said nothing of the sort. Quite likely, Miriam's assumption also includes related notions such as these: the princess will go against her father's decree; she will not order the child to be killed; she will face her father's probable wrath; she will choose to put her life in jeopardy to save this child; and she wants this child for her own.

Miriam's question also provides a way of escape for the princess, for the princess is unexpectedly faced with a situation requiring an immediate decision about what to do. This decision takes place in a public setting with her attendants and guards watching. Human nature being what it is, palace gossip would insure that her decision, whatever it is, would become palace knowledge within moments!

Both characters in this vignette, the unnamed princess and the unnamed slave girl, think quickly. The little girl's timely question buys time for the princess, giving her a chance to delay ordering or sanctioning the killing of the baby. While the slave girl runs off to fetch a wet nurse, a plan forms quickly in the mind of the princess. She will take the child when he is weaned. She will postpone until an indefinite "later" how she will inform her father. In an interesting side note, the text presents this princess as honorable in her financial dealings. Although she is the employer and negotiator, she makes it clear that she will pay the Hebrew midwife for the services rendered in her employ. The princess's shrewdness likewise becomes apparent in that she refrains from saying how much the wages will be. Quite likely, different wages were paid to her different employees, and she did not want them comparing amounts.

In her interaction with the princess, Miriam uses two persuasive techniques: incentives and empathy.[18] In her offer of support, Miriam provides the princess with the incentive to become a mother. The twist in this case is that an incentive most often comes from a superior (an employer) rather than from a subordinate (a child and a slave).

Miriam also employs the persuasive technique called empathy. A possible reading of the princess's exclamation, "This is one of the Hebrew babies" (Exod 2:6), is that she longs for a child. Perhaps there is compassion in her voice for a doomed, helpless infant. Perhaps there is outrage in her voice over the arbitrary injustice of murder ordered by her father. The text remains silent, as is usually its custom, about the thoughts, feelings, and motives of individuals. But the actions and words of this princess show that she desires the child to live and refuses to be part of his destruction.[19] Several characteristics of a skilled empathetic approach to persuasion are present in Miriam's interaction with the princess:

> The person employing empathy skillfully deflects attention from herself.[20] Miriam remains keenly aware of her goal and purpose—to save her baby brother's life—while she focuses attention on the needs of the infant and the assumed needs of the princess. Consequently, she, a little slave girl, remains very much the one in control of the situation. Her question, "Shall I go and get one of the Hebrew women to nurse the baby for you?" keeps the focus on the helpless, crying child even as it presses the princess to make a decision. Obviously, the child needs to be fed. That's common sense!

❧ The empathetic person cleverly pulls the person to be persuaded toward her own viewpoint.[21] Miriam's question employs one of the strongest strategies of empathy: she in effect says to the princess, "May I help you?"[22] Her actions and question also seem to say, "I would value your opinion on this: Don't you think the baby needs a wet nurse immediately?"[23]

❧ A persuasive style that stresses empathy also makes friends immediately. It instantly recognizes how important the other person is and creates a bond.[24] In this instance, a lifelong relationship indeed develops between this Hebrew family, this Egyptian princess, and the Hebrew people.[25]

❧ The empathetic person recognizes a deep need in another person. Here the deep need in the princess is not named. Possibly, because of the focus of Exod 1, it could be a sense of outrage against the order of her father, the pharaoh, for his decree of genocide. Perhaps she wishes to rebel against her father and uses this Hebrew baby to declare her independence. She may be sensing the need or desire to be a mother. Although the text does not specify the princess's marital status, the fact that she is surrounded with serving maids suggests that she is single, young, and of marriageable age. Perhaps her need may be nothing more than to deal with the immediate situation: she, as a princess, one to whom others look for authority, needs to make an immediate decision as to whether or not to follow Pharaoh's order to kill the male Hebrew babies. Whatever the need of this unnamed royal woman, Miriam's question—"Shall I go and get one of the Hebrew women to nurse the baby for you?"—meets it. Miriam intuitively understands the conflict that finding the baby presents to the princess. Miriam does not necessarily know what the princess's needs are. What is important is that Miriam offers a way out.

❧ The empathic approach to persuasion employs mutual respect. In this case, Miriam asserts herself honestly and forthrightly to someone she regards as a person of dignity. The response from the princess is returned respect. Miriam persuades the princess that it is in the princess's best interest to save the baby's life. The princess grasps the chance—indeed, the incentive—presented to her.[26]

The risk this mother and daughter, two unnamed characters born into slavery, take is significant, but it pays off. The princess accepts Miriam's way out. Miriam's solution buys the princess time. It saves face—her status and reputation among her serving girls is preserved. It meets the baby's immediate needs—no one enjoys hearing a crying child. It forestalls an immediate killing and saves a life. It creatively handles an unforeseen national incident and difficult personal situation. It allows a light-hearted spirit inherent in a bathing excursion to resume.

Significantly, the text remains silent about not only how the princess tells Pharaoh about her newly adopted son but also his reaction to her deed.[27] Other textual silences also are important in that they point to what Miriam, an able communicator, wisely avoids. First, by asking one direct question, Miriam avoids a long, complicated discussion. Second, she avoids making the princess choose among several Hebrew women or between an Egyptian and Hebrew woman; in other words, Miriam refrains from "either-or" questions. She presents one option: that of getting one Hebrew woman to nurse the child. Wisely, it is the option most favorable to Miriam and her mother. Third, she skirts guilt-laden questions such as "Surely you don't want to see an innocent baby killed?" or "Really, shouldn't you take the baby in?"

A HIDDEN YET ACTIVE GOD

Perhaps the most significant silence in the text concerns God: Where is God in this story? This is a common question in biblical narratives, which often focus on events in a matter-of-fact way, without providing a great deal of overt reflection on their meaning. Exodus 2:1–10 makes no mention of God at all, nor is there mention of prayer on the part of the slave family as they face a desperate situation.

What the text does record is a (seemingly) hopeless situation of ongoing slavery faced by Hebrews whose forbearers generations earlier had made an ongoing and generational covenant with and a vow to God (see the stories of Abraham and Jacob respectively, Gen 17, 28). It tells us of the (seemingly) immanent death of a fine Hebrew baby boy, and the might and apparent arrogance of Egypt, the prevailing world power. Yet the power and activity of the God of Abraham, Isaac, Jacob, and Joseph is conspicuously absent.

But if we look closer, we see that the text actually sets up a confrontation between powerless and powerful humans that vindicates God, allows divine character attributes to shine through, and demonstrates that God's covenant and vow hold true in a new circumstance faced by a new generation. In biblical narrative, human beings (in this case Miriam, her mother, and the princess of Egypt) consistently share in the unfolding of situations in which God (who may appear to be absent) ultimately gets the glory. From a human perspective, these are hard, dangerous, terrifying, and horrendous difficulties. From God's perspective, however, they serve to illustrate in new ways the established biblical principle that nothing is too hard for the Lord (Gen 18:14).

Exodus 2:1–10 resonates with faith, sparkles with audacity, and makes us cheer the underdogs and shout with joy when a helpless Hebrew baby is spared! But after the cheering, the text invites us to do some sweet reflection on the personal significance of the events recorded. Will not the covenant-keeping and vow-remembering God deliver us as he did little Miriam and baby Moses? Miriam's story is one among many in the Hebrew Bible that answers that question with a magnificent Yes! Exodus 2:1–10 shows that a point of critical need (in this case the sparing of the life of a baby boy under a death sentence) can become a means by which God delivers, saves, provides, and restores. Tears of fear become gasps of adoration and exclamations of joy. Our hearts find it difficult to contain such an amazing reversal. The proper response is worship.

On a basic level, the story of Miriam offers practical lessons for our lives: do as much as you know to do; do it quickly; do it without fear; expect good from others. On a deeper level, the witness of the text challenges us to the life of faith: do what you can, promptly and thoroughly, yet do it with prayer, keeping a cheery countenance; expect deliverance in whatever way God chooses, but be prepared for a period of waiting; expect God to receive the glory by bringing about salvation, for God is indeed a savior.

CONCLUSION

Miriam, at the age of six or seven years, was herself a miniature savior, at least in the realm of human affairs. This story's audacious, pint-sized heroine displays remarkable depth of character for one so young.

She listens intently, thinks quickly, acts decisively, preserves life, and even enhances her family's income! Emerging from the quadruple obscurity of slave, child, nameless person, and girl, she captures the imagination and hearts of generations of lovers of the Bible. It is significant that although the Hebrew Scriptures present Moses as the dominant character in the Pentateuch, elsewhere the Bible rightly gives Miriam equal footing and recognition with her brothers. In Mic 6:4 the Lord, speaking through the prophet, says, "I sent Moses to lead you, also Aaron *and Miriam*" (emphasis added). The basis for the Lord's good judgment is found in this beloved story.

QUESTIONS FOR FURTHER REFLECTION

1. What does the text reveal about the character of Moses' mother? Miriam? The princess? What clues in the text suggest or bring out these character attributes?

2. What strategies does Miriam use in her interactions with the princess of Egypt? How conscious or intentional do you think Miriam is in employing these strategies?

3. Do you think the encounter between Miriam and the princess was planned, spontaneous, or a bit of both? Give reasons for your understanding.

4. As is often the case in biblical narratives, God is not explicitly mentioned in this story. At what points and in what ways do you see God at work behind the scenes in this interaction between Miriam and the princess?

5. Take a moment to review the characteristics of empathetic persuasion mentioned in this chapter. Which of these characteristics would you most like to develop in your own character?

6. What lessons can you learn for your own life from Miriam's character and initiative in this passage?

3

RIZPAH
QUIET CATALYST IN KING MAKING

⁶During the war between the house of Saul and the house of David, Abner had been strengthening his own position in the house of Saul. ⁷Now Saul had had a concubine named Rizpah daughter of Aiah. And Ish-Bosheth said to Abner, "Why did you sleep with my father's concubine?"

⁸Abner was very angry because of what Ish-Bosheth said and he answered, "Am I a dog's head—on Judah's side? This very day I am loyal to the house of your father Saul and to his family and friends. I haven't handed you over to David. Yet now you accuse me of an offense involving this woman! ⁹May God deal with Abner, be it ever so severely, if I do not do for David what the LORD promised him on oath ¹⁰and transfer the kingdom from the house of Saul and establish David's throne over Israel and Judah from Dan to Beersheba." ¹¹Ish-Bosheth did not dare to say another word to Abner, because he was afraid of him.

2 Samuel 3:6–11

R IZPAH, A CRUCIAL FIGURE in the succession narrative,[1] appears twice in the Hebrew Scriptures (2 Sam 3:6–11; 21:1–14). Sex and violence, two major themes in modern literature and at times in the biblical narrative, surround her name.

In 2 Sam 3:7 Rizpah is introduced as the concubine of Saul and the daughter of Aiah.[2] She is defined in terms of her sexual and birth relationships to two men. Although she is silent—textually muzzled—and appears to be only a pawn in the succession narrative, Rizpah is highly significant. During a time of intense political turmoil, the mere mention of her name instigates a political upheaval. Men banter her name about as a magnet for testing loyalties. Men decide her fate as part of the spoils of war. Alliances form or crumble because of her. Court intrigues of a sexual nature swirl around her. Ultimately, her name sets in motion a chain of events that leads to a series of violent deaths and establishes David as king over all Israel. Rizpah indeed serves as a catalyst in king making.

The times are tense. Saul, the first king over Israel, has died by his own hand in battle (1 Sam 31). Israel now has two rival kings: David and Ish-Bosheth, the son of Saul.[3] A crucial difference exists in the paths these two men have taken in their rise to kingship. Abner, Saul's general and a self-appointed king maker, crowned Ish-Bosheth king over Israel (2 Sam 2:9).[4] David, however, rose to kingship over Judah through popular support (2 Sam 2:4). War eventually breaks out between the house of David and the house of Saul over kingly succession, with the former house steadily gaining the upper hand (2 Sam 3:1, 6). Part of the seamy side of the succession narrative and running parallel to it is the rivalry between Joab, the general over David's army, and Abner, the general over Saul's army. Just as the kingdom cannot support two kings, so it cannot support two generals with megawatt egos.

In 2 Sam 3:6–11, the eavesdropping biblical narrator brings the reader into a meeting between the two men of highest rank in Saul's house. Words and actions reveal motives and develop characterization.[5]

Ish-Bosheth accuses Abner, Saul's general and his senior in terms of age and experience, of sleeping with his father's concubine, Rizpah. The charge amounts to an accusation of treason, since Abner in bed with Rizpah equals Abner setting himself on Saul's throne.[6]

In his vehement denial of the charge, Abner uses crude and graphic language: "Am I a dog's head?" The meaning of this response is not quite clear. It may allude to the custom of calling male prostitutes dogs, or it may merely be self-debasement (cf. Deut 23:18; 1 Sam 17:43; Job 30:1).[7] What is clear is that Abner seeks revenge on Ish-Bosheth. He immediately vows to turn the kingdom over to David. The text then discloses Ish-Bosheth's lack of moral backbone.

Ish-Bosheth does not have the courage to rebuke Abner for his rudeness. Instead of responding to Abner with authority as the king, Ish-Bosheth "did not dare to say another word because he was afraid" (2 Sam 3:11). This brief quarrel may seem insignificant, but the destiny of a nation changes because of it. It serves as a "functional" event that effects the course of subsequent events.[8] Rizpah's pivotal status as concubine of the dead king instigates a quarrel, raises questions about gender roles at that time, reveals power struggles between men, and facilitates a permanent transfer of power.

BEING A CONCUBINE

In Hebrew, Rizpah is called a *pileghesh* (concubine), a term borrowed from Greek and Hittite words, and linked to the Latin *pelex,* a word for "mistress" or "male prostitute." In ancient Near Eastern society, concubines merited a social status lower than that of other women.[9] In the biblical text the term is associated most frequently with the tribes of Judah and Benjamin.[10] Caleb, David,[11] Solomon, and Rehoboam, all from the tribe of Judah, had concubines, for example.[12]

Throughout ancient history in the Near East, concubines were included among the spoils of war. Marriage to a former king's wife (or wives) or the taking of his concubine (or concubines) to bed legitimized the throne.[13] Furthermore, bedding both wife and concubine bestowed legitimacy on an aspirant who otherwise lacked a sufficient claim of succession.[14] Likewise, an heir's sleeping with his father's concubine constituted a political act, one that claimed the throne.[15] Arguably, this is what Abner, Ish-Bosheth, and Rizpah understood the alleged act to mean.

Concubines, however, differed from wives in several respects. First, unlike a matriarchal queen, they did not exercise legal power over the throne, even though they were included in the perquisites of the throne and went to whoever won it. While concubines were not negotiating parties in the development of any treaty, they were often one of the elements discussed in the treaty itself.[16] In ancient cultures, concubines like Rizpah were transferred routinely to the victor as one of the profits and responsibilities of war. The new sleeping or marriage arrangements afforded the women food, shelter, and protection. These cultural norms help explain Rizpah's silence in biblical narratives. While the silence may grate on modern readers because they interpret it to mean that Rizpah was thought to be less worthy and less important than the men who defined her life,[17] the biblical narrator has no reason to solicit or to record Rizpah's views.

POWER STRUGGLES BETWEEN POWERFUL MEN

The story in which the concubine Rizpah figures in 2 Sam 3:6–11 is clearly a tale about the struggle for power among three men: Abner, Ish-Bosheth, and David.[18] In this story, whoever beds Rizpah bids for the throne. Sexual access to her—real or alleged—provides the narrative's conflict.[19] Her status as concubine discloses the power issues among these men.[20] Yet in Israel it is Abner—son of Ner, kingmaker, Saul's general, and the most powerful man in the kingdom beside the king—who dominates 2 Sam 3.[21] The chapter mainly concerns his political maneuvers in the succession struggle between the house of David and the house of Saul. Significantly, it is Abner, not King Ish-Bosheth, who leads the house of Saul. The narrator adds intriguing information about battles and ancient equivalents of back-room deals.

The narrator highlights in particular the confrontation between Abner and Ish-Bosheth. The kindling of accumulated bad will between the two men seems ready to ignite, and Rizpah's name strikes the match. Abner up to now has supported Ish-Bosheth, but he apparently realizes that David's hold on the throne is tightening and that a divided Israel cannot stand. Ish-Bosheth initiates the quarrel with Abner with a blunt accusation (v. 7): "Why did you sleep with my father's concubine?"

Notice how impersonally and functionally Ish-Bosheth refers to Rizpah, whom the narrator has already introduced by name as Saul's concubine and Aiah's daughter. Ish-Bosheth omits her name, indicating perhaps that he sees her not as a woman with a name, feelings, and heritage, not as the mother of his half-brothers (as the reader later learns in 2 Sam 21:8), but only in terms of her relationship to the king. In Ish-Bosheth's eyes—and his words set the tone for the verses that follow,[22] Rizpah is a pawn in the great game of kings. Her life and future are caught in a power struggle between men. Like athletes in a locker room, Ish-Bosheth and Abner talk about a real or alleged sexual encounter with her. The passage plays on words. Verse six indicates that Abner was strengthening himself in the house of Saul, and the narrator subtly suggests various intrigues. In Ish-Bosheth's eyes, one of those intrigues included bedding Saul's concubine Rizpah.

Ish-Bosheth seems to have proof (which the narrator does not disclose) that the deed was done. The graphic choice of words stirs the reader's imagination.[23] The verb translated "sleep with" (lit., "to go into," from Heb. *bo'*) indicates that a sexual encounter has already taken place. Indeed, a harsh verbal exchange such as this one lends itself to the presumption that an actual sexual contact preceded it. The sexual act, therefore, is just as important as the confrontation between the two power-seeking men.[24] It is often the case in biblical texts that a story about sexual license frequently leads to another story about the murder of a stranger, friend, or brother.[25] True to form, this happens in 2 Sam 4.

Scholars offer a range of views about this sexual encounter. A. A. Anderson finds it plausible that Abner wanted the throne for himself and therefore probably slept with Rizpah.[26] However, he raises a more interesting possibility as a reason for Ish-Bosheth's angry accusation: Rizpah already had become Ish-Bosheth's wife, and therefore Ish-Bosheth was in effect accusing Abner of adultery.[27] Anderson's argument is persuasive since the narrative first identifies Rizpah as Saul's concubine and then Ish-Bosheth confirms this when he says, "Why did you sleep with my father's concubine?" (v. 7).[28] J. C. Vanderkam likewise believes Abner took liberties with Rizpah when she already had become Ish-Bosheth's concubine.[29]

The biblical narrator, however, chooses not to comment. His tone remains neutral.[30] He sides neither with Abner nor Ish-Bosheth. He neither champions Rizpah's innocence nor defends her virtue. He neither examines her opinions nor discloses her current marital status. Content with multiple ambiguities and nuances, the narrator lets the issue of the sleeping arrangements of the royals hang unanswered and left to the reader's imagination.[31]

Abner's angry response substantiates the view that Ish-Bosheth's words are accurate and confrontational and not merely tentative and curious. Ish-Bosheth upbraids Abner, and Abner takes umbrage, stressing under a self-imposed oath that he has not engaged in rebellious intrigue. (The reader may think he protests too much.) Abner obfuscates the issue with God-talk; he seems to take the higher moral ground. He appears to be looking for a reason to break his alliance with Ish-Bosheth. He seems eager to escalate a verbal fistfight with the new king and to pounce on the opportunity to do so. He declares, somewhat pompously, that he chooses to pursue the will of Yahweh in transferring the kingdom of Saul to David and establishing David's throne from Dan to Beersheba.

So despite his apparently neutral stance, the narrator stresses that even the hint of such an encounter with Rizpah represents a significant change in the relationship between Abner and Ish-Bosheth—it directly threatens Ish-Bosheth's throne and manhood. This alleged or actual sexual encounter provides the justification for a shift of alliance. Notice this: biblical narratives tend to present sexual matters straightforwardly. Often, when the text mentions sexual issues, the focus is more on the results of sexual activity than on the activity itself.[32]

Why does Ish-Bosheth confront Abner about his sexual encounters and pale at Abner's response? Because sexual encounters can be as important as military victories in the king-making process. How does Ish-Bosheth see Abner's deed? Ish-Bosheth sees it as a knife to the jugular—his jugular.

Although Rizpah appears passive in this story, she is politically important. Her name and status serve to reveal Ish-Bosheth's and Abner's character traits. Abner is a bully; Ish-Bosheth is a coward. Neither man is fit to be king.

Ish-Bosheth's loss in the verbal skirmish with Abner propels the plot by hastening his own death. Abner transfers the power of the state to David, and shortly thereafter assassins kill Ish-Bosheth (2 Sam 4). Ironically, Abner's actions regarding Rizpah likewise hasten his death at Joab's hands (2 Sam 3:22–27).[33]

For some time, Rizpah's name is not mentioned again in the Hebrew Scriptures. Then, during David's reign her name surfaces again in a story involving the Gibeonites (2 Sam 21:1–14). This second narrative will be the subject of the next chapter.

THE QUESTION OF GENDER

The syntax in 2 Sam 3:6–11 provides insight into gender roles in ancient Israelite society and culture. The narrator's syntax emphasizes who of the three named characters has status and import. The men act and speak. Ish-Bosheth starts the quarrel, but the language of the text indicates that Abner initiated an action even earlier, for it is he as the sentence's subject who "goes into" the woman. The woman, Rizpah, receives the action.[34] She does not initiate the act or dialogue about it, but is talked about. At least in grammatical terms, the narrator presents Rizpah not as an initiating subject, but as an object of the actions of Abner and Ish-Bosheth. She is kept silent and remains passive. This may be an intentional reflection of her status as a dependent woman; she clearly is not—at least not yet in the narrator's eyes—an independent force to be reckoned with or acknowledged.

Several significant points that shed light on Rizpah's status emerge from the quarrel in this narrative. First, while Abner strongly protests Ish-Bosheth's charge of sexual misconduct, he doesn't specifically deny the accusation. Second, while the violation of Rizpah is the topic of conversation, nothing is mentioned with regard to her well-being. Was she raped, or was she a willing partner? Was she merely doing her duty? What would having Abner or Ish-Bosheth as a bed partner (or husband) have meant to her? Does she grieve for Saul, who committed suicide rather than fall into the hands of the Philistines (1 Sam 31:4)? Third, Abner's response expresses disproportionate vehemence; it slurs Ish-Bosheth's manhood.

Abner's strong attack creates a smoke screen and makes one wonder about his deeper motives. He trumpets his virtues, but the sound is flat. Is he protecting Rizpah's reputation? Probably not. Is he obscuring other issues, wanting power for himself, deflecting blame from himself, and deciding that Ish-Bosheth is unfit to rule? Probably so. Whatever his reasons, Abner favors the old motto: *attack is the best defense.* This explains his "righteous anger and surprising volte-face" to David's camp.[35] Nonetheless, in the biblical stories about Abner, the narrators present him on the whole positively, depicting him as a mighty warrior, an Israelite loyal to the house of Saul and to Israel, and (most importantly) as the one who delivers Israel to David.

Yet by using a sexual slur involving the behavior of male dogs and perhaps comparing himself with male prostitutes, Abner degrades himself.[36] He goes on to break into a form of self-cursing that is characteristic of the books of Samuel and Kings.[37] One thing Ish-Bosheth's charge unexpectedly accomplishes, however, is to bring about Abner's switch of allegiance to David "this very day" (v. 8). With Rizpah's name and station as the catalyst, a new national coalition begins.

One doubts, however, the spontaneity of Abner's switch. This general is too seasoned, too cagey, for a spur-of-the-moment diplomatic change of heart. No, Abner's bedding (alleged or real) of Rizpah was arguably a coldly calculated move designed to produce a response from Ish-Bosheth that would enable Abner to do what he had already chosen to do—throw his allegiance to David. Abner appears to abide by this rule: Do whatever is best for Abner.[38]

Abner's decision to transfer the kingdom from the house of Saul to the house of David presents what appears to be an amazing claim. Can he deliver? By boasting that David's throne will be established over Israel and Judah from Dan to Beersheba, Abner flaunts his self-worth and power. Is he too cocky? Probably not, for as a general he knows how to lead and motivate an army, a key to securing any throne. Nowhere does the text show Ish-Bosheth as a man of war and prowess. In an age when might equals right, Ish-Bosheth lacks the manliness to stop Abner. And both Abner and Ish-Bosheth know it.

Consequently, this passage reveals some of the multiple power issues and tensions among three men. Clearly, one issue is the right to the throne. A second, more subtle issue is a deliberate slur on Ish-Bosheth's manhood. A third issue is who controls Rizpah's sexual favors. Yet a larger issue throughout biblical narrative and in the books of Samuel in particular is how God sovereignly controls and uses the power issues and tensions among individuals and guides them into his sovereign, good plan.

If Ish-Bosheth's charge were true, it would mean that Abner's sexual liaison with Rizpah had ridiculed Ish-Bosheth's manhood in a public and premeditated way. Men in ancient Israel were at least partially responsible for the sexual purity, honor, access to, and protection of the women in their household (see Judg 19; Gen 12, 20, 26). Protection of and access to women probably included wives, mothers, daughters, and concubines.[39] Arguably, Saul's honor depended on Rizpah's honor.[40] At Saul's death, responsibility for Rizpah, and specifically access to, or at least protection of, her sexuality, fell to Ish-Bosheth.

THE COWARDLY ISH-BOSHETH

Abner's reply to Ish-Bosheth, both because it is not a direct denial and because of its bellicosity, constitutes a frontal attack on Ish-
Bosheth's masculinity. Ish-Bosheth's honor as the leading, surviving
male of Saul's household is shamed because he cannot protect or control
the sexual practices of Rizpah and those who court her. By flaunting
Ish-Bosheth's impotency in these matters, the general also flaunts the
fact that Ish-Bosheth wears his shaky crown merely at Abner's whim.
Impotence in one sphere—logically or illogically—indicates impotence in another. Without Abner's support, Ish-Bosheth's throne will
wobble and crash like a house of cards. Provided with the excuse he
needs, Abner now defects to the house of David. Truly, at this stage in
Israel's national development, as Abner goes, so goes the kingship.[41]

Ish-Bosheth cowers before the angry bully Abner: "Ish-Bosheth,"
the narrator tells us, "did not dare to say another word to Abner, because he was afraid of him" (2 Sam 3:11).[42] If Ish-Bosheth emotionally and verbally quails in front of Abner in private, how can he face
him across the diplomatic table or on the battlefield? Clearly the answer is that he cannot. And because he cowers in a private meeting,
Ish-Bosheth demonstrates his unfitness to lead Israel as his courageous
father's successor. Ish-Bosheth's murder in his own bed comes as no
surprise (2 Sam 4). After all, Ish-Bosheth has shown himself to be incapable of protecting a woman of his own household. A man who cannot
protect the weakest member of his household—or himself—is not fit
to be king. Any man who wishes to become king must show himself to
be worthy of that position in the eyes of other men by demonstrating
those qualities that are thought to be essential in a king.[43] Second Samuel 3:6–11 shows that Ish-Bosheth is a spineless and unworthy leader
who lacks kingly qualities. Consequently, the reader expects his murder
and feels no regret at his death, violent and unjust as it is.

RIZPAH AND OTHER BIBLICAL CONCUBINES

Rizpah's story illustrates that kingdoms rise and fall around the
sexual and marital arrangements of the royals. While the narrator
never questions Rizpah's monogamous, exclusive relationship with
Saul while he lived, he shows that the death of her protector left her,

like many widows in countless cultures, vulnerable to public slander and sexual exploitation. A brief examination of two stories of other concubines—the Levite's concubine in Judg 19 and David's concubines in 2 Sam 16—shows that society and the narrators treat them the same way Rizpah is treated. Significantly, all of these women are silent—textually muzzled, which adds to their mystery and their apparent powerlessness.

In the Judg 19 narrative, the Levite's concubine remains mute while the men in the chapter—the Levite, her father, the old man in Gibeah, and the wicked men of Gibeah—all speak. Like Rizpah, she is the object rather than the subject of direct speech and action. Although, unlike Rizpah, she initiates some action (at the beginning of the chapter, she leaves the Levite and goes home to her father), the syntax here, as in the Rizpah account, suggests the woman's dependent status.

After a night of being gang raped, the concubine collapses and dies on the doorway of the house with her hands on its threshold (v. 27). By singling out her hands, the narrator emphasizes them. These hands say so much. Did she die pleading for help? Was she crawling to safety? Was the door blocked and bolted, forbidding sanctuary? Was she pointing accusing hands at those she blamed for her death, the Levite and the householder? Whatever the case, even in death her body speaks.

The text records nothing of the concubine's cries or pleas for help. Her night of rape receives no direct comment, although the narrator allows her body itself to convey a strong censure of the deed. Phyllis Trible argues that the concubine's body, immediately cut up in twelve pieces and sent by the Levite throughout Israel, continues to influence Israel's story.[44] How? Sadly, the concubine's dismembering perpetuates more violence against women because the Benjamites need wives and take the girls they want at Shiloh (Judg 21:15–23).[45]

Just as Rizpah serves as a pawn in a power game between Abner and Ish-Bosheth, the Levite's concubine becomes the playing field in a contest of male sexual dominance. Both stories raise disturbing questions related to gender. In the ancient world at large, and arguably in the culture of Israel at that time, men dominated women socially. Sexual penetration, indicating masculinity and social power, represented a palpable token of that domination. Rather than be overpowered in a homosexual way by the men of Gibeah, the concubine's supposed male protectors allowed the woman to be dominated, overpowered, raped repeatedly, and ultimately murdered.

Probably equally disturbing to modern readers is the story of Absalom's violation of his father David's concubines in 2 Sam 16. Here again their views, needs, wants, and rights remain immaterial, ignored, and overlooked in the text. During Absalom's rebellion, Ahithophel, David's counselor, defects to Absalom's camp and advises Absalom to have sex with his father's concubines, who have been left to guard the palace, in full view of all Jerusalem. Ahithophel tells Absalom: "Then all Israel will hear that you have made yourself a stench in your father's nostrils, and the hands of everyone with you will be strengthened" (2 Sam 16:21). The verb *ba'ash* (*to become odious, to make oneself odious*) is very graphic and used only two other times in the Hebrew Scriptures (1 Sam 13:4; 2 Sam 10:6).[46] A tent is set up, and Absalom performs. Absalom's display of sexual prowess serves to convince his followers that they have backed the right man as king in the rebellion. Unknowingly, however, Ahithophel facilitates the fulfillment of the prophetic words of judgment spoken against David for his earlier sin of adultery with Bathsheba and the murder of her husband, Uriah (2 Sam 12:11–12). The long-term result of Absalom's sexual display is not the crown but his own demise. Within days the battle goes against him. After gorgeous Absalom's heavy hair becomes entangled in a tree limb, Joab, acting yet again as a self-designated executioner in the best interests of the crown, pierces David's beloved son with javelins (2 Sam 18:9, 14–15).

POTENTIAL COMPLEXITIES IN DAVID'S MARITAL SITUATION

Rizpah's name and status indirectly raise interesting aspects of the interlocking family arrangements of the houses of Saul and David. Confusion, for example, surrounds the identity of Ahinoam, Saul's wife. The biblical text makes plain that Saul was monogamous in that he had one wife, Ahinoam,[47] and limited himself to one concubine, Rizpah. Yet David also had a wife identified as Ahinoam of Jezreel (1 Sam 14:50; 25:43; 27:3; 30:5; 2 Sam 3:2). Are there two Ahinoams, or did David take Saul's Ahinoam to wife *before* Saul's death? The text offers no comment on this, but the identical name raises the possibility that Ahinoam (possibly the mother of Ish-Bosheth, Jonathan, and Michal) became David's second wife.[48] Saul gave his daughter Michal to David, and she was his first wife (1 Sam 18:27).

Vanderkam calls the diverse references to Ahinoam a "tantalizing bit of evidence" that David may have taken Saul's wife. He posits that David assumed his Hebron throne five and a half years before Saul's death and did so in conscious opposition to Saul. "If Ahinoam was Saul's first wife and Jonathan's mother, it is difficult to escape the conclusion that David's act was meant as a political defiance against Saul," Vanderkam writes.[49] If David did take Saul's wife as his own, it would show both his political genius and his audacity. Furthermore, it would increase Rizpah's political importance as part of the booty of war and an avenue of succession to the throne.[50]

RIZPAH AND THE PURPOSES OF GOD

As with many biblical stories, God appears to be absent as an active participant in the narrative. In this text, Abner mentions God, but only in the context of an oath of allegiance to David (2 Sam 3:9). Yet this story shows God's guiding hand as it reveals the fulfillment of God's purpose: the establishment of David as the rightful king over all Israel (see 1 Sam 16:1–13). It is Rizpah who figures as the catalyst that catapults David to this position. Dehumanized by the inability to control even her own body, she seems incidental to the flow of the biblical narrative. Yet Rizpah is not incidental when it comes to the sovereignty of God over events. She furthers the purposes of God. The prophetic word of kingship given to Samuel, Israel's prophet, judge, and king maker, about David finally comes true (1 Sam 16:1).

On one level, Rizpah's story exposes the harshness of life in the ancient world. Sexual prowess and military might were seen as indispensable components of political success. On a deeper level, however, the narrator throughout the books of Samuel traces God's active, though largely silent, involvement in the affairs of state and in the lives of individuals. The narrator sketches God's greater purposes in the midst of personal anguish, social injustice, and political upheaval. Rizpah (and actually the mere mention of her name) serves as the connecting link, the vehicle, and the means by which power transfers irrevocably from the house of Saul to the house of David. She figures in a complex, deadly dance among men that on the surface is about male prerogatives, masculinity, sexual rights, and sexual practices. Consequently, though mute and muzzled in the biblical text and abused and used by selfish, powerful men, her significance in the larger purposes of God as seen in the books of Samuel is incredible. Quite likely in the anguish that surrounded her life, there is no reason to suppose that she understood her significance. But in 2 Sam 21, where Rizpah makes her second appearance in the Hebrew Scriptures, her courageous character captures a nation's heart.

⁓〽

QUESTIONS FOR FURTHER REFLECTION

1. Now that you have gotten to know Rizpah a little better, describe what you think she may have been like.

2. Why is Rizpah an important character in this story despite the fact that no words or actions are attributed to her?

3. Enumerate some of the ways in which Rizpah in various seasons of her life may have felt powerless or dehumanized as a woman in the ancient world.

4. If Rizpah could have participated in the conversation between Ish-Bosheth and Abner, what do you think she might have said?

5. What specific lessons have you learned from this story about Rizpah? How was God involved in her life?

4

RIZPAH
SILENT ACTIVIST IN NATION BUILDING

¹During the reign of David, there was a famine for three successive years; so David sought the face of the LORD. The LORD said, "It is on account of Saul and his blood-stained house; it is because he put the Gibeonites to death."

²The king summoned the Gibeonites and spoke to them. (Now the Gibeonites were not a part of Israel but were survivors of the Amorites; the Israelites had sworn to spare them, but Saul in his zeal for Israel and Judah had tried to annihilate them.) ³David asked the Gibeonites, "What shall I do for you? How shall I make amends so that you will bless the LORD's inheritance?"

⁴The Gibeonites answered him, "We have no right to demand silver or gold from Saul or his family, nor do we have the right to put anyone in Israel to death."

"What do you want me to do for you?" David asked.

⁵They answered the king, "As for the man who destroyed us and plotted against us so that we have been decimated and have no place anywhere in Israel, ⁶let seven of his male descendants be given to us to be killed and exposed before the LORD at Gibeah of Saul—the Lord's chosen one."

So the king said, "I will give them to you."

⁷The king spared Mephibosheth son of Jonathan, the son of Saul, because of the oath before the LORD between David and Jonathan son of Saul. ⁸But the king took Armoni and Mephibosheth, the two sons of Aiah's daughter Rizpah, whom she had borne to Saul, together with the five sons of Saul's daughter Merab, whom she had borne to Adriel son of

Barzillai the Meholathite. ⁹He handed them over to the Gibeonites, who killed and exposed them on a hill before the LORD. All seven of them fell together; they were put to death during the first days of the harvest, just as the barley harvest was beginning.

¹⁰Rizpah daughter of Aiah took sackcloth and spread it out for herself on a rock. From the beginning of the harvest till the rain poured down from the heavens on the bodies, she did not let the birds of the air touch them by day or the wild animals by night. ¹¹When David was told what Aiah's daughter Rizpah, Saul's concubine, had done, ¹²he went and took the bones of Saul and his son Jonathan from the citizens of Jabesh Gilead. (They had taken them secretly from the public square at Beth Shan, where the Philistines had hung them after they struck Saul down on Gilboa.) ¹³David brought the bones of Saul and his son Jonathan from there, and the bones of those who had been killed and exposed were gathered up.

¹⁴They buried the bones of Saul and his son Jonathan in the tomb of Saul's father Kish, at Zela in Benjamin, and did everything the king commanded. After that, God answered prayer in behalf of the land.

2 Samuel 21:1–14

THE PREVIOUS CHAPTER DEALT with Rizpah's first appearance in the Hebrew Scriptures. There, we saw how her name and status as concubine of a slain king served as a catalyst in king making. Triggered in part by her presence, political alliances changed, and David emerged as king over all Israel. Here, in her second appearance on Israel's stage (2 Sam 21–24), Rizpah appears as an activist. Her courage and defiance of David, now a sitting king, rivets a nation. In each passage she remains mute; the text muzzles her. Yet despite her silence and obscurity, Rizpah profoundly influences Israel's history. Here again she interacts with David from a distance. Here again the intersection of their lives changes Israel's history.

The Hebrew Scriptures characteristically present main characters in their humanity, recounting their strengths as well as their sins as a way of pointing to their need for a saving God. God, not a man or a woman or a nation, is the Bible's ultimate hero. Thus the Bible, as a realistic storyteller, records Noah's drunkenness (Gen 9:21), Abraham's cowardice and halfway honesty about Sarah, his wife and half sister (Gen 12:11–13; 20:2), Jacob's premeditated deceitfulness (Gen 27:18–24), and Israel's moral failures (Amos 2:6–16). But the Scriptures also hold Noah (Gen 6:22; 7:5), Abraham (Exod 3:6; 1 Chr 16:16; Rom 4:3), Jacob (Gen 24), and Israel (Isa 44:1) in high regard. Accordingly, the biblical text regards David as "a man after God's own heart" throughout his life, but there are passages that arguably show him less than favorably.[1] Second Samuel 21–24, which records Rizpah's second interaction with David in the affairs of state, is one of these. Here the text portrays David in a different role from that of the youthful giant killer, romantic lover, and gracious victor of earlier biblical history.

In 2 Sam 21 (as in 2 Sam 3), political intrigue swirls around Rizpah. Here again the text defines her primarily by her relationships to men: she is Aiah's daughter and Saul's concubine. But in this chapter, Rizpah acts.[2] An older, assertive, determined, courageous woman replaces the younger, flat, hazy character of 2 Sam 3.

Part of 2 Sam 21 involves an affair of state left unattended—a
proper burial for Saul and Jonathan, who fell during a battle with the
Philistines (1 Sam 31:1–7). Their bodies were not brought back to Israel but were left exposed to ridicule by the Philistines in Beth Shan.
However, the valiant men of Jabesh Gilead remembered Saul's heroic
action in saving them from the Ammonites (1 Sam 11).[3] They journey
by night to Beth Shan, take down the bodies, return to Jabesh, burn the
bodies, bury the bones under a tamarisk tree, and fast for seven days
(1 Sam 31:11–12). Yet despite their efforts, no natural mourning for
Saul and Jonathan takes place in Israel. Rizpah's grief and heroism in
this, her second appearance, address this omission.

Decades pass; rains cease; a famine ensues. David, now king, seeks
an answer from the Lord as to why. The Lord says that it is because of
"Saul and his blood-stained house; it is because he put the Gibeonites
to death" (2 Sam 21:1). So David summons the Gibeonites, who demand as recompense seven of Saul's male descendants "to be killed and
exposed before the Lord at Gibeah of Saul" (2 Sam 21:6). The seven are
the two sons of Rizpah (Saul's concubine), and the five sons of Merab
(Saul's daughter).[4] The Gibeonites slay the men. Spreading out sackcloth on a rock, Rizpah commences mourning (2 Sam 21:10). Months
pass. She tends the decaying bodies by beating off the scavenging birds
and wild beasts. Rizpah, by her public mourning, galvanizes a nation
to do its public duty for its fallen first king and fallen first prince of the
realm. Eventually, Saul and his male heirs receive a proper burial in the
family tomb. A contextual reading of 2 Sam 21:1–14 indicates that her
vigil over the bodies of the seven turns the hand of the Lord back from
the twin curses of famine and drought. In addition, her wordless action
rebukes David, the reigning, anointed king.

A NARRATIVE IN TENSION

As a narrative, 2 Sam 21:1–14 is so well constructed that a con-
ventional or surface reading, taking the events recorded at face value,
is natural. At an unspecified time in David's reign as king over all Israel, a three-year famine afflicts the land. David seeks the Lord, who
tells him it is divine punishment for an act committed by Saul and
his bloodstained house against the Gibeonites.[5] The Gibeonites were
a servile subculture in Israel,[6] yet the unjust murder of their people

must be avenged. *Lex talionis,* an eye for an eye, must be meted out. The Gibeonites, who want retaliation in kind (Exod 21:23; Lev 24:21; Deut 19:21), seem delighted at the prospect of blood vengeance. With alacrity they ask that seven of Saul's male descendants be handed over to them to be killed and exposed.[7] Apparently without much deliberation, David gives the seven to the Gibeonites. The executions take place at the beginning of the barley harvest. The Gibeonites slay Rizpah's two sons, Armoni and Mephibosheth, along with five unnamed sons of Saul's daughter Merab.[8] Their corpses remain unburied, and Rizpah fends off scavengers from them day and night for about six months. Arguably, because of her known affiliation with and allegiance to the defeated house of Saul, it is a rebellious action.

David (along with probably all Israel!) hears of her silent, solitary, ongoing vigil. It seemingly forces him to act. He brings the bones of Saul and Jonathan from Jabesh Gilead and the seven more recently slain Saulides to the tomb of Saul's father Kish at Benjamin and buries them there (2 Sam 21:11–14). A reading at face value portrays David as pious, righteous, and a great national leader. After all, the rains come and God answers prayers on behalf of the land (2 Sam 21:14).

A surface reading of the biblical narrative also rests on the premise that David alone hears from the Lord and competently carries out the word of the Lord.[9] However, unlike Nathan's earlier rebuke of David regarding his adultery with Bathsheba (2 Sam 12), no second party verifies the word of the Lord. David alone hears from the Lord that responsibility for the famine lies with Saul's bloodguilt. A surface reading accepts David's competence to hear from the Lord and act accordingly.

A more pragmatic and careful reading of the text, however, raises questions. For example, what are David's motives?[10] He certainly made some mistakes during his reign: he committed adultery and arranged a murder to cover it up (2 Sam 11). Could this not be another mistake? Does the biblical narrator reflect a tense ambiguity in the national assessment of David's reign? After all, tensions between the vanquished house of Saul and the triumphant house of David remain unresolved during David's reign. While the text shies away from directly saying that David's beloved place as the sweet psalmist of Israel and a man after God's own heart is erroneous, it nonetheless gives enough clues to warrant what Walter Brueggemann calls "a suspicious reading."[11] For example, who profits from the deaths of Saul's descendants? In a word,

David, for they are potential rivals for his throne; they threaten his house. Indeed David, in agreeing to the deaths of the seven may well be using what V. P. Hamilton calls a "hoax to create hell."[12]

The text speaks well, reinforcing David's favored status: the Lord both directly praises David (1 Kgs 14:8) and directly rejects Saul (1 Sam 16:1). Because First and Second Samuel and First and Second Kings reflect a generally positive view of David, it is probably safe to assume that any negative reference to Saul, and especially to any of his nefarious deeds, would have been recorded and preserved by the pro-Davidic editors. For example, the Bible never mentions elsewhere Saul's alleged killing of the Gibeonites, a key piece of historical background information, leading some scholars to doubt that it occurred. "If Saul had committed a grave offence against the Gibeonites," writes J. C. Vanderkam, "it is more than likely that it would have been a lively concern early in David's reign rather than toward the end of it."[13] The biblical text, however, content with both silence and ambiguity, refrains from editorializing.

A DEMAND FOR REVENGE

The second biblical narrative in which Rizpah figures begins with a national crisis—a severe famine.[14] Such crises were considered indications of God's displeasure and judgment. One rabbinic tradition holds that this famine occurred because Saul's remains had not been buried with the honor due a king.[15] This argument, while it differs from the text's claim that Saul's bloodguilt caused the famine, indirectly acknowledges Rizpah's role in alleviating the famine and ending the national crisis.

The narrative, however, provides no backup documentation for the Gibeonites' complaint of bloodshed against them at the hands of Saul. A principal irony is that Saul, whom the text presents as meticulous and observant, is an unlikely person to incur bloodguilt. Wrestling with this and trying to reconcile scriptures, some rabbis speculate that the Gibeonites were the servants of the priests of Nob, whom Saul had slaughtered (1 Sam 22:6–23), and that "the deaths of the priests brought about great suffering on the part of their servants and this was accounted to Saul as though he had brought about their deaths."[16]

Silence, however, blankets the biblical text. Perhaps via silence, the narrator suggests that the famine ably serves David's political purposes by providing an excuse to target Saul's survivors and a justification for extreme violence against Saul's house. After all, "Saul and his family," Brueggemann comments, "are endlessly problematic to David."[17] They threaten his reign and the longevity of his house.

However, to Saul's credit, the Bible traces his animosity toward the Gibeonites as originating not from personal hatred but from political motives stemming from a desire to benefit the people. David, the political savant, undoubtedly knows the checkered historical relationship between the Israelites (and Saul specifically) and the Gibeonites. After all, he inherited their political history with the kingship. Consequently, at their meeting, David and the Gibeonites engage in a delicate dance of crafty diplomatic language.

The Gibeonites, already shown in the text to be wordsmiths skilled in deception and in getting their way (see Josh 9), deftly maneuver David. They want blood, but blood vengeance exceeds their legal rights under their agreement with the Israelites. Evidently, as alien residents in territory assigned to the tribe of Benjamin, they had no right to legal redress against the Israelites at that time. H. Cazelles speculates that Saul never would have allowed the Gibeonites to achieve the *lex talionis* privilege.[18] Yet after hearing their complaint, David immediately makes special concessions.[19]

David agrees to the Gibeonites' demands and hands over seven of Saul's descendants.[20] The text emphasizes his sparing of Mephibosheth, Jonathan's son. David had promised Jonathan—his friend, comrade in arms, and Saul's princely son—his protection and loyalty (1 Sam 20:12–17), but he made no such promise to other members of Saul's household, and certainly not to Rizpah or Merab. Perhaps David chose Rizpah's sons for extermination because of cultural assumptions.[21]

Scholars debate the time and implications of the executions. According to the text, the execution takes place on the first day of the barley harvest in the month of Ziv, some time in early April. With the exception of the book of Ruth (1:22), no other biblical text mentions the barley harvest with such pointedness. Some speculate that the execution may have been a ritual act performed before Yahweh.[22] Perhaps it represented a seasonal ritual converted into an expiational rite.[23] Human sacrifice on the eve of a harvest may have been a carry-over from Canaanite religion, for 2 Sam 21 seems to present a picture of "non-Israelite religious attitudes and practices thinly veneered with Yahwism."[24] Rizpah's dressing in sackcloth, for instance, seems reminiscent of mourning rites associated with the annual death of Baal.[25]

How did the deaths take place? This question has long perplexed biblical scholars. According to verse 6, the Gibeonites wanted seven of Saul's male descendants handed over to them "to be killed and exposed." The NRSV renders the same phrase as "we will impale them." The Hebrew word used for the act of revenge is *yaqa'*, which is variously translated by words whose approximate meanings include "expose" (in the Septuagint), "crucify" (in the Targum and Vulgate), and "sacrifice" (in the Peshitta). Beyond this word, the text provides no clues as to the precise means of their execution.[26] However, the forcible seizure from their homes, the knowledge they would die at the hands of those who hated Saul, and the painful means of death all must have been excruciating.

RIZPAH ENTERS THE SCENE

After years or perhaps decades of obscurity, Rizpah once again enters the national stage. The scene shifts suddenly from David to this little-known woman. Casting her in a favorable light,[27] the narrator recounts Rizpah's actions. She initiates a means of protecting the bodies of her two sons and Saul's five grandsons from being eaten and defiled by scavenging birds and wild beasts. Perhaps she hopes (the biblical text as usual does not mention motives) that the bodies eventually will receive a proper burial. In the thinking of the ancients, exposure of a corpse to the elements, birds, and beasts equaled dishonor and punishment. Jewish tradition commends her for showing great respect to the bodies of the young men and to the house of Saul.[28]

Consider her courage, defiance, and character. As a widow, bereft of the protection of first a husband and now her sons, Rizpah faces destitution. Consider this scenario: As one intimately aligned with the house of Saul and now living under the rival reign of David, she is socially ostracized. As a political outcast, she expects no mercy from David. Indeed, defiance of the king merits death.[29] As an unprotected woman alone night and day with exposed corpses, she lives amid danger. The season of drought and famine requires her to scavenge daily an ever widening area for food and water. Since the seven male heirs of Saul were killed on a hill, she has to go up and down rocky terrain, fetching food and carrying water. As a twenty-four-hour caregiver, Rizpah enjoys no respite. No one from Saul's household—neither Merab nor Michal his daughters, nor Mephibosheth his remaining son, nor members of his tribe of Benjamin—helps her. Instead, the narrative points toward a grieving woman's isolation and loneliness and her feelings of hopelessness, grief, anger, and despair. As her vigil continues without abatement, it becomes the ancient equivalent of a stare-down contest with David. Who will blink first?

While the rabbis omit comment on the hardships inherent in Rizpah's long vigil, they offer Rizpah unequivocal praise and credit her with great kindness to the dead. They speculate that the Holy One spoke again to David, this time bringing to mind the fact that Saul, still buried outside the land of Israel, had not been mourned in accordance with required practice.[30] Although the rabbis stop short of suggesting that David received a divine reprimand, they acknowledge his slackness in correcting the injustice of Saul's improper burial. Consequently, Rizpah's actions shout across the nation! Her silent yet defiant protest compels the king to action. The rabbis record David's thoughts about her vigil as follows: "If she, who is but a woman, has acted with so much loving-kindness, must not I, who am a king, do infinitely more?"[31] Rizpah's action finally spurs David to declare national mourning for Saul, Jonathan, and the seven male descendents of Saul.

True, before he was made king, David publicly mourned Saul and Jonathan and even composed an eloquent eulogy for the slain (2 Sam 1), but the nation had not grieved corporately. This lack of public expression of grief violated Israelite cultural norms; the biblical text records seventy days of mourning for Jacob (Gen 50:3), thirty for Aaron (Num 20:29), and thirty for Moses (Deut 34:8). Samuel, the last great figure before Saul in Israel's pre-monarchic history, died and was mourned by all Israel as well, although the length of mourning is unspecified (1 Sam 25:1).[32]

The rabbis praise David for acting quickly, with grace and kingly authority. Summoning the elders and other eminent men of Israel, he turns the opportunity created by Rizpah's defiant act into a ceremony of state. Together he and his entourage cross the Jordan, find the bones of Saul and Jonathan (which according to rabbinic tradition miraculously had not decayed; see Ps 34:21), place them in a coffin, and give them a proper burial at Sela in the sepulcher of Kish on the outskirts of Jerusalem.[33]

Elaborating further on the text, the rabbis add that the procession carrying the coffins meandered through the territories of Israel. The tribes assembled "and showed their loving respect to Saul and his sons," and in doing so, "all Israel fulfilled their duty of showing loving kindness." The rabbis conclude that the loving kindness Israel showed to Saul and his family moved the Holy One to compassion, and "he sent down rain upon the earth."[34] Rain ends the cruel cycle of drought and famine. The biblical writer summarizes it this way: "God answered prayer in behalf of the land" (2 Sam 21:14).

Rizpah and Others

Like Rizpah, two other women—Abigail (1 Sam 25) and the wise woman of Tekoa (2 Sam 14)—prevail over David and maneuver him to do their will. Each studies him from afar and knows him at least by reputation. After all, he is a national hero. While Rizpah sets her face toward him in defiant silence, Abigail and the wise woman of Tekoa bombast him with words. A comparison of these three women highlights the different strategies each woman develops for getting through to David. Each woman (unbeknownst to David!) determines both what is in her best interest and what is best for David. Each makes these "bests" correspond to what she wants. Each presents the best course in such an attractive way that he succumbs to doing her will. In short, the outmaneuvered David is "bested"!

Abigail

The Hebrew Scriptures present Abigail favorably as one who uses her verbal skills to maintain control over the circumstances of her own life. Abigail, the only woman in the biblical text described as both intelligent and beautiful, is mismatched in marriage to Nabal, a prosperous Calebite whom the text describes as a brute and a fool (1 Sam 25:3). Refraining from commenting on their marriage, the narrator instead relates how Abigail disarms David's threat to annihilate her household. While he comes with a sword and four hundred men trained for battle, she counters with her own weapons—a lovely picnic, skillful use of body language, beguiling flattery, and wise words.[35]

The story in 1 Sam 25, which takes place while Saul is king, merits repeating. The scene is the rocky, rugged Judean countryside. David, on the run for his life from Saul, has amassed a vagabond following of debtors and malcontents (1 Sam 22:2). He and Joab forge them into one of the best fighting forces the world has ever known.[36] David's men run a protection scheme in the Judean wilderness. They watch the flocks of one of the Bible's wealthiest men, Nabal.[37] At sheep-shearing time, David sends a delegation to remind Nabal of his men's honest and faithful protection and asks to be invited to the post-shearing party.

Nabal replies with an insult: "Who is this David? . . . Why should I take my bread and water and the meat I have slaughtered for my shearers, and give it to men coming from who knows where?" (1 Sam 25:10–11). When David's servants return and relay Nabal's response, David, publicly humiliated, vows to kill all the males in Nabal's household before morning. Simultaneously, a household servant tells Abigail what has happened, and she orders a provision of food to be taken to David's men: two hundred loaves of bread, two skins of wine, five dressed sheep, five seahs of roasted grain, a hundred cakes of raisins, and two hundred cakes of pressed figs. The provisions are loaded on donkeys, and a caravan sets out with Abigail riding her own donkey (1 Sam 25:18).

Coming spontaneously from opposite directions, David and Abigail meet in a ravine. Abigail quickly dismounts and bows down with her face to the ground before David. From this position she delivers the longest speech made by any woman in the Hebrew Bible (one hundred fifty-three words!).[38] Fighting for the lives of her household, Abigail plays on word combinations to win David over. She calls him "my lord" or "my master" six times, calls herself his servant five times, and reminds David of the Lord six times (1 Sam 25:23–31). By cleverly using humility, gracious words, and their common covenant bond to the Lord, Abigail wins David's favor. She guides him to see that it is not in his best interest as the founder of a future dynasty to have innocent blood on his hands.[39] She honors him as Israel's rightful king.

Abigail's obeisance deflates David. He may be able to kill a giant, but he cannot slay a beautiful woman prostrating herself before him in supplication! By her defenselessness, she defeats him. By her gifts of food and provisions, she shows him that it is unnecessary to use violence to get them. By taking responsibility for Nabal's churlishness, she allows David to save face. David's men who witness this verbal interchange will not think him weak for forgiving a beautiful, unarmed woman. By her prophetic word that he will be king, she reminds David that his destiny is in the Lord's hands.[40] By her timely intervention, Abigail calms David, calling him to a higher standard than the violent course he and his four hundred men presently pursue.

David's response highlights her victory; her words win him over. With a characteristic abandon that no doubt endeared him to many throughout his life, David wholeheartedly praises the Lord, the God of Israel, for sending Abigail to meet him and to keep his hand from bloodshed! First Samuel 25 sounds a strong note of joy and acts as a respite between two chapters in which Saul relentlessly hounds David and tries to kill him.

THE WISE WOMAN OF TEKOA

In contrast to the narrative about Abigail, the story of David's interaction with a wise woman[41] from Tekoa carries no joy, for David is at another stage in his life. Perhaps he is weary of the duties that kingship imposes on him. Perhaps he is aware of his disciplinary failings as a father. Undoubtedly he awaits the fulfillment of the prophetic word of God delivered by Nathan against him for his actions of adultery and murder: "Now, therefore, the sword will never depart from your house, because you despised me and took the wife of Uriah the Hittite to be your own" (2 Sam 12:10).

In 2 Sam, the succession narrative extends into the second generation, with David's sons as stars. Who will be king upon David's death? Domestic troubles surface in David's household among the half-siblings. Amnon rapes his half sister Tamar. When David does nothing, Absalom, Tamar's full brother, slays Amnon and flees to Geshur (2 Sam 13). His exile lasts three years. Joab, as commander-in-chief of the army of Israel, instigates a plan to bring Absalom home; the text states that Joab "knew the king's heart longed for Absalom" (2 Sam 14:1). Joab brings in someone from Tekoa called a wise woman, tutors her, and sets up a ruse. This wise woman performs well, for she maneuvers David into reinstating Absalom, his handsome son, to royal favor.

The intriguing story continues. Dressed in mourning clothes, the wise woman of Tekoa approaches David in his role as kingly judge with a fabricated domestic problem (2 Sam 14:1–7). David hears her case, pronounces judgment in her favor, and tries to dismiss her. She persists, however, carrying the ruse to a higher level by making the king swear an oath to God. Once protected under David's vow, she accuses the king of harming the people by keeping a banished person (i.e., Absalom) away. She forces David to consider a new possibility, a new future, and an end to violence and vengeance.[42] Showing that she fully controls the conversation, she *allows* the king to talk. Roles switch when the king asks a question and she replies, "Let my lord the king speak" (2 Sam 14:18).

The wise woman designs her scenario to move the king's heart. She skillfully plays on David's love for his family . . . and his family guilt. She pulls his heart strings by sharing a tragedy similar to that in his own family: one son has killed another and justice demands the death of the survivor (2 Sam 14:5–8). David decrees mercy in the hypothetical situation, allowing the woman to press her real case: If the king can offer mercy to a woman he does not know, how can he not do the same for his son Absalom? The king immediately grasps the logic of her argument and decrees Absalom's safe return to Jerusalem. He perceives Joab's strategy behind the woman's speech, but refuses to let his son "see my face" and re-appear in court (2 Sam 14:19–24). The wise woman asserts herself and blesses David, calling him one like an angel of God who discerns good and evil (2 Sam 14:17). Her pronouncement stands as the only example in the Hebrew Bible of a woman blessing a king.[43]

THE WOMEN COMPARED

Rizpah, Abigail, and the wise woman of Tekoa share several characteristics in common. First, each woman faces a crisis. Second, while each one may not be able to control the events involved in the crisis, each develops a skillful response designed to achieve a specific purpose. Third, each woman knows David at least by reputation if not personally; each one has studied him before she acts. Fourth, each seeks to influence David's decisions and actions. Fifth, each plans and carries out her chosen strategy of attack. Sixth, each stands ready to confront David. Seventh, each is no less a warrior than the Philistines David usually faces.

None of these three women approaches David directly at first; wisely, none is overly or overtly zealous. They do not, for example, accost David the way Ish-Bosheth approached Abner with a direct accusation (2 Sam 3). In Rizpah's case, because the execution of the sons and grandsons of Saul takes place outside Jerusalem, she must use actions rather than words to pique David's attention. She relies on the buzz of national chatter and popular gossip to make her vigil known to the king. Encountering a different situation but the same man who is capable of murder, Abigail begins by humbling herself; she bows with her face to the ground, an action of homage reserved for kings and God. Perhaps knowing the king loves stories, the wise woman of Tekoa stages a ruse and graphically supports it by wearing mourning clothes.

Once each woman captures David's interest, sympathy, or intellect, he is pinioned. Like a skillful bass fisherman making a fish dance on the water, each woman holds before him what she knows to be in his best interest. Because each has studied David's character and credits him with being complex but magnanimous, self-serving but also God-honoring, she is able to reel him in, confident that he will decree in her favor and in his favor. He does so for Rizpah; he does so for Abigail; and he does so for the wise woman of Tekoa.

SUMMARY AND CONCLUSION

The Rizpah encountered in 2 Sam 21—a mature woman now bereft of sons, husband, and status—differs from the younger, more passive widow caught in the national turmoil over kingly succession in 2 Sam 3. She now has nothing more to lose. In the earlier passage, the reader does not know or understand Rizpah; as a character she remains flat and hazy. Over the years as the kingdom solidifies under David, Rizpah drifts into obscurity. As a member of Saul's house, she takes no part in the court of the new king. Away from the public eye, she raises her two sons by Saul. Yet in these intervening years, Rizpah changes and grows.[44] Gone is the passive character who nonetheless became a catalyst in king making. Gone is the compliant sexual pawn of the succession narrative. The woman David now encounters—again from a distance—is active, angry, assertive, determined, bereft, desperate, and morally courageous.

The story of the execution and burial of Saul's two sons and five grandsons invites a thoughtful probe of David's motives—and even a questioning of them. While the biblical text most often presents David in a positive light, it also reveals a tremendously complex man who is both brilliant and calculating, reverent and sinful. A pragmatic reading of the texts about David—and many modern commentators favor such a reading—suggests that spin doctors were at work even in the first millennium B.C.E.[45] Brueggemann, for example, bluntly says that the story of Gibeonites in 2 Sam 21 "jolts our expectations."[46] Drawing on David's earlier speech to the courageous men of Jabesh Gilead, who wrested the bodies of Saul and Jonathan from Philistine humiliation and buried them (2 Sam 2:4–7), Brueggemann adds, "We expect David to be a man of *hesed,* one who will keep his vows of loyalty to Saul and Jonathan especially."[47] Yet we find that David's loving kindness to others often coincides with what benefits his house in a practical way.

Because David's slaying of Goliath makes him a legend in his own time, the reader expects David to be consistently righteous, courageous, and noble. But the stories about David portray him in his humanity as both a loud praiser of God and a stealthy sinner in need of forgiveness. David is equally a political genius, a brilliant psalmist, a giant of Israel's faith,[48] and a man who profits throughout his life by the timely deaths of other contenders for the throne.

Regarding the story of the Gibeonites and their executions of Saul's two sons and five grandsons, at least two readings are possible. One strategy looks at a cardinal rule in solving any murder mystery: trace the trail back to the beneficiary. Whom will the deaths of Saul's male heirs benefit the most? Under this single criterion, the trail leads back to David. According to this reading, *realpolitik,* the advancement of national interest, becomes entangled with household politics and exposes David's desperate measures to secure his throne.[49] A second reading sees David as consistently taking advantage of situations that come his way at the hand of the Lord. Perhaps the executions of Saul's male descendants is God's way of solidifying the throne for David. Significantly, the narrator refrains from commenting on either of these two possible readings.

Jewish tradition discusses the issue and straddles the fence. It not only emphasizes David's righteous character but also acknowledges that David reaps unexpected national benefits from the deaths of Saul's sons and grandsons. The rabbis assert, however, that good came from the deaths of these seven because some 150,000 unbelievers saw justice administered and became proselytes.[50]

The final assessment on David's life comes from God more than fifty years later and is given to another obscure, silent woman, the unnamed wife of Jeroboam. Through the prophet Ahijah, the Lord compares her husband Jeroboam to David and finds Jeroboam wanting. The Lord tells her that David "kept my commands and followed me with all his heart, doing only what was right in my eyes" (1 Kgs 14:8).[51]

It is significant that 2 Sam 21 and 24, the chapters recounting the famine and the census, end in the same way: "After that, God answered the prayer for the land." Rain, a sign of God's blessing since the Flood, ends Rizpah's vigil.[52] With rain, the famine ceases. Other religions viewed rain as coming in response to a fertility rite whose purpose was to end a famine brought on by a drought.[53] But the Hebrew mind regarded rain as part of God's promised seasonal blessings (see Gen 8:22; Joel 2:2; Zech 10:1).[54] Throughout her vigil, Rizpah nobly shows her fidelity to the God of Israel, and in preventing the beasts and birds from devouring the remains, she demonstrates her contempt for the Canaanite practice of letting bodies rot in the open.

Rizpah's action rivets a nation; she may well be the foremost example of maternal loyalty in the Hebrew Scriptures.[55] Just as David is crowned king by a grassroots uprising first in Hebron and later throughout Israel, Rizpah's courage catches the nation's imagination and elicits respect. The nation needs an outlet for expressing national mourning, and David must respond.

In allowing the people a legitimate, open expression of sorrow for their slain first king, David probably does more politically to cement his claim to the throne than he did in all his earlier battles against Israel's foes. A government ultimately rests on popular support. Good will brings security. Approximately sixty years later, Rehoboam, David's grandson, ignores this fact, loses popular support, and watches his kingdom erode back along tribal lines (1 Kgs 12). Therefore, David's burial of Saul and his male descendants arguably serves somewhat as a patch to hold the kingdom together under a single house in a union that lasted for decades. In this way Rizpah, grieving mother, defiant widow, angry Benjamite, and silent activist, helps unify a kingdom.

By engaging in a self-appointed watch over her executed sons and Saul's grandsons, Rizpah demonstrates that God honors mercy, courage, and respect for others. Her lonely vigil clearly expresses the values of Mic 6:8:

> He has told you, O mortal, what is good; and what does the Lord require of you but to do justice, and to love kindness, and to walk humbly with your God? (NRSV)

Even though the text keeps her mute, Rizpah shows that one person acting righteously wields national influence. Rizpah, once a passive catalyst in king making, emerges in this second narrative as a fighter and a type of political savior. She is morally and politically courageous. As one who has lost everything, she fears nothing, certainly not death. A defiant, public action such as hers against the king merits death, but she does not die. As a biblical profile in courage, she illustrates how one person standing alone catches the imagination of a leader and a nation and propels that leader likewise to act righteously.

The rabbis, in commenting on this story, note further that Rizpah's courageous action inspired David's admiration—and more. Jewish tradition holds that David married Rizpah, thus affording her provision, protection, and status in her old age.[56]

$$\mathcal{T\!\!\!\!I}$$

QUESTIONS FOR FURTHER REFLECTION

1. Compare the profile of Rizpah in this chapter to the one in the previous chapter. What character qualities persist from the earlier narrative to the later one? In what ways do you see growth in Rizpah?

2. If Rizpah had been permitted to express her reflections on the slaying of her sons, what do you think she would have said?

3. Rizpah's actions could easily have been interpreted as running counter to those of the king. As you think about other biblical characters who opposed the legal authority of their times, what lessons can you learn? When is it justified to go against the status quo or to resist those who have authority?

4. This chapter raises questions about the character and motives of King David. How do you personally resolve the tension between David's reputation for devotion to God and the reality of his failures as a husband, father, and king?

5. What are some practical ways you can do justice and show kindness in ways that run counter to the status quo? How can you be more like Rizpah? Is it worth the risk?

5

THE WISE WOMAN OF
ABEL BETH MAACAH
WISDOM IN A TIME OF CRISIS

¹⁴Sheba passed through all the tribes of Israel to Abel Beth Maacah and through the entire region of the Berites, who gathered together and followed him. ¹⁵All the troops with Joab came and besieged Sheba in Abel Beth Maacah. They built a siege ramp up to the city, and it stood against the outer fortifications. While they were battering the wall to bring it down, ¹⁶a wise woman called from the city, "Listen! Listen! Tell Joab to come here so I can speak to him."

¹⁷He went toward her, and she asked, "Are you Joab?"

"I am," he answered.

She said, "Listen to what your servant has to say."

"I'm listening," he said.

¹⁸She continued, "Long ago they used to say, 'Get your answer at Abel,' and that settled it. ¹⁹We are the peaceful and faithful in Israel. You are trying to destroy a city that is a mother in Israel. Why do you want to swallow up the LORD's inheritance?"

²⁰"Far be it from me!" Joab replied, "Far be it from me to swallow up or destroy! ²¹That is not the case. A man named Sheba son of Bicri, from the hill country of Ephraim, has lifted up his hand against the king, against David. Hand over this one man, and I'll withdraw from the city."

The woman said to Joab, "His head will be thrown to you from the wall." ²²Then the woman went to all the people with her wise advice, and they cut off the head of Sheba son of Bicri and threw it to Joab. So he sounded the trumpet, and his men dispersed from the city, each returning to his home. And Joab went back to the king in Jerusalem.

2 Samuel 20:14–22

THE WISE WOMAN OF Abel Beth Maacah makes one appearance in the Hebrew Bible. Yet her words and deeds show that she comes well prepared for the single time she takes center stage in Israel's recorded history. In a life-and-death altercation with Joab (who shortly before their meeting had murdered Amasa and reinstated himself as commander-in-chief of the army of Israel), she not only quickly controls their encounter but also receives credit for the city's deliverance. Astute and to the point, this unnamed woman listens intently, weighs her options, thinks quickly, makes critical decisions, and saves her neighbors from a siege. She takes a textual bow as a political savior.[1]

The wise woman of Abel Beth Maacah remains beguilingly and mysteriously anonymous. She is defined only by her gender, her city, and her personal quality of wisdom.[2] The rabbis, however, fill in additional details about her from Jewish tradition. They say she is Serah, the stepdaughter of Asher, one of the twelve sons of Jacob, who was reared in the patriarch's household.[3] The Hebrew Scriptures mention Serah three times in genealogies as the daughter of Asher.[4] The repeated mention gives a strong indication of her significance, but there are no stories or any elaborations about her. The rabbis, however, say that "she walked in the way of pious children, and God gave her beauty, wisdom, and sagacity." She also escaped death and ranks as one of those who does not die.[5]

In common with other political saviors throughout Israel's history such as Deborah, Jael, Rahab, and Esther, the wise woman of Abel Beth Maacah acts quickly during a crisis that threatens the lives and destiny of God's covenant people. Her actions indicate her belief that their welfare is under her charge. She uses persuasive communication techniques instead of military force. As her community's leader, she sees beyond herself. She acts on a large scale for the good of her community and ultimately for the good of her nation. More specifically, she wisely aligns herself and her city with David in a time of civil war.

Unarmed except with acuity and wit, and focused on the right-
ness of her cause, the wise woman of Abel Beth Maacah pummels Joab
with logic. When facing a military force commissioned by David, she
defeats it with her intelligence, careful choice of words, and femininity.
Perhaps the absurdity of her physical powerlessness against the armed
might of Israel indirectly appeals to the soldiers. Perhaps it reminds
them of an earlier contest in their shared history—the pitting of the
youthful, righteous David against the blasphemous, seasoned, Philistine warrior Goliath (1 Sam 17).

There is no indication in the text that Joab and Abel Beth Maacah's
spokeswoman had previously met. In fact, the woman needs assurance
that the soldier standing below her is indeed Joab (2 Sam 20:17). The
text hints, however, that she knew him by reputation, as did all Israel.[6]
From afar she had studied the one with whom she now interacts. Summoned from obscurity, she comes ready for her cameo appearance on
center stage.

The wise woman of Abel Beth Maacah acts courageously. In the
face of death, she pursues a good larger than her personal safety. She
seeks to preserve the lives of those in her city, and to do so she is not
averse to shedding the blood of one person, Sheba. She judges between
the righteous and unrighteous. She makes a life-and-death decision to
call her townspeople to behead Sheba. No doubt she watches as the
deed is done.

The text treats her with respect. It backs up its double use of the
adjective *wise* (vv. 16, 22) by presenting her words and actions in a favorable light. The narrative—as it did with other political saviors who
happen to be women—lets stand her judgment call against Sheba.

Then, as is so common in the biblical text, the narrative moves on,
leaving unanswered any additional questions the reader and hearer may
have about the life of this remarkable woman. Wisely summoned from
obscurity, she returns to it.

THE HISTORICAL SETTING

The wise woman of Abel Beth Maacah appears at a time when
Israel faces internal disintegration. Civil war instigated by Absalom,
David's handsome, ambitious, and charismatic son, threatens to topple

the throne of David (2 Sam 15–18). But Absalom dies in a battle between his supporters and those of his father the king. The text recounts
the brutal way he died, hanging by his magnificent hair in an oak tree
and pierced by three javelins thrown by Joab. Family ties compound
the sadness of this civil war,[7] for Joab, the son of David's sister Zeruiah
and therefore David's nephew, slays his own first cousin. At that time,
Joab is David's designated commander-in-chief of the army of Israel, a
post he has held honorably, probably for more than thirty years (2 Sam
18:10, 14).[8]

David loudly mourns Absalom, disregarding the fact that his loyal
men had recently risked their lives for him (2 Sam 18:33–19:2). Joab,
outraged and immediately sensing that the king could lose his throne
because of a discouraged army, confronts his king with a stinging rebuke
and commands him to go out and encourage his men (2 Sam 19:1–8).
Significantly, the text lets the rebuke stand without comment.[9] David
obeys Joab, offering no counterargument.[10] But then David returns to
Jerusalem, fires Joab, and appoints Amasa, another nephew, as commander of the army of Israel (2 Sam 19:13).[11]

David's realignment of military authority is amazing, for he deposes
his victorious general, Joab, and appoints the commanding general of
Absalom's opposing army—Amasa! David then begins consolidating
his fractured kingdom by dealing with loyalty and inheritance issues
between Mephibosheth, Saul's son, and Ziba, Mephibosheth's servant,
and by seeking to patch up divisions between the ten tribes of Israel
and the two tribes of Judah (2 Sam 19:24–43). Meanwhile, since Jerusalem was an important city in the tenth century B.C.E.,[12] David also
needed to be concerned about external threats from Israel's neighbors.

Unfortunately, despite Absalom's defeat, the spirit of civil war still
reigns. Sheba, a Benjamite, expresses what must have been by then a
widespread, national discontent with David. Sheba instigates his own insurrection (2 Sam 20:1–2). David orders Amasa to muster Israel's forces
against Sheba, but Amasa dallies and fails. David then orders Abishai,
yet another of his nephews and Joab's brother, to take Joab's men and
pursue the rebel Sheba. Abishai's forces (under Abishai's command, but
probably still intensely loyal to Joab) catch up with Amasa and his forces.
Under the ruse of brotherhood, the ousted Joab greets an unsuspecting
and trusting Amasa and murders him. The biblical narrative lingers on
the trickery, brutality, and bloodiness inherent in the deed:

[9]Joab said to Amasa, "How are you, my brother?" Then Joab took Amasa by the beard with his right hand to kiss him. [10]Amasa was not on his guard against the dagger in Joab's hand, and Joab plunged it into his belly, and his intestines spilled out on the ground.[13] Without being stabbed again, Amasa died. Then Joab and his brother Abishai pursued Sheba son of Bicri. [11]One of Joab's men stood beside Amasa and said, "Whoever favors Joab, and whoever is for David, let him follow Joab!" [12]Amasa lay wallowing in his blood in the middle of the road, and the man saw that all the troops came to a halt there. When he realized that everyone who came up to Amasa stopped, he dragged him from the road into a field and threw a garment over him. [13]After Amasa had been removed from the road, all the men went on with Joab to pursue Sheba son of Bicri. (2 Sam 20:9–13)

After Amasa's murder, Joab immediately seizes and assumes his old position as commander-in-chief of the army of Israel. Sheba passes through all Israel, on the run and looking for fellow discontents. He and his forces take refuge in Abel Beth Maacah, a fortified town in Israel north of Dan.[14] Joab pursues Sheba literally to the city's outer fortifications, commences a siege, and begins battering the city wall to take it down (vv. 14–15).

THE WISE WOMAN EMERGES

The biblical text records no conversation, polite or otherwise, between Joab's army and representatives from the city. No account of Joab's approaching Abel Beth Maacah and asking for Sheba is mentioned. Why? Because it probably did not happen. Instead, the narrative conveys the sound of hammers and shouts, the smell of sweat and sawdust. Urgency dominates. Joab's army seeks forcibly to extract Sheba from Abel Beth Maacah.

Then suddenly the text introduces someone described only as a wise woman. She walks to the center stage of Israel's history without introduction as the city's representative.[15] From the wall, she summons Joab in a voice that all recognize as one accustomed to giving commands and being obeyed.

When Joab stands before her, she describes herself disarmingly as his servant and commands him to listen to what she has to say. She begins with a portion of what must be a parable or a proverb ("Get your answer at Abel"). She then asks why Joab attacks a peaceful city known in Israel as a seat of wisdom, one beloved as the Lord's inheritance. Joab responds twice with an oath: "Far be it from me!" He replies that Sheba has "lifted up his hand against the king, against David." He then offers a bargain: if she hands over Sheba, his forces withdraw from the city.

Willing to negotiate, the woman promises to deliver Sheba's head to Joab. Her townspeople comply and carry out the execution. Joab then sounds the trumpet, the army disperses, and Joab returns to Jerusalem. The text hints at what undoubtedly awaits Joab in Jerusalem— a hostile encounter with David and the need to justify his slaying of Amasa.

During the brisk public encounter between Joab and the woman, control of the situation and the siege switches from Joab and his army with their weapons of war to an obscure woman wielding only the weapons of common sense and insightful words. Joab wants Sheba. The wise woman promises even more: Joab will have his head! She retreats from the wall and counsels the townspeople. Their conversation, however, remains unrecorded by the narrator. After cutting off Sheba's head, they toss it over the wall. The army disperses. The woman's actions— although awful for Sheba—quell further community bloodshed and stop, at least temporarily, the fratricide within Israel. Although the narrator offers no evaluation of the woman's counsel and actions, he obviously regards them highly, for he introduces her as wise and backs up his assessment of her character with an account of her actions.[16]

In terms of contemporary communication theory, the wise woman of Abel Beth Maacah employs the technique of *logical persuasion*—she wins the siege using words as her weapons. One who employs logic to persuade uses facts and opinions and makes reasonable, logical connections between the two.[17] A logical person expects reason to win calmly, without bickering, shouting, or threatening. Indeed, logic uses reason and knowledge as a hammer. With her quick, sound, and rapid reasoning, the wise woman of Abel Beth Maacah knocks Joab flat!

EFFECTIVE COMMUNICATION

The setting of a story is a crucial part of biblical narration. It enhances a story and sets the scene to support its conflict.[18] Abel Beth Maacah faces a siege from fellow Israelites. The besiegers, bent on destruction, have the weapons to assail and the soldierly discipline necessary to accomplish destruction. It appears they have the advantage.

However, the presence of a superior military force apparently produces no panic in at least one of the city's residents. The city's wise woman sees assets the town possesses that others fail to notice. She knows she begins her counterattack with several advantages. The first is logistical—she calls out from atop the city wall, forcing all who reply to look up at her.[19] The second is her anonymity—never in the dialogue with the besiegers and then with Joab does she reveal her name. Third, she knows to summon the one in charge, Joab, commander-in-chief of the army of Israel. Fourth, she begins with a distinctly religious Hebrew word uttered twice: *shim'u, shim'u* (Listen! Listen!).[20] In only seven verses that prove pivotal for the political destiny of a nation (2 Sam 20:16–22), the wise woman employs logic as her primary persuasive technique. She quickly deploys a barrage of wordy weapons, including four commands, two questions, one proverb, an accusation, and a promise. Her efforts end successfully, as the army disperses, sparing the city.

R. Eales-White, a British communication specialist, describes logic as the heart of language and hence the heart of communication. When used as a persuasive strategy, logic expresses itself in phrases such as "You cannot do whatever you want to do, because it is illogical." This is essentially the woman's argument. Another phrase used in the logical approach is, "The facts speak for themselves." The wise woman employs facts in her use of questions, assertion, and promise. Essentially, she argues that besieging Abel Beth Maacah represents a stupid action because Joab assails a recognized national treasure, a city that is an inheritance from the Lord. And Joab is not stupid.[21] In the logical mode, the persuader presents facts; the persuadee agrees with the facts because he understands the logic that leads to the conclusion.[22]

The wise woman uses two other modes of persuasion as verbal reinforcements: incentives and empathy.[23] The incentive approach offers some kind of provocation to bring about a desired or hoped for response.[24] Using the incentives approach, she promises to deliver Sheba's head to Joab in exchange for his promise to leave Abel Beth Maacah. The persuader who uses empathy expresses an understanding of another person's personality and experience. The wise woman agrees with Joab that the rebel Sheba is an enemy of the state.

THE HANDMAID TAKES CHARGE

From her high point on the wall, the wise woman of Abel Beth Maacah begins by shouting to all who are in the process of building siege works below her to listen. She then requests a chat with Joab. She takes her time in her interchange with him.[25] Her actions and words recall Israel's heritage of matriarchs in Genesis. The textual legacies of Sarah, Hagar, Rebekah, Rachel and Leah portray women who are wise, learned, and highly developed spiritually.[26]

With Joab below her and looking up, the woman wisely delays in stating her purpose. She begins with a direct question: "Are you Joab?" The question suggests that she is the city's leader and designated representative and as such talks only with an opposing leader of equal rank. The question also suggests that she does not know him by sight. The specific summons of Joab by name and then the specific question to him flatter Joab publicly.[27] Her words and actions recognize Joab as commander-in-chief of the army of Israel and a man who is a legend throughout Israel, known on the whole for his fair dealings. There is no indication that she and her townspeople have heard of Amasa's murder.

After the question, the wise woman commands a fourth time: "Listen to your maidservant's complaint." By calling herself Joab's maidservant, or more specifically, Joab's servant or *handmaid* (Heb. אָמָה [*'ama*], 2 Sam 20:17), she humbles herself. Actually, she is not a maidservant; she is a leader. By using this term, she calls on a religious tradition that immediately builds on her description of herself as a mother in Israel and her city as the Lord's inheritance. As a chosen appositive of self-description, the term occurs twenty-two times in the Hebrew Bible. A number of other women in 1 and 2 Sam and 1 and 2 Kgs refer to themselves this way, including Hannah, Abigail, the witch/medium of Endor, Tamar, the wise woman of Tekoa, the wife of Elisha's friend the prophet, the queen of Sheba, the widow of Zarephath, the honest prostitute who sought counsel from Solomon, the Shunammite, and the Israelite girl who became the servant of Naaman's wife.

The first woman to use the word *handmaid* in Samuel is Hannah (1 Sam 1:11). Three times in her fervent prayer to the Lord she describes herself as his servant, his handmaid. This denotes her complete confidence in the Lord and her unswerving faith in his willingness to help.[28] In 2 Sam, Joab uses this technique of overstated humbling of himself to get Absalom back from exile, when he falls on his face before David and says, "Today your *servant* knows that he has found favor in your eyes" (2 Sam 14:22; italics added). Similarly, the term *handmaid* signals women who use their subservience to get what they want. Although on the surface the term shows deference and humility, the words of a handmaid invariably are forceful, specific, and self-assertive. While veiled by a deferential tone, the words reveal a fine mind, critical thinking skills, and deference to the Lord. While it would be unfair to call these women manipulators, they nonetheless do play their roles and achieve their purposes effectively.

Kathleen Robertson Farmer points out that commentators such as Jack M. Sasson, Edward F. Campbell, and Illona Rashkow believe that *'ama* connotes a higher status than the Hebrew *shifhah* (servant) and is the more familiar, more intimate term of the two.[29] The narrator of Genesis uses the term *shifhah* to describe Hagar, Zilpah, and Bilhah (Gen 16:1, 25; 29:24, 29; 30:4; 35:25, 26). A *shifhah* can perform sexual services, but these services are controlled by her mistress.[30] This appears to have been the case with Sarai regarding her husband Abram's union with Hagar, and with Rachel and Leah regarding their husband Jacob's unions with Bilhah and Zilpah.[31]

Throughout 2 Samuel, subservient-sounding terms like "servant" and "maidservant" are loosely spoken by confident and powerful men and women when they seek to exert their influence. Often when a woman uses the phrase "your handmaid" in the biblical text, the tables turn on the man in charge, and the man loses the verbal confrontation. Thus the term "your handmaid" should have alerted Joab that something momentous was about to happen. Indeed, in his verbal exchange with the woman he appears to know the verbal game already and agrees to play along.[32] He replies to the woman on the wall, "I am listening" (v. 17).

Some texts show a progression in the interchange of the terms *servant* and *handmaid* when applied to a woman. For example, when Boaz first speaks to Ruth (Ruth 2:13), she answers using the term *bondslave;* but later, when she meets him at the threshing floor, she calls herself his handmaid and asks him to spread his mantle—symbolic of his name and marital protection—over her. Clearly the reticent bondslave at the beginning of the barley harvest becomes the bold handmaid by the end of the wheat harvest! Farmer argues that Ruth's use of the word *handmaid* makes her "eligible for marriage with her master

(Ruth 3:9)."[33] While the wise woman of Abel Beth Maacah's purpose obviously is not marriage to Joab, her choice of the word *handmaid* suggests recognition on her part of his fame throughout Israel and her equality with him. Again, in the verbal parrying between David and the wise woman of Tekoa, the woman begins by calling herself his *slave* and then switches to calling herself a *handmaid* midway through the chapter, when she asks the king to perform her request (2 Sam 14:6, 15). She reverts to the more formal and subservient *bondslave* in her last words to David, after he discovers the hand of Joab has guided their interchange (2 Sam 14:19).

Abel Beth Maacah's wise woman addresses Joab in three terse sentences. She begins with what seems to be part of a proverb.[34] She points to the city's well-known reputation for wisdom and good counsel:[35] "Long ago they used to say, 'Get your answer at Abel,' and that settled it" (v. 18).[36] The proverb the woman cites reminds Joab of a long-standing tradition in Israel, namely, that Abel Beth Maacah has a reputation for being a seat of justice. It enjoys national goodwill for its ability to settle disputes, for its arbitration skills, and for seeking peace between brothers in Israel. In this chapter, however, the city graduates from settling disputes between individuals to settling disputes between the house of David and Sheba, a Benjamite. Abel Beth Maacah itself suddenly becomes the center of dispute.[37] Clearly, a locale known as a peacemaker within a province or area for so long is too valuable to all Israel to be wiped out.[38] Her double use of the word *Israel* indicates her loyalty to her country. Her allegiance transcends the tribe of Benjamin or Judah. She and her city remain true to a cause larger than tribalism: they stand neutrally as a national seat of wisdom for all Israel.

PROTECTING A MOTHER IN ISRAEL

In her next verbal weapon against Joab, the wise woman purposefully equates herself with Deborah, a mother in Israel, by calling her city a mother in Israel.[39] This phrase, "a mother in Israel," appears only one other time in the Hebrew Scriptures (Judg 5:7).[40] The phrase raises problems for scholars, for they admit that the original readers and hearers knew a context now lost to modern ears.[41] J. Cheryl Exum's work on the phrase proves helpful here. A mother in Israel, she argues, brings liberation from oppression and ensures the well-being and security of her people. A mother in Israel provides counsel, inspiration, a safe haven, and leadership.[42]

A closer look at the two passages where the phrase "mother in Israel" appears shows that similarities dominate over differences. In Judg 5, Deborah refers to herself. Here, the wise woman refers to her city—or possibly to herself.[43] Both are spoken in contexts that show favorable circumstances. In both cases, the phrase employs the mother image purposefully to connote a place of honor. Both indirectly bring to mind the sixth commandment, the first one with a promise attached to it: "Honor your father and your mother that your days may be long in the land the Lord is giving you" (Exod 20:12).

Both uses of the phrase "a mother in Israel" occur in contexts of extreme need. In Judg 5, Israel needed a deliverance from the Canaanites.[44] In 2 Sam 20, Abel Beth Maacah, which in peaceful times was a center where disputes were settled, now is itself the center of a dispute. Deborah and the wise woman rise up as the deliverers of a nation and of a city. In both instances, the phrase signals a turn in the story's action. In Deborah's Song, it serves a priestly function, separating a theophany about God's prowess and a description of the tribes that acted as his agents in the war—or failed to do so. In 2 Sam 20 it causes Joab to swear an oath, explain his position, and offer a plan (vv. 20–21).

In both cases, the phrase introduces the possibility of rebuke. Deborah, in her role as a mother in Israel, rebukes the rich who ride donkeys and the tribes of Reuben, Gilead, Dan, and Asher for not following the other Israelites (notably Ephraim, Issachar, Zebulon and Naphtali) in the holy war against the Canaanites (Judg 5:5, 15–17). Similarly, the wise woman rebukes Joab for trying to destroy a city that is a mother in Israel, one known as the Lord's inheritance (2 Sam 20:19). On both occasions, the phrase touches on death. Deborah, the judge and military leader, faces death at the hands of the Canaanites. The wise woman faces death from Joab's besieging army.

The words "a mother in Israel" directly affect their hearers. The use of the phrase unifies Israel on both occasions. All Israel recognizes Deborah as a judge for all Israel, not just as a judge for her region, Ephraim. The wise woman presumably speaks loudly enough that the citizens of Abel Beth Maacah and the army of Israel on the other side of the wall hear her. Her use of the phrase seeks to alleviate any possibility of pitting tribe against tribe.

The wise woman's question—would Joab destroy a mother in Israel and swallow up the Lord's inheritance?—begs a negative reply. She first compliments Joab on his intelligence and then immediately questions it. How could someone with Joab's astuteness and brilliant record wish to level a city so long beloved in Israel? Naturally, she seems to say, it would be stupid to acerbate tensions in Israel by destroying so renowned a national treasure. And again, Joab is not stupid.

GUARDING THE LORD'S INHERITANCE

The wise woman continues her verbal attack with a provocative question to Joab: "Why do you want to swallow up the Lord's inheritance?" (2 Sam 20:19).[45] Most scholars concentrate on the phrase "mother in Israel" but gloss over the city's other appositive, "inheritance of the Lord." The Deuteronomistic[46] writer or writers, however, employ this phrase a number of times, and it bears closer examination.

The woman's use of the word *inheritance* arguably refers to the people of Israel themselves (see 1 Sam 10:1). The word appears five times in 1 and 2 Sam (1 Sam 26:19; 2 Sam 14:16; 20:1, 19; 21:3).[47] In 2 Sam 20, Sheba's rally cry, "We have no inheritance in David!" (v. 1), exposes a vein of popular sentiment and amounts to strong criticism of David.

The wise woman personifies the city. Her words indicate that Joab, in attacking the city, attacks her, and in attacking her and the city, he quite logically attacks God. The woman deftly maneuvers Joab to deny his wrongdoing and by denying it to change his actions. "Why are you swallowing up an inheritance of Yahweh?" she asks. Joab must deny such the charge—to do otherwise admits that when he fights against Abel Beth Maacah, he fights against Yahweh.[48] The woman's attack suddenly becomes personal and theological. She denounces Joab's attempt to attack her and her city and to kill its inhabitants. The woman brings in a moral element in her argument: this city is sacred; it is an inheritance of Yahweh.

By skillfully identifying herself with the city, with Deborah the great judge and prophetess, and with a good gift from the Lord, the wise woman puts Joab in a difficult position in a public setting.

She continues her verbal barrage of logical armaments by appealing to Joab's stature in Israel and to his honor as an Israelite. She indicates that she (and not he) is the one who is the peacemaker, the one who is faithful in Israel. She also appeals to Joab's sense of manhood. Her words imply that when he strikes Abel Beth Maacah, he strikes her—and striking a woman and killing her is beneath his manhood as an Israelite.

A Skillful Prosecutor

By her request from the wall to talk to Joab, her command to him to hear, and the three rapid sentences that follow, the wise woman seizes control of the situation. She speaks like a prophet. She speaks with authority and exercises power effectively.[49] In not revealing her name she remains a woman of mystery, and this contributes to her strength in this deadly verbal game. She quickly turns the verbal tables on Joab. Showing her skill at reasonable discourse, she quells for a moment the battering ram against her city.[50] In the story thus far, Joab has been the attacker with weapons, but now an unnamed woman successfully attacks with words.

The wise woman's logic moves quickly from compliment to complaint to indictment.[51] Amid the present altercation at her gates, the woman displays her ability to prosecute. She calls Joab forth, lays a charge upon him, and convicts him.[52] Because of her logic and skill, the woman's indictment of Joab rings true. She proves herself to be one qualified to judge. The judgment leaves Joab dumbfounded. Elsewhere the Hebrew Scriptures record no one else except the king ever speaking to Joab in this way.[53]

Most importantly, the wise woman's words show her deep devotion to the Lord. She claims the city as an inheritance of the Lord and appears amazed that Joab even entertains the thought of exterminating it. She argues against a *herem*—a wholesale slaughter of inhabitants and a burning of the city.[54] If, as the rabbis believed, she was Serah, the daughter or stepdaughter of Asher, she knew Israel's patriarchs and matriarchs well. If she was a typical woman with a typical lifespan for that time, she knew by tradition and personal experience Israel's covenant relationship with God. In either case, the wise woman of Abel Beth Maacah presents a public example of a living faith in a covenant-keeping God.

Although the wise woman mildly rebukes Joab for not following the law of Moses, she wisely avoids arousing his anger. She apparently assumes Joab already knows the good reputation of the city and the propensity of its inhabitants toward wisdom and peace. She assumes that he is well aware of the rule of law in Deut 20:10, which requires an invader attacking a city first to make its people an offer of peace. Holy war against such a city, an innocent city, the woman reasons, represents an error.[55] Perhaps even stammering, Joab returns the woman's rebuke with a mild oath,[56] "Far be it, far be it from me." A modern translation is, "It is not as you say."

An analysis of the textual background of the phrase, "Far be it from me," provides insight into Joab's strong declaration.[57] In Deuteronomistic literature, God uses the phrase first in an oath concerning the house of Eli to signal strong displeasure (1 Sam 2:30). Jonathan employs it regarding his father Saul's good will toward David (1 Sam 20:9). Ahimelech the priest uses it in an oath to Saul, swearing David's loyalty to Saul, an oath that cost Ahimelech his life (1 Sam 22:15). Joab uses it twice in 2 Sam 20:20, proclaiming his reasonableness and innocence regarding his motives in attempting to destroy Abel Beth Maacah. In 2 Sam 23:17, the story of one of David's earlier encounters with the Philistines, David's champions, known as The Three (Adino the Eznite, Eleazar the Ahohite, and Shammath the Hararite) risk their lives to break through the Philistine lines and bring David water from Bethlehem (2 Sam 23:8–11). David, honored and humbled by their courage, refuses to drink the water but pours it out as an offering to the Lord with this same oath: "Far be it from me" (2 Sam 23:17). The phrase consistently occurs in life and death situations and in rebukes. It heralds significant change. It carries the exclamatory sense of "God forbid!"

The woman's sound reasoning makes Joab pause. Although he fails to apologize for his assault, he explains that he pursues Sheba, one who has lifted up his hand against the king, against David (v. 21). By saying "against the king, against David," Joab lets the woman and the city know of the failure of Absalom's rebellion and that David still reigns. Since rumors run rampant when a country faces the turmoil of civil war, Joab clarifies who sits on the throne. By naming David as king, he in effect asks if the city is loyal to David or is part of the insurrection. He volunteers to withdraw if the city hands over one man, Sheba.[58]

A DECISIVE WOMAN OF ACTION

At this point the wise woman makes a quick, executive, logical decision. She agrees to do as Joab asks. Yet she retains overall control by saying the city will do more than Joab requests—its inhabitants will send Sheba's head over the wall. By convincing the city to execute Sheba, she shows Joab—and ultimately David—the city's clear loyalty to David. At the same time, the glory of the battle and the credit for quelling the rebellion go to the wise woman and to the city rather than to Joab.[59] Throughout this verbal exchange, the woman exhibits the confidence of one who rationally and routinely exercises authority. She negotiates directly as one who is equal, or even superior, to another leader. Joab recognizes her as someone exercising effective and legitimate power.[60] The woman promises something; then she goes back to her constituents and convinces them to deliver it. Her past with her fellow citizens gives her the standing necessary for her argument to prevail. She acts as judge, counselor, prosecutor, and leader.

The woman's conversation with her townspeople is not recorded. Yet her public speech and her private communication with her townspeople show her high standing in the city. She is accustomed to listening, to defending, to seeking answers, and to being an arbitrator. Joab's threat (backed by his army) remains clear: sacrifice the town for one man, or let that one man pay for his own rebellion against David. Evidently Sheba garners no support from the townspeople of Abel Beth Maacah for his life. In this case, the people conclude that it is better that one should die so that many should not perish. A millennium later Caiaphas, the high priest in Jerusalem during Jesus' time, also used this reasoning in deciding to seek the execution of Jesus (see John 11:50).[61]

The wise woman's swift reversal of roles via words from the one besieged to the one who judges comes as a surprise to the reader and to Joab. It represents the turning point in the confrontation, for it simultaneously quells two rebellions: Sheba's insurrection against David and Joab's siege that threatens to continue pitting Israelite against Israelite.[62]

JOAB, A STUDY IN CONTRASTS

In contrast to the wise woman, the broader narrative presents a detailed portrait of Joab over a period of about forty years. Ambitious Joab is a complex character whose life parallels that of David.[63] A driving force in his life seems to be love of his position as commander-in-chief of the army of Israel. He attained that job heroically (1 Chr 11:6) and served his king loyally by never coveting the throne (2 Sam 12:26–

28). The king fires Joab at the summit of his career (2 Sam 19:13), yet Joab remains powerful enough to murder the new commander and successfully take back his old job. Joab defies his king—and lives to tell it (2 Sam 20:10, 23).

Joab acts both rashly and wisely in 2 Sam 20. A man of war, he enters the chapter by killing for yet a fourth time.[64] By this time in the succession narrative, his personal and political fortunes apparently merge too closely with his view on the best course for the state. He violates the sixth commandment by committing murder to regain his position as commander-in-chief of the army of Israel.[65]

Still, 2 Sam 20 shows much about Joab that is positive, including his practical side, his ability to command troops, his confidence, his loyalty to the throne, and, in this encounter, his willingness to treat a woman as an equal leader. His troops hold him in awe. Arguably, his political acumen surpasses David's abilities, for he sees the direction the house of David must take to survive. His military prowess made him, like David, a legend in his own lifetime.[66] Once Sheba's head lands at his feet, Joab keeps his word to the wise woman of Abel Beth Maacah and disperses his troops. By choosing to rescind the siege without more bloodshed, Joab chooses to share credit with or even accede credit to the wise woman for ending Sheba's rebellion.[67] Once again, Joab's actions rescue David's throne. Once again, Joab receives no thanks from David.[68]

THE WISE WOMAN IN BIBLICAL HISTORY

The wise woman of Abel Beth Maacah emerges as a surprising national leader. Her verbal encounter with Joab portrays her as an able negotiator who thinks fast on her feet. She upholds the reputation of her city as a mother in Israel and herself as its designated speaker.

The story of the wise woman of Abel Beth Maacah and Joab propels the succession narrative forward by showing the virtually bloodless stoppage of Sheba's rebellion; only Amasa and Sheba lose their lives. An uneasy peace ensues. The story, occurring near the close of David's reign, exposes the animosity of Benjamin, the tribe of Saul, toward the house of David. The raw rancor between the victorious house of David and the vanquished house of Saul festers for generations and contributes to the division of the kingdom during the reign of David's grandson, Rehoboam. The biblical text, because of its list of officials (2 Sam 21:23–25), ends with recognition that the rebellions of Absalom and Sheba produce no structural change in the kingdom. The story of the wise woman and Joab leads to a lull in the succession narrative and the political history of Israel. The land enjoys peace, and the house of David remains in control of the kingdom. David, though old, still reigns. The text, however, concludes with an uneasy silence, leaving unanswered how and if David will punish Joab for Amasa's murder. In addition, the narrative leaves unanswered the question of whether David realizes the political debt he owes to an obscure but very wise woman.

BECOMING A WOMAN OF WISDOM

The story of the meeting of Joab and the wise woman of Abel Beth Maacah reinforces the biblical principle that wisdom comes from the Lord.[69] Deliverance from a besieging army comes not by the intervention of a stronger army rushing over the horizon to the rescue but by the prudent words and actions of a wise, vulnerable woman standing atop a wall.

Aside from providing a vivid example of the value of wisdom, 2 Sam 20 contributes significantly to the biblical definition of wisdom. What constitutes a wise woman? It would seem that a wise woman guides a situation or a person in a righteous way. A wise woman plans ahead. She achieves her goals by using well-chosen words and employing profound psychological insights. She works to get people on her side. Avoiding animosity, she wins support and cooperation. A wise woman senses hidden emotions and realizes that concealed agendas are a part of everyone's life. She turns these insights to her advantage. She thinks quickly and adapts. She knows human nature and exhibits finesse at word games.[70]

How does one become wise? The Scriptures indicate that wisdom not only can be taught and sought (Prov 8) but is also a gift from the Lord (Jas 1:5). Wisdom is sought in secret and refined in the normal intricacies of life. In a modern sense, wisdom comes with spending hours of time with the Lord.[71] Early on in the Hebrew Scriptures the Lord establishes the principles of wise leadership: three times in Josh 1 the Lord and then the people (!) tell Joshua how to succeed:

Be strong and courageous, because you will lead these people to inherit the land I swore to their forefathers to give them. Be strong and very courageous. Be careful to obey all the law my servant Moses gave you; do not turn from it to the right or to the left, that you may be successful wherever you go. Do not let this Book of the Law depart from your mouth; meditate on it day and night so that you may be careful to do everything written in it. Then you will be prosperous and successful. Have I not commanded you? Be strong and courageous. Do not be terrified; do not be discouraged, for the Lord your God will be with you wherever you go." (Josh 1:6–9)

The Scriptures remain silent on the years of time the wise woman spent with the Lord. Instead they give a succinct account of what amounts to a test of that wisdom and an evaluation of it. The woman meets a life-threatening situation calmly, asks relevant questions, works for the common good, presents a solution, and delivers what she promises. Her past history, marital status, and patrimony remain unknown. She is presented without introduction, save for the adjective *wise*. Her words and actions validate, substantiate, and expand the meaning of the adjective. Her words and actions glorify the Source of her wisdom.

QUESTIONS FOR FURTHER REFLECTION

1. As you think about the confrontation between the wise woman of Abel Beth Maacah and the military general Joab in 2 Sam 20, compare and contrast the personalities of these two individuals. What traits do they have in common? How are they different?

2. What specific strategies did the wise woman use to help resolve the tension of the moment and to redirect the actions of Joab and his army?

3. At some points in her conversation with Joab, the wise woman takes a commanding tone. Why was this an appropriate response in this situation? How did the woman do this without offending Joab?

4. Averting the peril the wise woman's city faced at the hands of Joab's army required swift and decisive action. What was the wise woman's solution to the crisis at hand? Have you ever been in a situation that called for difficult yet decisive action to avert a crisis? How did you resolve the situation? What can you learn from this woman that might be helpful in resolving future crises?

5. The book of Proverbs emphasizes that wisdom can be taught and learned. If you were standing in Joab's shoes, what lessons of wisdom might you have learned through this interaction with the wise woman? Are there recent situations in your own life that have taught you wisdom?

6

THE WIFE OF JEROBOAM
ABUSE AND OBEDIENCE

¹At that time Abijah son of Jeroboam became ill, ²and Jeroboam said to his wife, "Go, disguise yourself, so you won't be recognized as the wife of Jeroboam. Then go to Shiloh. Ahijah the prophet is there—the one who told me I would be king over this people. ³Take ten loaves of bread with you, some cakes and a jar of honey, and go to him. He will tell you what will happen to the boy." ⁴So Jeroboam's wife did what he said and went to Ahijah's house in Shiloh.

Now Ahijah could not see; his sight was gone because of his age. ⁵But the LORD had told Ahijah, "Jeroboam's wife is coming to ask you about her son, for he is ill, and you are to give her such and such an answer. When she arrives, she will pretend to be someone else."

⁶So when Ahijah heard the sound of her footsteps at the door, he said, "Come in, wife of Jeroboam. Why this pretense? I have been sent to you with bad news. ⁷Go, tell Jeroboam that this is what the LORD, the God of Israel, says: 'I raised you up from among the people and made you a leader over my people Israel. ⁸I tore the kingdom away from the house of David and gave it to you, but you have not been like my servant David, who kept my commands and followed me with all his heart, doing only what was right in my eyes. ⁹You have done more evil than all who lived before you. You have made for yourself other gods, idols made of metal; you have provoked me to anger and thrust me behind your back.

¹⁰"'Because of this, I am going to bring disaster on the house of Jeroboam. I will cut off from Jeroboam every last male in Israel—slave or free. I will burn up the house of Jeroboam as one burns dung, until it is all gone. ¹¹Dogs will eat those belonging to Jeroboam who die in the city, and the birds of the air will feed on those who die in the country. The Lord has spoken!'

¹²"As for you, go back home. When you set foot in your city, the boy will die. ¹³All Israel will mourn for him and bury him. He is the only one belonging to Jeroboam who will be buried, because he is the only one in the house of Jeroboam in whom the Lord, the God of Israel, has found anything good.

¹⁴"The Lord will raise up for himself a king over Israel who will cut off the family of Jeroboam. This is the day! What? Yes, even now. ¹⁵And the Lord will strike Israel, so that it will be like a reed swaying in the water. He will uproot Israel from this good land that he gave to their forefathers and scatter them beyond the River, because they provoked the Lord to anger by making Asherah poles. ¹⁶And he will give Israel up because of the sins Jeroboam has committed and has caused Israel to commit."

¹⁷Then Jeroboam's wife got up and left and went to Tirzah. As soon as she stepped over the threshold of the house, the boy died. ¹⁸They buried him, and all Israel mourned for him, as the Lord had said through his servant the prophet Ahijah.

1 Kings 14:1–18

A T THE HEART OF the narrative in 1 Kgs 14 is a silent, obscure, yet significant woman, identified only in terms of her function and status: she is the wife of Jeroboam, king of Israel. The other four characters in the narrative are Jeroboam, the first king of Israel in the divided kingdom; Abijah, his young son who is desperately ill; Ahijah, a blind prophet; and God, who speaks through the prophet. Although the text does not state explicitly that the unnamed woman is the mother of Abijah, it is safe to assume so.[1]

Three named characters—Jeroboam, God, and Ahijah—have speaking roles; Abijah and his mother do not. The narrative unfolds in three scenes: a private meeting between Jeroboam and his wife (presumably in the royal palace at Tirzah); a second private meeting between the prophet Ahijah and the wife of Jeroboam at the prophet's lodgings in Shiloh; and the death of the child Abijah in Tirzah that occurs as soon as his mother returns home and crosses the threshold. The text provides no details about the journey of the wife of Jeroboam from one place to the other.

Unquestionably, the wife of Jeroboam provides a connecting link that holds together this threefold tale of doom. To her comes the first prophetic word of another triad of destruction: the upcoming disaster on the house of Jeroboam, the imminent death of Abijah her son, and the impending uprooting of Israel.[2] God's riveting prophetic word to her raises her from obscurity to prominence in the biblical text. The ways Jeroboam, Ahijah, and God treat her showcase her character, identity and motivations—and at the same time reveal some incredibly tragic aspects of her marriage. The cameo appearance of the silent, anonymous, and obscure wife of Jeroboam carries a surprisingly contemporary message.[3]

THE HISTORICAL CONTEXT

First Kings 14 forms part of what for convenience I will call the "Jeroboam cycle." It begins positively, when Jeroboam is introduced in

1 Kgs 11 as a man among men, a competent worker.[4] Solomon, no-
ticing the young man's skills, puts him in charge of the labor force of
the house of Joseph. The biblical narrator pays Jeroboam a significant
compliment, calling him a *gibbor hayil*—a mighty man of standing
(11:28).[5] The prophet Ahijah tells Jeroboam that God plans to tear ten
of Israel's twelve tribes from Solomon and give them to Jeroboam. If
Jeroboam will walk in God's ways and do what is right, God will build
a dynasty for Jeroboam as enduring as the one he built for David. In
Jeroboam a new era begins.[6]

Subsequent stages in the Jeroboam cycle, however, recount how
Jeroboam falls into disobedience. He changes from a *gibbor hayil* to a
man whose name and character become bywords for insult and a yard-
stick for measuring infamy (2 Kgs 3:3; 13:11; 17:22). There are several
important parallels between the Jeroboam cycle and the earlier story of
Saul and the failure of his house to rule Israel. Both Saul and Jeroboam,
for example, lose their thrones because of disobedience, their houses
are decimated, and God's favor departs from them (see 1 Sam 16:1;
31:1–7; 2 Sam 4). Yet Jeroboam seems to have started his reign with a
decision to follow the Lord, for he gave his son the godly name Abijah,
which means "my father is God."[7]

In 1 Kgs 12, the kingdom of Israel divides into Israel (also called
the Northern Kingdom) and Judah (also called the Southern Kingdom). Rehoboam, the southern ruler, begins with little popular support and has to run for his life to escape being stoned. Nevertheless, he
eventually manages to unite the tribes of Judah and Benjamin under
his leadership (1Kgs 12:18–21). Jeroboam, the northern king, quickly
fortifies the towns of Shechem and Peniel (v. 25). These were probably wise tactical moves, for Jeroboam as a new king quite likely felt
the threat of an immanent Judahite attack from the south and inces-
sant Aramean incursions from the north.[8] Fearing that the people's annual pilgrimages south to the temple of the Lord in Jerusalem will lead
to their returning their allegiance to Rehoboam, he establishes rival
worship centers in the north by setting up golden calves in Dan and
Bethel.[9] His blatant idolatry foreshadows his ultimate downfall.

The narrative of Jeroboam's reign continues in 1 Kgs 13, surely one
of the strangest texts in Deuteronomistic History.[10] Someone referred
to singularly as a "man of God" prophesies against the altar at Bethel.
When Jeroboam orders the prophet seized, the king's hand shrivels and
the altar splits (vv. 4–5). Terrified, Jeroboam commands the man of

God, crying, "Intercede with the Lord your God and pray for me that
my hand may be restored" (v. 6).[11] The man of God intercedes for Jeroboam, and God heals the king's hand. The man of God, however, subsequently is deceived by an older prophet, disobeys God, and is killed
by a lion (vv. 11–24). This prophetic event, the only one singled out in
detail in Jeroboam's twenty-two year reign, provides a prelude to the
downfall that comes in the subsequent chapter.

In the Hebrew Masoretic Text of 1 Kgs 14, dialogue predominates;[12] the narrator moves to the background, serving only as a sum-
marizer and bridge between direct speeches.[13] In the midst of this
dialogue, the wife of Jeroboam functions as a silent conduit, an un-
speaking emissary between the more prominent characters, Jeroboam
and Ahijah. The chapter splices together a tragic human drama and a
prophetic word from God.[14] Theologically, the narrative chronicles
the catastrophic results of Jeroboam's unwise choices. Death and destruction, the inevitable consequences of Jeroboam's earlier disobedient actions,[15] ripple out toward his son and his house and eventually
shatter his kingdom.

JEROBOAM'S COMMAND

In 1 Kgs 11, the blind prophet Ahijah sought out Jeroboam. Now,
in 1 Kgs 14, Jeroboam seeks out the man of God. In the intervening
years, Jeroboam's setting up rival places of worship away from Jerusalem at Dan and Bethel[16] caused him to forfeit his favorable standing
with God and Ahijah. Like Saul, who desperately sought advice from
a medium when facing a potentially devastating battle with the Philistines (1 Sam 28), Jeroboam seeks to discover the fate of his son. Will
the lad live? The dreams of his dynasty depend on this boy.

The narrator begins the chapter by drawing the reader into a private conversation between the royals, presumably taking place in their
private quarters in the palace in Tirzah. This kind of literary eavesdropping is a fine example of a narrator who is omnipresent but not
omniscient. The listener soon discovers that Jeroboam enjoys dictating
instructions. Just as he had formerly commanded men to seize the man
of God and expected them to obey (1 Kgs 13:4), he now commands
his wife to seek an audience with the prophet. Jeroboam does not address her by name, and the narrator leaves her unnamed as well.

The king's instructions come in a series of terse imperative verbs: rise up, disguise yourself, go to Shiloh, and take specific provisions. Robert Alter notes that when a sequence of verbs is attributed to a single speaker, the message conveyed is one of intensity, rapidity, and purposefulness of activity.[17]

Jeroboam wastes no time with courtesies. Rather than offering comfort or tenderness, he commands his wife, treating her as if she were one of the slave laborers he used to supervise, or as one of his military subordinates (cf. 1 Kgs 11:28; 13:4). Just as laborers and military personnel were expected to obey without question, Jeroboam's wife offers no protest. The scene is a cold one, with no mention of the couple's shared grief over the child they conceived together. No kind words escape the king's lips in response to this mother's natural suffering and anguish.[18]

Jeroboam's attitude toward his wife reveals his character. Ignoring any needs she may have, he selfishly manipulates and uses her to his own advantage. His attitude emphasizes that he believes she exists for his purposes. His refusal to engage in direct dialogue with her and his willingness to hide behind her as he seeks sensitive information from the alienated prophet portrays his essential cowardice. He in effect ignores her as a person. He treats her as one of his servants. Verses 1–3 reveal multiple discourtesies; they raise a red flag about the marital relationship of the royals.

Earlier, the prophet Ahijah had torn his new cloak into ten strips, symbolic of the ten tribes of Israel that were to be torn away from the house of David and given to Jeroboam. Perhaps in a way reminiscent of this more favorable occasion, Jeroboam now commands his wife to take ten loaves of bread to the prophet. More hopeful than confident, Jeroboam then utters the self-fulfilling prophecy that Ahijah will tell her what will happen to their son (14:3).

One can only surmise Jeroboam's reasons for choosing not to visit Ahijah in person: fear of another unfavorable prophetic word, fear of another shriveled hand, or fear of an even worse fate. Jeroboam acts like a man who knows he deserves judgment—and fears it. Jeroboam's motive in ordering his wife's disguise may have been to deceive the prophet and thereby to obtain a more sympathetic revelation.[19] Here again the narrative reminds us of the earlier actions of Saul (1 Sam 28:8), who went in disguise to seek information from the medium at Endor.

Biblical dialogue often allows individual traits to become apparent even through fragmentary language.[20] In Jeroboam's case, his specific instructions to his wife reveal more than craftiness, discourtesy, abruptness, and an abrasive command mentality. Despite his confidence that the prophet has revelatory powers, he believes he can manipulate the prophet, now blind and old, and get whatever he wants. Jeroboam in this respect also reminds the reader of crafty Jacob. But unlike Jeroboam, Jacob wrestled with God, bargained with God, and acknowledged God. In wrestling with God, Jacob wrested a blessing from him (Gen 32:22–32). Sadly, the Jeroboam cycle (1 Kgs 11–14) never records a time when Jeroboam sought the Lord.

The quiet acquiescence of Jeroboam's unnamed wife suggests that she may have been used to her husband's rude treatment. The couple's lack of conversation may indicate her hopelessness and sad resignation regarding the futility of trying to talk things out with him. Perhaps her silence indicates scorn, her chosen form of retaliation. Like Abraham, who remained silent and did not question God when told to take a journey and sacrifice his son Isaac (Gen 22), Jeroboam's wife prepares to fulfill her husband's wishes without dispute. As she begins her journey, one can only speculate as to whether she traveled out of mere compliance to Jeroboam's wishes or with confidence in the God of Abraham. Sadly, by the end of her journey, there is no mention of any initiative on her part to seek the God of Abraham.

Ahijah's Prophecy

Although the text says that Ahijah's eyes are gone because of age (1 Kgs 14:4), the Lord acts as his eyes, showing that the prophetic word comes with a seeing and a knowing that are independent of human senses.[21] Although Jeroboam's wife disguises herself, her disguise, like Saul's, proves futile. Ahijah hears the woman's approach, invites her in, and immediately identifies her as the wife of Jeroboam. By addressing her in terms of her function as the wife of Jeroboam, the prophet acknowledges that she comes as Jeroboam's emissary and not as an independent woman. Although the prophet's salutation expresses kindness to her, he nevertheless has harsh prophetic words to deliver. When she returns home, she returns as the prophet's emissary.

Ahijah first asks why she has come in disguise.[22] Without waiting for her reply, he suddenly switches pronouns. She has not come to him; *he* has been sent to *her!* The narrator uses irony here, for logistically Ahijah has not moved and the wife of Jeroboam has indeed come to him. Yet when Ahijah says he is the one sent, he adopts the prophet's authoritative role as the commissioned one. The tables suddenly turn, reminding the reader and the woman that God controls the destinies of royals, prophets, and readers. Jeroboam, king of Israel, cannot control God, the king of the universe.

Furthermore, the prophet announces that he has been sent to her with bad news.[23] The prophecy comes swiftly, directly. Even as Jeroboam had ordered her to rise up and go (v. 2), Ahijah now orders her to return to Jeroboam with specific words. The prophetic word contrasts God's goodness in electing Jeroboam with Jeroboam's ungrateful response to it (vv. 7–9). Speaking in the name of the God of Israel, Ahijah recounts how God tore the kingdom from the house of David and raised up Jeroboam to be king over God's people, Israel. The Lord, speaking through the prophet, adds, however, that Jeroboam is not like "my servant David who kept my commandments and who followed after me with all his heart" (v. 8). Here Jeroboam resembles Saul, Israel's first king: God called Saul to lead Israel but later rejected him because of his disobedience (1 Sam 15).

Like a prosecutor reading a list of indictments, Ahijah specifies the charges. By promoting wholesale idolatry, Jeroboam has done more evil than all the others who came before him (v. 9). God's charge through the prophet does not dignify these idols with names. By turning the people from the living God to graven images, Jeroboam has "thrust God behind him." The Hebrew term *shalah,* here translated "thrust behind," means "to cast off or throw away" and speaks of the outright rejection of a person or thing.[24] In this context the term signifies a momentous event, like Moses' action of hurling down the tablets of the Law in anger (Exod 32:19; Deut 9:17; cf. Mic 7:19).

Verses 10 and 11 merit more detailed scrutiny. The Hebrew phrase *'atsur ve 'azuv* (v. 10) contains a pair of parallel words translated either "slave and free" or "helpless and abandoned." The phrase represents a narrative alliteration "of utter loathing";[25] both renderings indicate the annihilation of Jeroboam's house. The prophecy shows great contempt for Jeroboam's house by defining it dramatically and deliberately in terms of male urination practices. The prophecy about Jeroboam's house follows the pattern of other prophecies against the house of Baasha and the house of Ahab (1 Kgs 16:1–4; 21:20–24). Because a verbatim fulfillment follows immediately, it promotes an underlying view of historical causality. The prophecy serves as a sharp narrative device pointing to the unswerving authority of a monotheistic God who at this instant chooses to communicate his will via the words of the prophet Ahijah. Furthermore, the prophecy reinforces the view throughout Scripture that God controls the destinies of nations (see Jer 1 and Amos 1–2, among many examples).

God says he will burn away (Heb. *ba'ar*) Jeroboam's memory and influence from the land. The verb *ba'ar* carries the sense of relentless pursuit of all that is Jeroboam's. Burning away, when accompanied by God's wrath, terrifies! Will God's wrath come? Jeroboam made the grave mistake of making God his enemy, as did others before him: the priest Eli, Saul, the Canaanites, and the Amalekites.[26] The prophetic word notes that God keenly felt Jeroboam's rejection. "You thrust me behind your back" (v. 9), God says through Ahijah.

God returns Jeroboam's rejection and contempt by confirming that his household will be eaten by dogs and birds (vv. 10–11). The reference to birds echoes a curse in the treaty of Esarhaddon, king of Assyria, with Baal of Tyre. One of its entries announces that eagles and vultures will eat the treasonous flesh of any who break the treaty.[27] The reference to dung emphasizes God's abhorrence of Jeroboam. The judgment of no decent burial echoes the fear of public humiliation common to peoples in the ancient Near East. Jeremiah delivers a similar curse to Jehoiakim (Jer 22:18–19). Even as God was able to tear ten tribes from Solomon and give them to Jeroboam, God has the power to cut off the house of Jeroboam. Significantly, God's judgment is not arbitrary; it responds to Jeroboam's willful, prolonged choice of disobedience and idolatry.[28]

Ahijah's rapid-fire prophecy leaves no room for the wife of Jeroboam to respond. Quite likely it renders her speechless, riveting her to the spot. She may be overcome and perhaps even collapses, because Ahijah tells her to rise up (Heb. *qumi*) and go home. Even as she departs, the prophetic word continues. The boy whose fate she sought to know will die as soon as her feet enter the city, and all Israel will grieve.[29] Yet grace pervades even in judgment: Abijah alone of the house of Jeroboam has found favor with the Lord and will receive a proper burial (vv. 12–13).

THE PROPHETIC WORD TO ISRAEL

So far, the prophetic word concerns Jeroboam and his house. With 1 Kgs 14:14, the prophetic word begins to mete out punishment more broadly to the kingdom of Israel for its misdeeds against God. The prophetic word works from the family house (micro level) to the house of Israel (macro level). God will strike, uproot, and scatter Israel (v. 15).

With its three verbs in the active voice, 1 Kgs 14:15 is the first prophetic word in Deuteronomistic History announcing judgment on the northern kingdom of Israel. This incredible word to an unnamed woman acts as a fulcrum marking a change of direction in Israel's path. Just as Jeroboam made God angry, so Israel has incited God's wrath by making Asherah poles for worship. As a result, the nation will be scattered and destroyed (1 Kgs 14:9, 15). Significantly, the verbs recur in God's later prophetic word through Jeremiah to Judah—God will scatter and smite Judah (Jer 49:32; 21:6). The sins of Jeroboam become a standard by which all other kings of Israel are judged.

To this silent, unnamed woman, the wife of Jeroboam, God reveals his will and plan concerning the northern kingdom, Israel. This obscure character receives riveting, history-changing news. God does not ignore her. The prophetic word of striking, uprooting, and scattering a nation is placed in the context of a much smaller, more intimate personal consultation. A mother arrives seeking her son's fate and hears of the destruction of her husband's shameful dynasty and the larger destruction of Israel. No time frame—months, days, or years away—accompanies the prophecy. But its veracity and immanence coincide with the prophetic word about her son: he does die as soon as she returns home.

The words of the prophet concerning her son are fulfilled with the slight alteration that the boy dies when she crosses the threshold of her home and not when she enters the city (1 Kgs 14:12, cf. v. 17). Like Saul, who faced his last battle with the Philistines knowing he would die (1 Sam 28:19), she knows the deadly, heartbreaking, and ultimately horrific outcomes of her return home. Yet she goes back. Initially when she went to the prophet Ahijah, she represented Jeroboam. Now when she returns home, she represents Ahijah. As an intermediary, she links the two men and sets in motion the prophetic word on both the micro (family) and macro (national) scenes.

ANONYMOUS WOMEN

The wife of Jeroboam is one of a number of anonymous women in 1 and 2 Kgs who are tragically connected to one another by the untimely deaths of their sons. The wife of Jeroboam shares space with the prostitutes who approach Solomon (1 Kgs 3:16–28); the widow of Zarephath (1 Kgs 17:8–24); and the Shunammite (2 Kgs 4:8–37). As anonymous women, they are narrative antonyms—opposites—of the major characters, the named prophets and kings in the stories; this is a typical feature of Deuteronomistic History. But in the Hebrew Bible, anonymous women consistently break out of molds.[30] They emerge with distinct personalities and definable characteristics.

Anonymous women like the wife of Jeroboam in this story accomplish two narrative purposes. First, they direct attention to the named male characters with whom they interact. Second, their anonymity deflects attention from them as people and highlights their roles.[31] The narrative tradition emphasizes dialogue and allows actions to attest to character traits. Their functions as wife, slave child, prostitute, queen, widow, or wise woman define them.

Unlike the anonymous women who have speaking roles, the wife of Jeroboam remains both anonymous and silent. Nevertheless, her silence sheds light on Ahijah's and Jeroboam's character traits. By muting her, the narrator shows Jeroboam's propensity toward manipulating events, people, and God. He is a biblical example of what today we would call a control freak. His tendency to control may be based on fear. Earlier, in order not to lose control of the kingdom, he erected golden bull calves at Dan and Bethel. Then he led people in offering illicit sacrifices, a sin that two generations earlier had cost Saul his kingdom (1 Sam 15).[32] Jeroboam's maneuver of sending his wife as an undercover ambassador indicates that he thinks he can hoodwink God and God's prophet—both fatal actions in themselves.[33]

The silence of the wife of Jeroboam sheds light on Ahijah's character by showing him to be a prophet who obeys God. In literary terms, he stands in stark contrast to the disobedient prophet of chapter 13. Knowing disobedience brings death, Ahijah expresses no such tendency! Instead, like Samuel to Saul, he renders the words of doom to the wife of Jeroboam without sweetening or editing them.[34] The wife of Jeroboam came for a word from God and got it. Her silent return sets in motion God's word to her son, her household, and her nation.

First Kings 14 has both political and theological significance. Politically, Jeroboam's disobedience decides the fate of his house, just as Saul's disobedience sealed the fate of his house. Throughout the history of Israel and Judah thus far, naming a royal successor has remained God's right exclusively. Through the prophetic word, God reveals his purpose to raise up a new king whose purpose is to cut down Jeroboam's family (1 Kgs 14:14). Theologically, Jeroboam's evil, which builds on the disobedience of Saul and Solomon, becomes the standard of evil for the rest of the kings of Israel, and the prophecy against him turns up in the prophetic curses on other households. Baasha, another evil king of Israel, receives a similar prophecy: like Jeroboam's house, his house will end up as dog food and bird pickings (1 Kgs 16:4). Likewise, Ahab's house soon will fare the same (1 Kgs 21:24).

The blame the text places on Jeroboam for the disastrous events soon befalling Israel typifies ancient Near Eastern literature because it attributes Israel's destruction to the sins of its leader.[35] First Kings 14:1–18 solves a dilemma for the narrator—it justifies the northern kingdom's ultimate destruction and exile.[36]

The theme of obedience always figures prominently in Deuteronomistic History. The prophet Samuel tells Saul that obedience is better than sacrifice (1 Sam 15:22). Solomon disobeys by seeking other gods outside the covenant. Certainly disobedience prevails as a theme in the Jeroboam cycle. In 1 Kgs 13, the man of God dies because he violates God's command not to eat or drink before returning home. Jeroboam erects idols of metal, and he too will die. Choice, certainly, factors in these events. Saul, Solomon, the man of God, and Jeroboam each choose disobedience. The meaning for Israel is clear: follow Saul, Solomon, the man of God, and Jeroboam in their disobedience and perish. If that is Israel's choice, then just as Jeroboam's family will be judged, so will Israel. With the Jeroboam cycle, the narrator sets the stage for a contrast in kings. Jeroboam's disobedience and evil become a foil for good kings—Asa, Hezekiah, and Josiah, all of Judah. Ironically, the lad Abijah merits the only favor the Lord gives to the house of Jeroboam, and Abijah dies long before maturity. Ironically, the only adult family member in 1 Kgs 14 in the house of Jeroboam who obeys God is the unnamed, overlooked, ignored wife of Jeroboam. Ironically, obedience finds its home in this obscure woman—but brings no joy or reward.

Passive, yet Significant

Defined solely in terms of her relationship to Jeroboam, the wife of Jeroboam seems a passive, flat character. Yet despite her silence and anonymity, she holds her own between two strong, dominant, named male characters in chapter 14—Jeroboam and Ahijah. She enters the text when Jeroboam summons her and commands her to go disguised to the prophet Ahijah to learn the fate of their son. She leaves the text when the prophet, after saying her son will die, commands her to return home. She obeys both commands.

To her come the first prophetic word of the upcoming destruction of her house and—far more important—the first prophetic word of the upcoming destruction of Israel. The wife of Jeroboam, an obscure character at first glance, holds an important literary position because of the significance of the words spoken to her. Like an arrow in flight, this silent messenger returns home bearing the prophetic words and inaugurates their fulfillment in the death of her child and the destruction of her household and her nation.

The woman appears in all three scenes. Although she is referred to generically as the wife of Jeroboam throughout the chapter, the text enlarges her character by casting her as the mother of the ill child. She bridges the chasm between Jeroboam, their son, and Ahijah.

The woman's passivity piques the reader's curiosity. One wonders, *Is she stupid?* Does she not understand the prophetic word? Perhaps someone with more spirit would repent, try to delay the prophecy, circumvent it, or see if God might relent! Ahab tries this effectively (1 Kgs 21:29). The reader wonders why she remains unresponsive and why she dutifully heads home, having been told her entrance will bring death. The narrator leaves these questions unanswered, choosing instead to focus on the sins of Jeroboam. Perhaps, however, she understands the prophetic word all too well and knows it will inevitably find fulfillment.

EVIDENCE OF ABUSE

There is yet another way of understanding the woman's passivity. The wife of Jeroboam and her marriage indicate the classic signs of spousal abuse. Granted, the verses about her reveal no physical beating. But other textual evidence suggests that she is an abused wife and that Jeroboam is the abuser. Evidence that the wife of Jeroboam experienced abuse includes the following:

- her isolation
- her passivity
- her instant obedience
- her unquestioning return
- her lack of response to Jeroboam and Ahijah

Evidence that Jeroboam is an abuser includes the following:

- his command mode and manner of addressing his wife
- his use of emotional control over his wife
- his lack of compassion toward her when their son becomes ill
- his insecurity over going to Ahijah himself
- his lack of courage
- his earlier violence toward the man of God (1 Kgs 13)
- his persistent choice to do evil

As part of the law governing the covenant community, women were to be treated well in Israel and were not to be abused.[37] For instance, if a man took a second wife, he was not to deprive the first one of "her food, clothing, and marital rights" (Exod 21:10). If Jeroboam was in violation of these provisions, the judgment of evil against him (1 Kgs 14:9) and the later pairing of his sins and evil (see 2 Kgs 13:2; 13:11; 14:24; 15:9, 18; and chapter 24, for example) as the evaluative standard of the character and activities of the kings of Israel enlarge the definition of evil to include an indictment against wife abuse.[38]

JEROBOAM: AN ABUSING HUSBAND

Jeroboam, chosen by God to be king of Israel, recipient of a covenant covering his house for generation after generation if he obeys God, is a man who becomes a byword and definition for evil (1 Kgs 11:26–40; 2 Kgs 3:3). In one of the most startling downward spirals in the Hebrew Bible, Jeroboam falls from being described as a *gibbor hayil,* a man of standing (1 Kgs 11:28), to becoming the standard for measuring evil and sin (1 Kgs 14:9). Jeroboam also fits the pattern (for lack of a better word) of an abuser. Abuse is a modern word for the age-old condition of excessive physical and/or mental and emotional control over another.

In her book on domestic violence, Margi Laird McCue[39] provides a comprehensive character sketch of an abusive male. Traits of an abuser include low self-esteem, a belief in male superiority, the tendency to blame others for one's actions, a pathological jealousy, a dual personality, severe stress reactions, the frequent use of sex as an act of aggression, and a refusal to believe that one's actions may have negative consequences. An abusive man is jealous and possessive of his wife's time. He stalks her, eavesdrops on her, puts her under surveillance, and monitors her activities.

The biblical narrative substantiates that Jeroboam possesses a number of these characteristics. He monitors and directs his wife's activities. His reaction to the man of God's decree against him (1 Kgs 13) is severe anger over his withered hand. He refuses to believe that his setting up golden calves in Dan and Bethel will have severe consequences. Although given several opportunities, he expresses no repentance or remorse.[40] He sends his wife on a potentially dangerous errand totally alone and without protection.

A person like Jeroboam, who demonstrates marked leadership characteristics, may be an abuser in the privacy of one-on-one encounters. According to James Alsdurf and Phyllis Alsdurf, men who batter their wives are often articulate, function successfully in their jobs, and are competent in their roles outside of marriage. They come from all walks of life, and many hold positions of leadership.[41]

An abuser is typically both bully and coward. Jeroboam's actions indicate he wants to control all situations.[42] He displays his feelings of insecurity as a leader by erecting golden calves at Dan and Bethel (1 Kgs 12:26–30). Hunger to keep his position reveals a desire to have and to

wield power as king.[43] Jeroboam is jealous of Jerusalem's position as
the center of Israel's festivals, hence his building of shrines, installation
of priests, offering of sacrifices, and institution of rival festivals (1 Kgs
12:31–33). If this trait of jealousy extended toward his wife, this too
would fit the profile of an abuser.[44]

Jeroboam's lack of remorse raises the further question of whether he
was psychopathic. Most normally-socialized men go through periods
of remorse if they abuse their wives.[45] Psychopathic men, however, do
not suffer normal pangs of conscience. Jeroboam displays no remorse
about any of his actions. Instead, throughout the lengthy textual space
devoted to his twenty-two-year reign (1 Kgs 11–14), he intensifies his
counter-covenant actions with innovative religious reforms that are
subsequently described as evil.

Because Jeroboam acts in an emotionally uninvolved way, he may
fit the profile of a severe personality disorder called ESS (Extremely
Self-Serving). According to Gary Hankins and Carol Hankins,[46] a husband with this disorder is so self-centered that he believes he has every
right to do whatever he wants to his wife. An ESS husband regards his
wife as his personal property.

The isolation of Jeroboam's wife bears additional scrutiny. It shows
that Jeroboam regards her as one who must obey, perhaps even as one of
his servants. He purposefully isolates his wife. His mode of communication with her permits no response. His treatment of her shows that he
views her as someone who deserves to be ordered around, as one who
lives to meet his needs. Issuing commands would seem to be his normal
method of communication and operation toward her.[47] He keeps her in
her place, and her place—as he views it—is to be subservient to him.[48]
At his command, she journeys deceitfully disguised and dangerously
unaccompanied to the prophet.

THE MARRIAGE OF THE ROYALS

Although outwardly Jeroboam and his wife play the role of a married couple, inwardly their marriage has come to an end long before
they appear together in 1 Kgs 14.[49] The small vignette recording their
encounter abounds with evidence of the deterioration of their relationship. We find no evidence of a personal connection between them.[50]
Jeroboam treats his wife with abruptness. His treatment indicates he
views her as one whose purpose is to meet his demands. He takes no

personal responsibility for the quality of their marriage. In the command mode, he portrays no tenderness, no respect, and clearly no love toward her. The wife of Jeroboam exudes lifelessness. Her passivity makes her seem emotionally dead inside. Unlike other women in Kings—the widow of Zarephath, Jezebel, Athaliah, and Jehosheba,[51] strong women portrayed as good and bad—the wife of Jeroboam exudes no self-confidence.

In any marriage, the partners assume roles that if not comfortable are at least habitual. Often a woman living in an abusive situation functions as the heroic martyr, concealer, placater, rescuer, and victim. In doing so, she can become an unwitting enabler of the abuse:

> A classic victim didn't ask for this situation, whatever it is. The victim could be happy if only all this weren't happening. She is the soul most to be pitied because she is so very nice down inside and none of this was deserved. The victim who is the enabler is a self-pitying person, but a true victim does not perceive of herself in this self-pitying way.[52]

In the marriage of the king of Israel and his wife, Jeroboam acts as the decision-maker, the one who orders others around, the commander. The wife of Jeroboam is a concealer and a resigned enabler of her husband's cowardice.

THE POSSIBILITY OF VIOLENCE

The terse, strained interaction between Jeroboam and his wife raises the possibility of violence in their marriage. Research stresses that a wife's actions are not the cause or precipitator of violence.[53] Quite the contrary: violence is a specific choice made by an abusive husband.[54] A man's violence is a man's choice of behavior.[55] At the heart of violent actions is the condition of the heart. Until this heart condition is changed and sin is acknowledged, violence will continue.[56]

The question of power in a relationship appears to play a significant role in battering. Some studies show that this begins before marriage.[57] There are attempts to dominate one's partner via financial, social, and decision-making control. Some researchers theorize that because men of lower socioeconomic status are more likely to batter, they do so to assert the power they lack economically and/or socially. Violence becomes the tactic that compensates for the control, power, independence, and self-sufficiency these men lack in other areas.[58] Although

Jeroboam as king of Israel enjoyed financial security, he may have used domestic violence to bolster his personal insecurity.

According to popular culture, violence is a response to stress, the result of poor family modeling, and the outcome of failure to be aware of one's feelings. However, this is not an adequate discernment of where the battle lies. Alsdurf and Alsdurf argue that battering and violence are expressions of evil and must be confronted on a spiritual level because they are spiritual problems.[59] The prophetic word charges Jeroboam with making for himself other gods, idols made of metal. Instead of seeking the God of Israel, Jeroboam provoked the God of Israel to anger (1 Kgs 14:9).

Violence by the batterer is violence done on the batterer's own behalf. It is violence designed to serve oneself and attain power over others. It is violence based on a lust for power, a lust that destroys.[60] Jeroboam's violent behavior toward the man of God (1 Kgs 13) and his treatment of his wife (1 Kgs 14) show that he gears his actions to attain power over others.

Battering denotes elements of control and a fight for pre-eminence in a hierarchy. Battering also involves terror, power, ownership, and entitlement.[61] The problem of wife abuse is not one of feminism, secular humanism, or a lack of leadership in the home. It is the problem of evil—unseen and unopposed.[62]

RETURNING TO ABUSE

After hearing Ahijah's prophesy, why does the wife of Jeroboam go back? Indeed, if she is an abused wife, then why does she stay? These are excellent questions, and research on abuse again provides the needed perspective.[63] The wife of Jeroboam returns home, and her return sets in motion the chain of events leading to the death of her son, the extinction of the house of Jeroboam, and the extinction of the Northern Kingdom. Recent research on domestic violence finds that an abused woman who returns home after a battering session most often has been married for a long time; she is not a newlywed. Judging from the age of Abijah and the placement of the story of his illness, his parents have been married for a minimum of ten years.

The primary reason an abused woman stays in an abusive relationship is fear—either fear of the abuser or of the future consequences of leaving.[64] According to recent research, the long-term effect of the repeated and unpredictable situations of terror to which battered women are subjected is that they become afraid of staying in their marriages and yet are more terrified of leaving.[65] In the case of the wife of Jeroboam, where could she go? Who would take her in? The arm of the king extended throughout the kingdom. Quite likely she does not know what to do because she does not know if her actions will bring her what she longs for the most—safety.[66]

A closer look at fear reveals that it also involves extensive loss. An abused woman fears the loss of her family, the loss of her reputation and status, the loss of her children, the loss of her home, the loss of her income. Consequently, many an abused woman in the modern world faces the cultural pressure and economic necessity to "stay put."[67] Surprisingly, research reveals that women of higher socioeconomic status tend to turn inward when encountering spousal aggression.[68] Arguably, the silence of the wife of Jeroboam is not because she is stupid but because she has turned inward. She seeks safety from a frightening exterior world by turning inward to a quiet place inside where at least she can control the silence.

Interviews with abused women indicate that they repeatedly return to abusive relationships because they retain a naïve hope of resolving the conflict and avoiding personal and marital failure. Even those who have sought outside help go back to their abusers once the tension has subsided.[69] Perhaps the wife of Jeroboam returns because she is familiar with the cycle of abuse (a build-up of tension, anger, rage, explosion, a "honeymoon period," a renewed build-up of tension, etc.).[70] She knows the habits of her husband and calculates that the timing in the cycle of abuse favors a time of relative peace. Whatever her reasoning, the wife of Jeroboam reenters her abusive world and continues to act in a passive, non-provoking way.[71]

It is significant that the narrative in 1 Kings gives no background information about the wife of Jeroboam. We read nothing about where she came from or who her parents were.[72] Although we lack specific evidence in her case, social learning psychologists theorize that women who grow up in a home where they witness their mothers being beaten are more likely to become victims themselves.[73] In an ironic twist that emphasizes the passivity of the wife of Jeroboam, Jeroboam's mother and her status are mentioned (1 Kgs 11:26). The text introduces Jeroboam as an Ephraimite, the son of Nebat, and an official of Solomon who rebels against the king and describes his mother as a widow named Zeruah.

In a sense, the text slights the wife of Jeroboam by excluding details about her. Economic standing is no safeguard against abusive relationships. An affluent woman today may be married to a man at the top of his career, have children, and be active in her community. She may entertain guests regularly in her home, yet privately her life may be a nightmare.[74] Faced with social embarrassment and shame, she may not feel that she can go to family or friends for help. The husband may manage the credit cards, or as a couple they may have jointly owned assets. Despite her affluence, she may feel helpless in her abusive situation.[75] Her abusive husband's money only enhances his power, and she faces the prospect of losing custody of her children as well as her home and her social status.[76] Although Jeroboam's wife lived in Israel in c. 915 B.C.E., it is likely that she faced the same dynamics that keep affluent wives in abusive relationships today.

Although it may seem that the simplest solution to the problem of domestic abuse is for the woman to leave, studies show that women separated or divorced from their abuser actually increase their likelihood of encountering further abuse.[77] The cold reality is that women who try to escape the cycle of abuse are often beaten or killed for it.[78] A Florida study showed that fifty-seven percent of men who killed their wives were living apart from them at the time of the killing.[79] Another study revealed that fifty-five percent of assaults against separated women were perpetrated by males they knew and that more than fifteen percent of assaults on married women were domestic.[80] If it is true that the wife of Jeroboam lived under the tyranny of a powerful abuser, it seems likely that she also would have understood that the consequences of escape could be fatal.

WAS SHE ABUSED?

The biblical text shows that the wife of Jeroboam, like modern women in abusive situations, adopts a strategy for coping with abnormal and unusually frightening situations.[81] Her strategy involves silence, denial, passivity, instant obedience, isolation, and minimalizing herself.[82] Denial and minimalization enable an abused woman to live with what is happening and to avoid feelings of terror and humiliation.[83] Battered women may suffer a range of psychosocial problems not because they are sick but because they are battered.[84] The wife of Jeroboam's silence may indicate a pattern in her marriage of being blamed for everything. She may be reasoning that if she says nothing, maybe Jeroboam won't affix blame to her. Research finds that the abuser blames the woman because he feels a loss of control.[85]

Although the wife of Jeroboam arguably sees few alternatives to her loveless and possibly abusive situation, she is a survivor. It is important to give abused women credit. Victims of domestic violence are survivors. Many find various ways to contain the abuse until they are able to leave the relationship. The coping strategies they work out enable them to put their feelings on hold so that they can deal with the day-to-day challenges of living in a violent and dangerous home. An abused woman may adopt survival strategies like learned helplessness. She may dissociate, self-hypnotize, and emotionally distance herself from her situation.[86]

Often a woman in an abusive situation thinks she has only two choices: physical death or psychological death. If she leaves, she fears the reprisal of the abuser. But if she stays, she runs the risk of psychological death. The wife of Jeroboam, if indeed she is the victim of domestic violence, chooses psychological death, and the price, as indicated by her silence, is depression. As victims of violence, abused women may, like the victims of post-traumatic stress syndrome, experience prolonged depression.[87] Her silence may likewise indicate disintegration anxiety, in which the victim shows a serious loss of initiative, a profound drop in self-esteem, and a sense of total meaninglessness.[88]

Again, the woman's silence also may indicate her intense suffering. A woman's sense of self and self-worth are often determined by the input and opinions of others.[89] Jeroboam's treatment of his wife arguably indicates a contempt for her and a deliberate devaluing of her as a person.

Perhaps the most tragic note in the lives of Jeroboam and his wife is that the biblical text gives no hint of any statement of faith, no sign that they sought God together. They pursue God's prophet to gain information about the outcome of their son's illness, but there is no indication that they seek to deepen their relationship with God. It is possible that along with her low self-esteem, the wife of Jeroboam also has a low estimation of God and his concern for her plight. Nancy Leigh DeMoss believes that the central problem of many modern women is not low self-esteem or a poor self-image, but a poor image of God. "Our need is not to love ourselves more but to receive His incredible love for us and to accept His design and purpose for our lives," DeMoss writes.[90]

Her counsel is good advice for women struggling with difficult or even abusive domestic partnerships.

SUMMARY AND CONCLUSION

In 1 Kgs 14, the prophet Ahijah assesses the reign of Jeroboam and finds it lacking. He then delivers two harsh words of judgment from God against the house of Jeroboam and the first word of destruction against Israel. This three-pronged prophecy toward a house and a nation reinforces the biblical principle that God's covenants are conditional, requiring obedience on both individual and national levels. The story of Eli the priest and his sons represented for Jeroboam an important precedent (1 Sam 2:27–36). The prophetic word against Eli provides a stern warning of God's wrath against those in positions of authority who persistently and wilfully disobey. Ironically, the histories of Eli and Jeroboam contain sad similarities: the prominence of two boys, Abijah and Samuel. God earlier promised Eli "that your house and your father's house would minister before me forever" (1 Sam 2:30), but Eli's sons degraded the Lord's presence at Shiloh, and Eli failed to reprimand them. So God decreed destruction through a prophetic word given through the boy Samuel (1 Sam 3:11–14).

Through the prophet Ahijah, God had earlier given Jeroboam a similar promise of blessing when he was one of Solomon's workmen: "You will rule over all that your heart desires; you will be king over Israel. If you do whatever I command you and walk in my ways and do what is right in my eyes by keeping my statues and commands as my servant David did, I will be with you" (1 Kgs 11:37–38). God's subsequent counter-message of humiliating destruction to the house follows the principle established with Eli and continued under Solomon—the necessity of unswerving obedience to the Lord.

The houses of Eli and Jeroboam resemble each other in yet one more telling aspect. The prophecy against Eli's house comes through a child, Samuel; the prophecy against Jeroboam's house comes about because of the illness of a child, Abijah. Both prophecies predict a thorough annihilation of the houses. Both children are the only ones with whom the Lord is pleased.

The wife of Jeroboam, the mother of Abijah, is a colorless character muzzled in the text. The chapter does not enlarge upon her role as queen, her physical appearance, any emotions she experiences because of her son's illness, or her reaction to Ahijah's catastrophic prophecy. In the way her husband orders her around, the text hints that her marriage is unhappy and perhaps even abusive. She obeys her husband, the prophet, and God, but without any deep sense of purpose. Although she is a major participant in the chapter and the link connecting Jeroboam and Ahijah, the wife of Jeroboam herself appears flat; she lacks personal impact.[91]

Yet, like a placid pond, her character provides a clear reflection of the two men named in the story, Jeroboam, king of Israel, and Ahijah, the prophet who prophesied he would be king (1 Kgs 11:30–39). In his interaction with her, Jeroboam emerges as one accustomed to command, as one used to things going his way, as one insensitive to the emotional needs of his wife, and perhaps even as one who routinely and abusively tramples on those emotional needs. The way he orders her around shows that he treats people—even his wife—as objects and as means to achieve his ends. Jeroboam fears no human—but he does fear circumstances he cannot control: a shriveled hand and the potentially fatal illness of his son, Abijah.

The blandness of the wife of Jeroboam also allows the character of the prophet Ahijah to come more clearly into focus. Ahijah's interaction with her when she visits him disguised shows him to be one who listens to and obeys God. Ahijah, though blind, sees through her disguise because the Lord had told him to expect her arrival. Although she is the one who has journeyed, disguised, to see the prophet, he greets her by saying that *he* is the one who has in fact been sent to *her*.

Despite the predicted disaster, perhaps the prophet's choice of the verb "sent" opens up a possible means of repentance, for Ps 107:20 says, "He sent his word and healed them and delivered them from their destructions."[92] Yet Jeroboam and his household fail to repent. Israel fails to repent. So the prophetic word instead propels the plot forward toward household and national destruction. Years later, in 722 B.C.E., the prophecy achieves fulfillment when the Assyrians trample Israel. The annihilation of Jeroboam's household comes much sooner. Baasha assassinates Nadab, Jeroboam's son and successor, and systematically kills off Jeroboam's whole family (1 Kgs 15:25–30). Jeroboam reigned from about 930 to 909 B.C.E., and his household was exterminated probably by 907.[93]

The prophecy to the wife of Jeroboam illustrates a persistent theological theme in the Bible: God often starts a great work in a small way, with a woman or with a child. Usually this is a good work, as in the births of Isaac, Joseph, Moses, Samson, and Samuel. Each birth comes with much rejoicing and ultimately signals deliverance, the fulfillment of a promise, or an upcoming great move of God. This time, however, a boy's illness and death signal national death rather than national deliverance. Through Ahijah's prophecy to this unnamed woman, God chooses to announce Israel's upcoming destruction. The prophetic word does not come to the public at large in a public setting but rather to a mother concerned about her son, to a wife sent on an errand by her cowardly husband, to a queen ordered to go disguised on a journey by her king. The prophetic word Ahijah gives sends her home (1 Kgs 14:12). But the one to whom she returns, the one who currently leads Israel into sin, fails to repent. The text remains silent on Jeroboam's reign after the prophetic word. It merely recounts its end in a formulaic expression.

The wife of Jeroboam is important in the flow of biblical history because of the prophecy she receives. God's plan to uproot and scatter Israel is revealed first to this unnamed woman. Her return home sets in motion events that lead to her son's death, the destruction of her household, and the overthrow of Israel. Obedient, mysterious, and mute, she nonetheless figures prominently in Israel's history because of the significance of the prophetic word she transmits. If indeed she is an abused wife, God's judgment against Jeroboam (1 Kgs 14:9) significantly expands the concept and definition of evil beyond idolatry. Seen in this light, the text—and God—accord the wife of Jeroboam significance and dignity. The text—and God—hold Jeroboam accountable.

QUESTIONS FOR FURTHER REFLECTION

1. As you reflect on the events of 1 Kgs 14, focus on the main characters in the narrative. What was Jeroboam like? How would you describe Jeroboam's wife? What was Ahijah like?

2. The first three verses of the chapter describe the detailed instructions Jeroboam gave his wife in order to find out what would

happen to their son. What do these instructions suggest to you about Jeroboam's motives and character?

3. Why do you think Jeroboam's wife complied with her husband's commands? Why do you think she went along with his attempt to deceive the prophet of God?

4. Do you think the wife of Jeroboam was an abused woman? Give reasons for your opinion.

5. Jeroboam's wife also obeys Ahijah's command to return home. What might have motivated her to obey the prophet's request even though he had predicted that her return would trigger her son's death? In answering this question, consider the range of emotions that might have wrestled in her heart, among them fear, anger, resignation, desperation, and hatred. How might you have responded in similar circumstances?

6. Ironically, the boy Abijah, described as the only one in the house of Jeroboam who found favor with the Lord, is doomed to die as soon as his mother returns home. She must return, knowing that she will lose her son. How would you react in similar circumstances? What advice would you give this woman if you were to accompany her on her return journey?

7. Overall, do you think the wife of Jeroboam serves as a positive or negative role model for women today? Tell why you think so.

7

THE WIDOW OF ZAREPHATH
VALIDATING GOD'S PROPHET

¹Now Elijah the Tishbite, from Tishbe in Gilead, said to Ahab, "As the LORD, the God of Israel, lives, whom I serve, there will be neither dew nor rain in the next few years except at my word."

²Then the word of the LORD came to Elijah: ³"Leave here, turn eastward and hide in the Kerith Ravine, east of the Jordan. ⁴You will drink from the brook, and I have ordered the ravens to feed you there."

⁵So he did what the LORD had told him. He went to the Kerith Ravine, east of the Jordan, and stayed there. ⁶The ravens brought him bread and meat in the morning and bread and meat in the evening, and he drank from the brook.

⁷Some time later the brook dried up because there had been no rain in the land. ⁸Then the word of the LORD came to him: ⁹"Go at once to Zarephath of Sidon and stay there. I have commanded a widow in that place to supply you with food." ¹⁰So he went to Zarephath. When he came to the town gate, a widow was there gathering sticks. He called to her and asked, "Would you bring me a little water in a jar so I may have a drink?" ¹¹As she was going to get it, he called, "And bring me, please, a piece of bread."

¹²"As surely as the LORD your God lives," she replied, "I don't have any bread—only a handful of flour in a jar and a little oil in a jug. I am gathering a few sticks to take home and make a meal for myself and my son, that we may eat it—and die."

¹³Elijah said to her, "Don't be afraid. Go home and do as you have said. But first make a small cake of bread for me from what you have and bring it to me, and then make something for yourself and your son. ¹⁴For this is

what the LORD, the God of Israel, says: 'The jar of flour will not be used up and the jug of oil will not run dry until the day the LORD gives rain on the land.'"

¹⁵She went away and did as Elijah had told her. So there was food every day for Elijah and for the woman and her family. ¹⁶For the jar of flour was not used up and the jug of oil did not run dry, in keeping with the word of the LORD spoken by Elijah.

¹⁷Some time later the son of the woman who owned the house became ill. He grew worse and worse, and finally stopped breathing. ¹⁸She said to Elijah, "What do you have against me, man of God? Did you come to remind me of my sin and kill my son?"

¹⁹"Give me your son," Elijah replied. He took him from her arms, carried him to the upper room where he was staying, and laid him on his bed. ²⁰Then he cried out to the LORD, "O LORD my God, have you brought tragedy also upon this widow I am staying with, by causing her son to die?" ²¹Then he stretched himself out on the boy three times and cried to the LORD, "O LORD my God, let this boy's life return to him!"

²²The LORD heard Elijah's cry, and the boy's life returned to him, and he lived. ²³Elijah picked up the child and carried him down from the room into the house. He gave him to his mother and said, "Look, your son is alive!"

²⁴Then the woman said to Elijah, "Now I know that you are a man of God and that the word of the LORD from your mouth is the truth."

1 Kings 17:1–24

F IRST KINGS 17, THE first chapter of the "Elijah cycle,"[1] traces the coming of age of a new prophet in Israel. Elijah enters the stage of Israel's history without any introduction, thus setting a new literary precedent for how God chooses and announces a prophet.[2] The majority of this first chapter in the cycle deals with Elijah's sojourn in the home of an unnamed widow and her unnamed son. By her pressing needs and her dramatic words, this non-Israelite widow validates the man who became known in his lifetime as Israel's most flamboyant and dramatic prophet. Miracles and a statement of faith bring this woman, identified solely as a widow in Zarephath (v. 9), out of obscurity and into the light. The narrator's use of an anonymous Gentile[3] as a means to establish and affirm Elijah's prophetic credentials is an unusual textual tool, yet consistent with other events in Elijah's career.

The narrator in this chapter continues various Deuteronomistic themes laid down in the preceding books in the Hebrew Bible through the following means:

- giving evidence of God's consistent character as one who "defends the cause of the fatherless and the widow, and loves the alien, giving him food and clothing" (Deut 10:18)

- showing how God desires to bring "outsiders"—foreigners and those born outside the covenant—into a relationship with him

- telescoping events that highlight developing themes, among them the totality and universality of Yahweh the God of Israel's power

- emphasizing the intercessory prayer life of a prophet rather than a priest's duty of sacrifice

- proclaiming Yahweh the God of Israel's exclusivity and power over all rivals

The events associated with Elijah's stay in Zarephath—the regional drought and famine and the boy's illness and death—lead to two major

miracles: the replenishment of the widow's flour and oil and the raising of the widow's son from the dead.[4] These miracles, especially raising the boy from the dead, validate Elijah as a prophet. The unnamed
boy is the first person in the Hebrew Bible to be restored to life once
dead. Significantly, the narrator confirms both the boy's death and his
restoration to life by ending the chapter with the widow's exultant and
extemporaneous thanks: "Now I know that you are a man of God and
that the word of the Lord from your mouth is the truth" (1 Kgs 17:24).
The anonymous widow carries tremendous weight because the narrator develops Elijah's character through his interaction with her and her
son, and establishes his credibility as a prophet through her pressing
needs and her bold words.

The events of this chapter establish Elijah's credentials as the preeminent prophet in Israel at the time. They present irrefutable evidence
of Elijah as the minister of Yahweh, the God of Israel.[5] Furthermore,
his success at the height of Ahab's and Jezebel's political power equips
him for mortal combat against the prophets of the rival gods Baal and
Asherah, recorded a chapter later.[6] The events bolster Elijah's self-confidence and self-assurance, qualities clearly needed for the upcoming
public confrontation against the prophets of the rival deities.[7]

Throughout much of this chapter, the widow acts as a foil as the narrator explores and unfolds the development of Elijah's character. And
as the widow interacts with Elijah, she too emerges as clearly drawn,
feisty, humorous, and likable. The modern adage, "Behind every great
man is a great woman," accords well with this ancient story of Elijah
and the widow of Zarephath. History universally acknowledges Elijah
as a great prophet, and Jewish tradition lists the widow among twenty-
two women of valor in the Hebrew Bible.[8]

A STRUCTURED NARRATIVE

Although the widow is not introduced until v. 8, her difficult circumstances and the miracles associated with them dominate the chapter.
Her importance, however, cannot be understood without first looking
at the context. First Kings 16:29–18:2 begins and ends with Ahab, king
of Israel.[9] First Kings 16:29–33 summarizes his reign and lists his sins.
In 18:1–2, God instructs Elijah to return to Ahab. Drought and rain
serve as secondary brackets that enclose the text (17:1; 18:1).[10]

The main text, chapter 17, can be viewed and approached from several different standpoints: as a play, with a set of scenes with openings and conclusions; as a section with recognizable patterns; or as a series of escalating crises. Considering the narrative as a succession of escalating crises provides the most practical framework for the discussion of the widow and Elijah.[11] The widow and her needs constitute six crises: her lack of oil, flour, and water; her sense of the inevitable starvation of herself and her son; her fear; the death of her son; her faulty theology; and her sense of sin. Because the narrator shows that God responds to crises at exactly the time of highest need, the tension associated with each crisis builds and then abates when the need is met. The story moves forward with expectancy to the next crisis. Although the form each crisis takes and the kind of victory that will be won are not immediately discernable, we as readers and hearers know that Elijah, the one whom the text presents as the rugged hero, will prevail. We smugly and confidently await the "how to's" of his victory.

Moreover, as the multiple crises unfold, the text credits the God of Israel with constantly supplying temporal ways to save all concerned and theological ways to demonstrate to Israel, to other nations, and to the widow herself, that Yahweh alone is God. As God, Yahweh can declare what sin is (apostasy) and confirm its punishment (no rain or dew). Thus the narrator presents events in Ahab's reign so that through them a biblical principle emerges: *apostasy always leads to death*.

A prologue consisting of five verses at the end of 1 Kgs 16 (vv. 29–34) leads into the narrative of chapter 17. These verses list Ahab's sins and provide the reason for the drought as punishment. The prologue's sixth verse (16:34) merits close scrutiny.

> In Ahab's time, Hiel of Bethel rebuilt Jericho. He laid its foundations at the cost of his firstborn son Abiram, and he set up its gates at the cost of his youngest son Segub, in accordance with the word of the Lord spoken by Joshua son of Nun.

The placement of this verse, proclaiming the fulfillment of Joshua's prophetic word (Josh 6:26), at this point in the narrative jolts readers and puzzles scholars. But by abruptly including the information here, the narrator heralds success for others who like Joshua (and more significantly, in the manner of Joshua) speak the prophetic word.[12] In mentioning the prophecy of Joshua, the text arguably makes several announcements:

✍ the commencement of a new prophetic era, one bringing a season of unusual miracles

✍ the emergence of a new prophet[13] who in some ways follows
and emulates Joshua[14]

✍ a shift in focus from physical warfare against the Canaanites to
spiritual warfare against their gods

✍ the possibility that a woman outside the covenant again will be
influential in the upcoming saga (as Rahab was in Josh 2 and 6)

Furthermore, the disruption in the flow of the text, caused by the in-
sertion of v. 34, alerts the reader to expect a narrative section full of
surprises.

First Kgs 17:1 also jolts the reader, for the immediately preceding
verse provides no logical transition from the summary of Ahab's reign
to the introduction to the main part of the Elijah cycle. Yet because of
the otherwise tight and even predictable structure of 1 and 2 Kgs, the
placement and abruptness of these verses must be taken as deliberate.
From a structural standpoint, 1 Kgs 16:29–34 provides a "kingly" transition from the important Jeroboam to the similarly important Ahab,
whose notoriety prepares the reader for the prophetic stories about Elijah to follow.[15]

Elijah's formal introduction consists of the obscure adjective *Tishbite*. Elijah is called *Tishbite* six times in the Hebrew Bible (1 Kgs 17:1;
21:17, 28; 2 Kgs 1:3, 8; 9:36). *Tishbite* is a word of uncertain meaning.
It could be a place, an origin, a social category, a clan, a play on the
similar Hebrew word for *settler,* a resident of Gilead, or a combination
of all of these. Or it could refer to a location east of the Jordan and
south of the Yarmuk, a wild, forested, and largely unsettled region.[16]
Cornfeld believes that Elijah the Tishbite came from the pasture region of Gilead, eighteen miles north of the Jabbok.[17] With no mention
of his patrimony, without any history of his experience or theological
credentials, Elijah literally explodes onto the stage and into Israelite
history. His sudden declaration that no rain or dew will fall until he
says so signals how unprepared Ahab and the rest of the nation are for
his message of judgment. Elijah apparently offends Ahab, renders him
speechless, and triggers a crisis.[18] Beginning with the drought, the lives
of Ahab and Elijah become intertwined, and their ties to one another
are not severed until Ahab's death (1 Kgs 22:40).

The prologue's terseness, coupled with Elijah's abrupt announcement, present structural difficulties for the larger narrative.[19] The suddenness of the prophet's entry and the lack of introduction to or foundation for his ministry require that his ministry be validated throughout the Elijah cycle. In this way, the cycle represents a significant digression from earlier narrative patterns, notably the extensive background information given about Moses (Exod 1–3) and Samuel (1 Sam 1–3). Instead, the narrator chooses to fill out the drought's three years with selected information about Elijah's whereabouts and doings at the Wadi Kerith and in Zarephath. The widow provides the needed foil for details about Elijah's activities after his sojourn at the wadi and before his next confrontation with Ahab. Throughout chapter 17, Elijah eludes Ahab.

At God's command, Elijah hides from Ahab at the Wadi Kerith. There, ravens feed him and he drinks from the brook. The rabbis consider the feeding of Elijah one of the great miracles of God. Jewish literature ranks it in the same list with the parting of the Red Sea, the sun standing still for Joshua, the lions doing no harm to Daniel, and the fish spewing forth Jonah.[20] When the wadi dries up, God issues a new order: "Go at once to Zarephath of Sidon and stay there. I have commanded a widow in that place to supply you with food" (17:8). Elijah obeys.

In contrast to when he spoke to Ahab, Elijah speaks to the widow directly as God's emissary. The text indicates not only a change in the way Elijah addresses people but also a change in his character, namely, growth in his knowledge that he is a prophet and in his acknowledgement of his responsibilities as a prophet. Where the readers and hearers justifiably may have regarded Elijah as cocky when he confronted Ahab, when he speaks to the widow he speaks as one having compassion and even a sense of humor. In both encounters, however, he speaks with authority. To the widow he presents himself as a seasoned, confident, controlled man of God.

Elijah meets the widow at the city gate. Perhaps she wears special clothing and is identifiable by them.[21] He talks to her while she gathers sticks. He asks for water and bread, and she replies that she has no bread, only a little oil and flour. Soon she will go home, cook her last meal for herself and her son, and prepare for their death. Elijah intervenes to stop this horror. He proclaims a word from the Lord full of hope to her: her oil and flour will not be used up until the Lord sends rain upon the land!

Elijah lodges with the widow. As time passes, her son becomes ill and dies. The widow, convinced that God is punishing her by killing her son, blames Elijah for exposing her sin to God. Elijah asks for the dead child and takes him to his chamber, an upper room. He alternately challenges God and prays to God to restore life to the boy. As is consistently found in the Psalms, Elijah commands God to intervene immediately![22]

Elijah stretches himself over the boy, and the boy's life returns to him. He then presents the lad to his mother. In uneven Hebrew that conveys the sense of wonder, awe, jubilation, and thankfulness one would expect in such a situation, the widow exclaims the chapter's key verse, "Now I know that you are a man of God and that the word of the Lord in your mouth is the truth!" (17:24).

COLORFUL CHARACTERS

The human characters in 1 Kgs 17, like those in the larger Elijah cycle, are presented as archetypes. There is the proud king whose sinful ways lead to a nation's suffering and eventual downfall. There is the impoverished, hungry, yet hospitable widow who, while preparing her last meal before she and her son die, expresses feisty, detailed opinions about her lack of provision and talks back to an odd-looking stranger. There is the forceful zealot, a seemingly bombastic braggart, who claims to hear from and speak for God, and whose predictions come true. Two of the narrative's characters are silent—Ahab and the widow's son. Three have speaking roles—Elijah, God, and the widow.

AHAB AND THE UNNAMED SON

Although Ahab is a king, the narrator treats him with no favoritism. Instead, like a lawyer reading charges, the narrator lists a dismal summary of Ahab's life and reign, condemning him as one who "did more evil in the eyes of the Lord than any of those before him" (1 Kgs 16:30).[23] Throughout the Elijah cycle, the character of Ahab presents a negative foil against the character of Elijah. Depicting evil and good respectively, the king and prophet lock in combat over the destiny of Israel.[24] The text indicates, however, that they represent a much larger contest—the divine conflict between Yahweh, the God of Israel, and

Baal, the god of the Sidonians.[25] Ahab and his consort, Jezebel, along with their particular forms of paganism, were Elijah's constant target.[26] Yet Elijah's persistent confrontations with Ahab also portray God's constant and confrontational means of reaching out to an apostate king. A Jewish tradition records one such possible outreach by maintaining that Elijah earlier challenged Ahab and his god, Baal, to a test to end the famine.[27]

The narrator does not link Ahab and the widow's son, also a minor character, but the two present a study in character contrasts. Ahab remains static in the present passage but grows and shows remorse in a later portion of the cycle. At that time he tears his clothes, puts on sackcloth, and fasts (1 Kgs 21:27). The boy remains passive and acted upon.[28] He dies, but God restores his life; Ahab later dies but is not restored to life. While Ahab receives horrible written condemnations for his sins, the text treats the boy neutrally and refrains from talking about his character and life.[29]

Though otherwise strikingly different, both Ahab and the widow's son receive God's mercy, although arguably only in proportion to the merit of their deeds. God notices Ahab's humbling of himself and delays his penalty of destruction so that it falls on his son Ahaziah (1 Kgs 21:28–29). The lad receives God's mercy by being restored to life (1 Kgs 17:22).

Elijah

Throughout the narrative, Elijah dominates.[30] Yet the text surrounds the prophet with mystery, revealing few details about the man himself. As a pre-classical prophet,[31] he caught the public's imagination and had a profound influence on his time and on later Jewish and Christian thought.[32] The text presents him as the foremost prophet during the reigns of Ahab and Ahaziah (874–853 and 853–852 B.C.E. respectively).[33] He may have been a member of the Kenites or Rechabites, sects that led a nomadic existence,[34] or the Nazirites. But what kind of man was he? The answer is complex.

First Kings 17:1–7 establishes certain characteristics about Elijah, and his interaction with the widow adds to and embellishes them. A folk hero in part because of his nonconformity, unusual dress, directness, and courage, Elijah lives a life of confrontation. He confronts those, like Ahab, who oppose Yahweh, the God of Israel, and these confrontations show his mercurial, fiery temperament.[35] He deals directly with those concerned, refusing to triangulate or bring in third parties. When the widow's son dies, he deals first directly with the widow, then directly with God, and finally directly with the widow again.[36]

The narrative portrays another side of Elijah as well. Alexander Rofé wisely advises readers to consider carefully how the narrator portrays the prophet.[37] Elijah sounds abrupt, angry, and forceful with Ahab, yet straightforward, kind, and even humorous with the widow when he first meets her, and compassionate and bewildered when she later presents her dead son to him. The text also reveals Elijah's sense of humor and playfulness. In his first encounter with the widow, for example, Elijah seems to tease her by asking (presumptuously!) for a little water (v. 10). Once she takes the bait, so to speak, by turning to get him some water, Elijah asks her to bring him a little piece of bread as well (v. 11). If he is indeed egging her on to an outburst, she accommodates him royally!

Verses 1–7 show that Elijah favors secrecy regarding his whereabouts and his inner thoughts. While he at times hides from Ahab and Jezebel (vv. 2, 9; 18:21; 19:3), he also makes a disconcerting habit of popping up when Ahab does not want to see him (v. 1; 21:20–24). Elijah habitually vanishes just as unexpectedly as he appears (see 1 Kgs 18:12).[38] The opening verse suggests that Elijah plans and seeks the confrontation with Ahab that ensues.

Unlike Amos, Isaiah, and Jeremiah, Elijah refrains from describing himself either emotionally or professionally.[39] Only rarely does he express himself in writing.[40] Throughout the cycle, he travels extensively. Although he serves primarily as the prophetic witness in the northern kingdom, he lives for a season east of the Jordan at the Wadi Kerith, then resides in Zarephath (vv. 3, 8–24), and then flees to the mount of God at Horeb in Sinai (1 Kgs 19:8). The text gives him no settled home but recounts his wanderings around the countryside. Single and solitary, Elijah neither roams with the bands of roving prophets nor attends a school for the prophets.

Elijah's name, which means "Yahweh is my God,"[41] aptly summarizes his life and his special mission—to proclaim Yahweh as his God and the only God of Israel.[42] The prophet's first words, "As the Lord, the God of Israel, lives, whom I serve" (v. 1), announce his philosophy: he teaches the preeminence of the God of Israel.[43] Elijah's driving purposes are to discredit Baal and to show Yahweh as the true God of Israel.[44] His uncompromising stand brings him into constant contact and conflict with Ahab and Jezebel, both polytheists. Anger and hatred strong enough to jeopardize his life flare against him from both monarchs. In today's vernacular, Elijah plays verbal hardball with Ahab. Yet during his confrontations with the king, the prophet exhibits a mocking control.[45]

In contrast, Elijah treats the widow with deference in the remaining two-thirds of the chapter. When the two meet, Elijah calls out first for some water and next for a palmful of bread (vv. 10, 11).[46] He listens carefully to her lengthy reply in which she juxtaposes the motifs of eating and dying. The narrator presents her in a kindly way, letting her brassy words and hospitable heart describe her.

The subject of death dominates the widow's thoughts. She, her son, and now this stranger in front of her will eat a last meal together and die. The widow defines her life in terms of what she has and does not have. She has a son, but she has no bread. She has enough flour and oil for one more meal for herself and her son but lacks additional supplies. She has no means of getting more sustenance. Finally, without being asked, she freely expresses to Elijah her suspicion that he has come to remind her of the upcoming slow death by starvation of herself and her son.

Undaunted and perhaps even amused, Elijah answers her kindly. "Do not be afraid," he says (v. 13). He first responds to her fear, although she has not mentioned it by name. In this way, God speaks through Elijah, although Elijah does not use the familiar formula of Moses and the prophets, "Thus says the Lord," until later (v. 14). His compassion in addressing her fear marks him as a prophet even more clearly than his proclamation about the lack of rain and dew.[47] Elijah speaks not to her difficulty but to her heart. Her real problem isn't a lack of food and water, the essentials of life, but fear.[48]

If the cessation of rain and dew is considered the chapter's first miracle, and the feeding of Elijah by the ravens is the second, then a third miracle occurs here—the widow's oil and flour replenish themselves. Just as drought means death, so a supply of oil and flour means life. During the drought, Elijah lodges with her and her son. Because of the prophet's presence in her household, she comes under God's microscope, so to speak. As time passes, the special attention that brings blessing and provision to her household also highlights her needs, fears, and sins. When the widow's son grows ill and dies, she reasons that God punishes her for her transgressions with his death.[49]

Elijah never argues with her. He declines to discuss the accuracy of her theology and beliefs.[50] He lets pass her accusation that God brought him to her home to expose her sin. He does not debate with her whether the death of her son represents God's punitive hand against her household. Instead, Elijah remains silent,[51] an action showing his wise counseling skills and his compassionate heart. He knows her distress over the boy's death has pushed her beyond reason; throughout the chapter she vacillates between faith and unbelief.[52] Elijah simply asks her for her dead child. "Give me your son," he says.[53] The woman complies, handing the child over to the prophet. The child becomes symbolic of and synonymous with the word of God: Is each alive or dead?[54]

Elijah and the widow both confront the finality of death, but they do so in different ways. The woman reacts in anger, anguish, and terror. She sees Yahweh, the God of Israel, as the one who sees sin, reveals sin, punishes sin unfairly, and destroys the perpetuator of sin. Her words show that she believes in the finality of death. His words show that he believes the God of Israel controls both life and death.

Holding his tongue with the woman, Elijah nonetheless responds vociferously to God. Alone in his room with the dead boy, he peppers the ceiling with anger and prayer. The prophet's confusion manifests itself. He suddenly switches roles with the widow, speaking to God in the way the widow has just spoken to him. He hurls blame at God. He demands action from God. His tone seems resentful, much like the widow's. Echoing the widow's accusation, he questions why God has slain her son. But unlike the widow, Elijah, even in his anger and confusion, has the faith to draw on God for a miracle. Putting his faith in action, he utters the text's single prayer and also takes part in its implementation.[55] He beseeches God in one of the most heart-wrenching texts in Scripture: "O Lord my God, let the boy's life return to him" (1 Kgs 17:21).[56]

Elijah's prayer expresses a range of approaches and emotions: honesty, directness, supplication, anger, need, and bewilderment. First he releases his immediate feelings by charging Yahweh the God of Israel with the child's death. Simultaneously, his appeal contains a moral urgency: *God, act now!*[57] Mirroring Job in their anguish, both Elijah and the widow ask questions. They direct their questions, anger, puzzlement, and helplessness toward God. They ask, Why did the lad die?

Why is this happening? On these, surely some of the great questions facing all humanity, God remains silent.

Perhaps most appealing of all, Elijah's interaction with the widow and God at this moment shows his humanity. The boy's death leaves him in a theological predicament (how can a good God permit this?) and in a domestic mess (the widow blames him—with her peculiar logic—for bringing God into her house and exposing her sin). For the first time in the text, Elijah appears baffled and caught unawares. The boy's death makes him look inadequate as God's representative. More importantly, it makes his God look inadequate. Elijah clearly wants the boy to live and he both upbraids God and beseeches God to do something![58]

Elijah prays and acts. He actively and even bodily continues his intercession for the boy.[59] Verse 21 says, "Then he stretched himself out on the boy three times." Stretching out over someone was a typical, symbolic act familiar among the prophets of Israel. It was a way of saying, "Let his lifeless body become a living body."[60] In keeping with his role as a prophet, Elijah intercedes, and God accepts and answers his prayer.[61] The narrator's reticence to comment editorially points to his expectation of a miraculous event because Elijah merely did his job: intercession.[62] A hint, however, of Elijah's joy and compassion comes when he presents the son—alive—back to his mother (v. 23).[63]

The text repeats Elijah's name twice in these verses, thus stressing the personal victory of Elijah as God's agent of life over death.[64] The jumbled, spontaneous dialogue between Elijah and the widow hints at their confusion regarding the boy's death and their joy over his recovery. For the first time in the narrative, the widow stops complaining. She validates Elijah as a man of God. She witnesses and now is holding a miracle in her arms—her son restored to life!—and she gives every evidence of now believing in the God of Israel.

First Kings 17:8–24 clearly establishes Elijah as a man of intercessory prayer. It verifies his special position with God as one to whom God listens. It sets the stage for the upcoming showdown with the prophets of Baal and Asherah.[65] The narrative recounts how God immediately answers Elijah's forceful prayers. God withholds rain, thereby backing up Elijah's shocking decree; God restores life to the boy, thereby answering Elijah's entreaty. Throughout Elijah's career, this interesting pattern presents itself: Elijah orders or prays, and God obeys or answers in ways that bring either life or destruction (1 Kgs 17:22; 18:36–38; 2 Kgs 1:9–14).[66]

The Widow

The unnamed woman in this section of the Elijah cycle is described only as a widow and a resident of Zarephath. The Jewish legal definition of widow is a woman who was once married but no longer has a means of financial support. Her husband is dead, and she has no sons or children to care for her.[67] In this instance, the text uses the widow's situation and her words as its most significant means of affirming Elijah as a prophet. An analysis of her character entails looking at her side of the conversations with Elijah that dominate their initial encounter. Although they spar verbally, their interaction reveals both the widow's feistiness and the prophet's empathy and understanding.[68]

Two-thirds of this chapter focuses primarily on the developing relationship between Elijah and the widow.[69] Arriving in Zarephath after apparently walking the width of Israel, Elijah no doubt appears travel-worn.[70] Furthermore, a side effect of a drought is no extra water for baths! The brief description of the prophet later—as a man wearing a garment of hair and a leather belt (2 Kgs 1:8)—denotes a fearsome, extreme appearance.[71] Wild, gaunt, and stern, Elijah looks like one un-accustomed to luxury.[72] Lately, he has camped out near a drying-up wadi and enjoyed ravens as his companions. But his demeanor toward the widow is not one of a highwayman or a beggar or an accoster. His address to her contains no hint of the accusative, combative manner he displayed toward Ahab. With the widow, Elijah reveals a meek, playful, nonargumentative side of his personality.

The widow treats Elijah with what today would be called an attitude. With the exception of their last recorded conversation, her words show a brash, feisty nature. She expresses opinions without hesitation. Later she unequivocally blames Elijah and Elijah's God for killing her son. Perhaps her words demonstrate that the people of Tyre looked down on their neighbors, the Israelites. Yet her sharing what she believes is her last meal with a stranger shows her hospitable heart.

The text also employs humor as it records the developing relationship between these two starkly different characters. Elijah knows that God has commanded a widow to feed him. Apparently by divine revelation, the widow also knows of her assignment. But which of the many men in town is the one the Lord has sent? The situation, desperate as it is because of the famine, has a touch of comedy as each seeks to find the other. Elijah faces a problem much like Abraham's servant when he was sent to find a wife for Isaac (Gen 24). A humorous reading of the text is further reinforced when the widow presents herself as a thoroughly inadequate source of provision. Elijah's request catches her between the societal demands for hospitality and her inability to meet those demands.[73] Caught off guard, she displays a range of attitudes.

The text describes the widow sparsely. The narrator remains silent about her name, status, or history; nothing is recounted except the brief interlude in which her life intersects with that of Elijah.[74] We as readers and hearers don't know if she is physically young, beautiful, and strong, or old, wizened, ugly, and frail. We must supply these details mentally. The text does however sketch the widow well enough through her words to show her "utter disheartenment and forlorn poverty."[75] Still, as a woman versed in the social mores of her times, a woman with a reputation to maintain before her neighbors, she grants hospitality to a stranger. Not even famine and drought permit the cultural breach of refusing hospitality. Nothing—not even the certainty of death—allows her to demean herself by refusing to minister to a traveler in distress.[76]

The widow and Elijah meet at the town gate in Zarephath, a public place. He begins the conversation, and they talk while she gathers firewood. In a situation of extreme drought, the prophet brazenly asks her for a favor tantamount to asking for her life—he wants her to bring him a little water in a jar so that he can drink! Although the narrator remains silent regarding her internal reaction, she loses no time in going off to get water for him. While she is still within earshot, Elijah calls out again, seeming purposefully to provoke her by asking for even more—a piece of bread!

Given the extreme famine, Elijah's request to the widow is peculiar—even audacious. Why does he ask her to share her last morsel plus water with a stranger, a traveler, a man of another culture, and a servant of another god?[77] Is he testing her? Is Elijah trying to figure out if this woman is the one God has appointed to feed him? Although the text remains silent on this, the situation recalls a similar test Rebekah faced when she volunteered to draw water for Abraham's servant and his camels (Gen 24:17–19).

The widow's reaction to the prophet's requests hints at her bristling indignation. Oh, the audacity of the man! His cockiness! His rudeness to intrude even more on the universal rules of hospitality, especially in a time of drought and famine! Yet her indignation quite possibly also conceals her acute embarrassment over her inability to provide suitable hospitality. The famine cuts into her ability to give to another and therefore compromises her social standing.

Yet her words also show that she recognizes something different about Elijah. The narrator does not explain how she knows Elijah is different, but her reply lets us as readers and hearers know that she perceives that he does not follow her gods but follows the single God, Yahweh.[78] This acknowledgment gives the reader a favorable attitude toward her.[79] Because of the widow's initial unselfishness in sharing her family's last meal with a stranger, we want this needy, spunky widow and single mother to succeed. In a very real sense, she already is part of the historic community of faith because of the hospitality she extends.[80]

Certainly, responses other than generosity were open to this anonymous widow. She could have chosen to ignore Elijah, mock him, run away in terror, hurl rocks at him, or call the city's guards. But the widow surprises us. She responds generously to Elijah's outrageous request for water and food,[81] willingly sharing what she considers her last meal with a stranger.[82] According to Rofé, she passes the tests and gets the reward of miraculous provision from Elijah.[83] She gives from her own need, willingly sharing even her son's portion.

Elijah goes home with her. Perhaps his bizarre appearance is enough to ward off any scandalous gossip from her neighbors.[84] Although they presumably eat meals together with her son,[85] in her two-level home they have separate bedrooms, separate lives, and separate gods. Yet they are joined together in enjoying the God of Israel's miraculous provision and in being called together by him for some purpose only he fully knows. The tone of the text indicates that for the time Elijah sojourned with the widow and her son, the home's atmosphere was one of peace, unity, and safety—a marked contrast to the outside world where chaos, danger, and death prevailed because of the famine and drought.[86]

Although the widow has a strange man living in her home, no hint of impropriety emerges. The text makes clear that the relationships within the household remain formal but cordial. Although first names are never exchanged in the text, for example, the widow in her distress knows Elijah well enough by the time of her son's death to rail at him. Her upbraiding of the man of God comes across as a frantic appeal.[87] Though the widow connects the boy's death with her own sin, the text graciously remains silent on whatever sins she claims to have committed. The mother's speeches start in bitter accusation and end in a bewildered, halting, but definite confession of faith.[88]

GOD

Among all the stories in this book in which two girls and five women appear, God is most active as a character in the narrative in 1 Kgs 17, where Elijah encounters Ahab and a widow in Zarephath. Yet this chapter noticeably lacks God's verbal endorsement and assurance that Elijah is a prophet.[89] Instead, the text presents God, a speaking character, as going to extraordinary lengths to show himself as backing Elijah's judgments and portraying himself as a mighty savior to the Gentile widow. The text presents the extraordinary possibility that the whole situation involving the drought is part of God's larger plan to demonstrate *to the widow* that Yahweh alone is God.[90] God sends Elijah to evangelize the widow, to turn her from Baal, and to make her a convert to Yahweh, Israel's God. To do this, God as a character always directs Elijah with succinct orders: "Leave here . . . You will drink from . . . Rise. Go to Zarephath . . . Go and present yourself to Ahab" (1 Kgs 17:3–4, 9; 18:1). Significantly, God speaks only twice to Elijah (1 Kgs 17:8–9; 18:1); as is usual in the Hebrew Scriptures, God's remarks come as commands. But God also speaks to the widow (although the words remain unrecorded), for he tells Elijah he already has spoken to a widow in Zarephath about providing for Elijah's needs (1 Kgs 17:9).

The text, as usual, foregoes any physical description of God but recounts the words and deeds that serve to reveal God's character. The appearance of Yahweh the God of Israel as a character and the use of his name infuse any biblical story with moral dimensions. In 1 Kgs 17 the text demonstrates God's active interest in the safety and actions of Elijah. God involves himself through Elijah in the larger political situation in Israel—the apostasy of Ahab and Israel. The text shows God's watch care, God's ability to provide sustenance, God's willingness to perform miracles, God's control over national and international events, and God's primacy over rival gods. The text presents God's attributes in this story as consistent with previous accounts in other stories.

First Kings 17 offers yet another textual twist: Elijah introduces God.[91] Usually in biblical stories God takes the initiative in introductions. Furthermore, God does not comment on Elijah's statement of no

dew nor rain falling until Elijah says so. The text—and God—let that
statement stand unchallenged. Does Elijah try to control God by issuing a decree of no rain?[92] The text remains silent, but God does respond
to Elijah's declaration with a plan for saving Elijah's life. He commands
Elijah to journey eastward to the Wadi Kerith east of the Jordan and
hide.[93] Next he establishes his first form of provision, clearly a very creative mode—ravens will fly in bread and meat.[94] When the wadi dries
up, he soon finds an equally novel way of provision—a heathen widow
living in Zarephath, a city in Jezebel's home territory.[95] Through Elijah, God promises a widow, traditionally one of the poorest and most
overlooked in a society, that he will feed her and her household.[96] By
providing for his prophet and an unnamed, heathen widow and her
unnamed heathen son, the God of Israel establishes that he responds
to the needs of his covenant followers in Israel (in this case Elijah) and
to those outside Israel whom he is inviting to covenant membership
(in this case the widow and her son). The text thereby enlarges God's
character. God's workings with those outside the covenant are clear
throughout the Hebrew Bible: with Melchizedek in Gen 14; with Abimelech in Gen 20; with Job in the book of Job; and with the Cushites,
Philistines, and Arameans in Amos 9:7.

The text establishes God as one who listens. God listens to Elijah's
bold words decreeing no rain and responds to the situation Elijah arguably himself creates by providing for his prophet (1 Kgs 17:1–2). God
listens to the widow's angry confession of sin and to Elijah's accusative, petulant cry to restore the boy's life (1 Kgs 17:22). In his listening,
God proves to be both gracious and decisive. The text portrays the God
of Israel as the one who controls both life and death, the one who withholds and sends rain, the one whose jurisdiction extends beyond the
boundaries of Israel, the one who provides for his zealous spokesman
in creative ways, and the one who looks after the well-being of the least
in society, the fatherless and the widows.

ESSENTIAL THEMES

The obscure widow of Zarephath figures prominently in the narrator's development of three themes that are crucial to the establishment
of Elijah as the preeminent prophet in Israel: miracles, obedience, and
evangelism.

MIRACLES

This short narrative abounds with miracles, containing more than almost any other chapter in the Hebrew Bible. These wondrous deeds and events include the withholding of rain and dew, the ravens' feeding of Elijah, the replenishment of the widow's oil and flour, and—most remarkable of all—the restoration of life to the widow's son. While the narrator does not take these miracles for granted, he recounts them with detachment, as though they were normal. Put another way, the narrator expresses no surprise when miracles occur.

No less astounding than these tangible miracles is the wonder of the widow's changed heart: she abandons her belief in a foreign god or gods and turns toward the God of Israel.[97] The miracles demonstrate God's *hesed* toward her—the type of love that occurs when one of superior rank helps one of lesser rank. If the help had not come, the one of lesser rank would have perished.[98]

The miracles that take place in this chapter have significance on both the macro and micro levels. Regarding the former, the several miracles expose a king's helplessness and the inability of the god Baal (who is, ironically, the storm god) to provide rain or life.[99] Instead, the miracles exhibit the power and personality of the God of Israel. The God of Israel is the God of life, rain, and nature. The God of Israel controls the elements. The God of Israel forces death to relinquish its prey. On the micro level the miracles show that the God of Israel cares for the physical, emotional, and spiritual needs of his servant Elijah, but more particularly, that he cares for the widow and all aspects of her life because she is the more needy one.

Elijah's actions and the miracles performed through him can be viewed as promulgations of the knowledge of the character of the true and only living God. The wonders in Chapter 17 showcase God's ability to sustain and give back life.[100] God displays himself as a mighty provider for Elijah, the widow, and her son.

This chapter serves as a reminder that daily situations present opportunities for the miraculous. When the water dries up in the wadi, God (not bereft of ideas!) comes forth with a plan. We as readers and hearers commonly call a response to an insurmountable crisis a miracle, for we define miracles as happenings outside the ordinary. The biblical text, however, presents miracles as normal—even ordinary—to God and easy to accomplish.[101] The multiplication of flour and oil at the widow's house is consistent with God's other multiplication miracles in the Hebrew Bible.[102] The biblical theme is clear: *God takes something natural and multiplies it.* In the widow's case, the replenishment miracle takes place silently, day after day after day.

Through the widow's location and needs, the narrator also introduces a theological concept that was seen earlier in God's dealings with Rahab and Ruth: *God's miraculous power and his invitation to fellowship with him extend outside Israel,* in this case to Zarephath, to a woman outside the covenant.[103] But has God not shut up the heavens there, too? Even so, can he not sustain his prophet and his prophet's new household with an unusual form of miraculous replenishment? The story progresses to answer both questions affirmatively. The widow's house experiences no lack. Why should we as readers and hearers be surprised at that? The prophet, after all, symbolizes God's presence.[104]

The miracles in 1 Kgs 17 refute the magic that predominates in the surrounding culture by pointing to God. According to Rofé, the Elijah narrative "deliberately assaults the belief in the magical origin of miracles."[105] The miracles illustrate that God's sovereign power—not the widow's provision, not her son's gift of new life, not even Elijah's newly found status—is a primary focus of the passage. The widow's statement when she receives her son alive, "Now I know that you are a man of God and that the word of the LORD from your mouth is the truth" (v. 24), affirms her belief that her son's restoration to life is not an event produced by magic but a miracle wrought by the God of Israel. Furthermore, the miracles accomplish their deeper purpose of evangelism.[106] The widow's exclamation represents not only a recognition that Elijah speaks for God, but also "a full and explicit avowal of faith in God."[107]

OBEDIENCE

The narrator also explores the concept of obedience that is displayed between the various characters and forces within the narrative. Elijah, the widow, the ravens, the oil, the flour, the dew, the rain, the son, and even God, carry out the will of others in the story. Ahab alone disobeys.[108] Verses 5 and 15, almost identical except for the actors, record that Elijah went and did what the Lord commanded and the widow went and did what Elijah commanded. The repeated language confirms the fulfillment of a word of God and highlights another biblical theme—*God's word is fulfilled through human obedience.*[109]

Obedience to Yahweh the God of Israel and obedience to his prophet Elijah are so closely tied in this passage that sometimes things get confused. At times within the text, obeying Elijah becomes the equivalent of obeying God. In this way the text uses the concept of obedience to firmly establish Elijah as God's prophet. The narrative, moreover, recounts how obedience to the word of Yahweh the God of Israel precedes the fulfillment of any promise.[110]

Obedience, upon further examination, involves both activity and passivity, both acting and letting God act. After Elijah's active role of assigning a drought, he actively obeys the instructions of Yahweh the God of Israel to go to the wadi.[111] Soon he passively enjoys an almost vacation-like atmosphere that flows from his obedience.[112] He drinks fresh water from the brook and ravens cater to him, bringing him meat and bread twice a day.

But Elijah's "vacation" is short-lived. When the wadi dries up, he again immediately obeys a new word from the Lord by traveling to Zarephath. Although the widow, in an outward display of obedience, responds to Elijah's request and makes him a meal, she breaks the pattern of passive obedience reflected in Elijah's life by expressing her incredulity at his initial request to share her last meal. Yet despite her ambivalence, she obeys. Later, the close connection between the obedience of the various parties and the fulfillment of God's will emerges again as even God obeys (or at least actively responds to) Elijah's urgent prayer to restore life to the widow's son. The widow honors God by befriending the prophet, and God rewards her obedience by restoring her son to life.

EVANGELISM

The 1 Kgs 17 narrative uses the widow to reinforce a pattern established early on in the biblical corpus: *God builds a major work slowly by working with individuals, one at a time.* In this chapter God establishes an important model for extending the covenant outside the physical boundaries of Israel. Obedience to God's invitation to join the covenant community is never mandatory. The lone widow in this chapter voluntarily changes her faith, abandoning Baal's domain and aligning herself with the God of Israel.

The raising of the widow's son points likewise to the chapter's emphasis on evangelism. The ethical meaning of the revival-from-death experience further expands the scope of God's goodness since the boy

is a Gentile. Rofé rightly points out that the return of life to the boy
would have been much easier to understand if he had been an Israelite.[113] But here Rofé fails to grasp the significance and scope of God's
broader outreach to the nations.[114]

In addition, this chapter further demonstrates how God goes to
extreme measures both for little people and big people, for the unimportant and the socially prominent. He uses drought and hardship to
spur repentance. They succeed with the widow and fail with Ahab. The
story ends with the widow's confession of faith, only the second recorded in the Hebrew Bible from among the worshipers of Baal.[115] Although the account focuses on the widow and Elijah, in it God sets up
a model for bringing others into the wonders of his covenant: go and
live among the people, and as their needs arise, proclaim God's provision and pray for God's miraculous power to meet those needs.[116]

SUMMARY AND CONCLUSION

First Kings 17 sets the tone for the rest of the Elijah cycle. By the
beginning of 1 Kgs 18, the narrator's goal has been fulfilled—we as
readers and hearers believe without question that Elijah is a prophet,
the preeminent prophet in Israel. After all, not much can top a progres-
sive succession of miracles that ends with life returning to a dead boy.
We look forward to Elijah's further adventures!

One reason Elijah's life story captivates the imagination is that
chapter 17 establishes the narrative pattern for the rest of the Elijah
cycle. Elijah goes from one exciting adventure to another. And yet, by
the narrator's use of the character of the widow, the prophet retains
his humanity throughout his adventures. Because the stories associated
with his sojourn in her house show his confusion and humanity, he
really never becomes larger than life. In a sense, she brings him down
to size; she makes him human. The way she treats him by talking back
to him at their initial meeting and then by railing at him when her son
dies reveals a restrained side of Elijah. Elijah rebukes a murdering king
and queen but remains silent—even henpecked and a bit cowed!—
before a feisty, self-confident widow with an attitude!

The widow's input helps prepare us as readers and hearers for even
more astounding stories about the prophet's life and work. Uriel Simon
succinctly characterizes the prophet's growth:

He who was answered with flour and oil in Zarephath will be answered with fire and rain on Mount Carmel; he who stretched out on the child and overcame death will stretch out on the soil of Mount Carmel and bring a speedy end to the drought; he who could move the Phoenician woman, who was on the verge of evicting him from her house, to declare that 'the word of the Lord in your mouth is truth' will move the Israelites after their earlier sullen refusal to respond to him, to proclaim that the Lord alone is God, the Lord alone is God.[117]

First Kings 17, the account of Elijah's introduction to Israel, operates on both the micro and macro levels.[118] The text shows God's interest in the micro (a small household in an alien god's territory) and to a lesser degree in the macro (the larger story of what is happening in Israel). The three stories depict an escalation of problems from drought to famine to death. The narrative concentrates on the two main characters, Elijah and a widow, but allows a king, Ahab, to loom large in the background. The chapter opens with an unspoken but assumed question: Who does Elijah think he is? It proceeds to answer this question forthrightly: Elijah is a mighty prophet, one sent by God to tell the people of their sins.[119]

According to Claudia V. Camp, 1 Kgs 17 concerns itself "with a prophetic recognition and authorization as much as with prophetic power."[120] The verification of Elijah as a man of God and as a prophet comes through the words of a widow, a non-Israelite, a resident of Jezebel's territory, a woman "insignificant" in a patriarchal religious society, an unnamed Gentile widow.[121] Her confession is twofold. First, Elijah is a man of God with divine power; second, he truly does speak the word of the Lord.[122] What trust and prominence the narrator gives an unnamed foreigner, a person initially outside the covenant![123]

Although unusual, this chapter's way of confirmation is consistent with how God often operates. He frequently begins a significant, new move with small things and delivers his people in mighty ways through them. The woman's confession proclaims Elijah's rise to full prophetic maturity.[124] She and her son experience nothing short of God's "scandalous mercy."[125] Her statement of awe and wonder publicly voices her gratitude over the provision of oil and flour and the overwhelming joy of receiving her son back to life. Knowing her sin and recognizing that she lacks merit within herself, she nonetheless acknowledges that the mercy of Yahweh the God of Israel has in a sovereign, surprising way embraced her household.[126]

The widow's crises—by necessity—contribute to the text by enlarging Elijah's faith. Elijah already has faith that the drought will commence and cease at his word (1 Kgs 17:1). He proclaims that the oil and flour in her house will not run dry (1 Kgs 17:14). These two miracles equip him with faith for another, larger project: the raising of the dead boy to life.[127]

In addition, the raising of the widow's son highlights other biblical themes. For instance, a "first" has just occurred. The prophet Isaiah quotes the Lord as saying, "Behold, I do a new thing" (Isa 43:19). Throughout the Hebrew Bible, God repeatedly does new things. The raising of the lad from death, the first such miracle in the biblical text, offers another verification, stronger than the miraculous withholding of rain and dew and the miraculous provision of oil and flour. It confirms God's emphasis on life.[128]

Clearly, without his sojourn in Zarephath with the widow and her son, Elijah's credibility would remain minimal. Without the story of the return of life to the lad, the text presents no substantiation that Elijah has the moral fiber, resolute courage, and bold, persistent faith needed to stand alone against the four hundred and fifty prophets of Baal and the four hundred prophets of Asherah. Following the account of the boy, we as readers and hearers (and arguably the narrator, too), experience confidence in Elijah's ability to face whatever comes his way in subsequent adventures. Consequently, the widow's input reveals to all the secret Elijah already knows: truly, he is a prophet of Yahweh the God of Israel. His adventures are assignments from God. The feisty, self-assured, amazed, awestruck, and now thankful widow speaks for everyone—the narrator and readers and hearers alike—when she says so succinctly, "Now I know that you are a man of God and the word of your mouth is true" (v. 24).

QUESTIONS FOR FURTHER REFLECTION

1. In Elijah's interactions with Ahab and with the widow of Zarephath, two sides of his personality emerge. On the one hand,

Elijah is a wild-looking, fiery, confrontational prophet of the Lord, ready to take on God's enemies. On the other hand, Elijah is the compassionate man of God, quiet even when rebuked, able to interact caringly with a grieving widow. In what ways does God use this obscure widow to help Elijah maintain a balance of toughness and tenderness? What can you learn from this narrative about balancing strength and sensitivity in your own life?

2. What elements of humor do you find in Elijah's interaction with the widow? Why is it significant that the text introduces humor even in the midst of crises? What can you learn from this?

3. The death of the widow's son is clearly unexpected and bewildering to both the widow and the prophet. What do their reactions to the death have in common? In what ways do their reactions differ? What do we learn about Elijah from this crisis? What do we learn about the widow? What lessons can you derive from this incident for crises or tragedies you might face?

4. Why do you think God led Elijah to the home of a non-Israelite woman? What personality traits in this woman make her an unlikely candidate to be a hostess for an exiled prophet? What qualities make her a good candidate to see Elijah through the days of famine? How can you better prepare yourself to be God's instrument in times of crisis?

5. Why is "Do not be afraid" (1 Kgs 17:13) such an important admonition in this chapter? The command is carried over in the New Testament as an announcement that God is at work (see Luke 1:13, 30; 2:10). How does its use give an indication that Elijah is indeed a prophet and one through whom miracles can be worked? How do you respond to this command?

6. The story of Elijah and the widow presents an important model for evangelism: *go and live among people and as their needs arise, proclaim God's provision and pray for God's miraculous power to meet those needs.* What are some ways in which you can implement this model in your present situation?

8

THE ISRAELITE SLAVE GIRL
OVERCOMING OBSCURITY THROUGH FAITH

¹Now Naaman was commander of the army of the king of Aram. He was a great man in the sight of his master and highly regarded, because through him the LORD had given victory to Aram. He was a valiant soldier, but he had leprosy.

²Now bands from Aram had gone out and had taken captive a young girl from Israel, and she served Naaman's wife. ³She said to her mistress, "If only my master would see the prophet who is in Samaria! He would cure him of his leprosy."

⁴Naaman went to his master and told him what the girl from Israel had said. ⁵"By all means, go," the king of Aram replied. "I will send a letter to the king of Israel." So Naaman left, taking with him ten talents of silver, six thousand shekels of gold and ten sets of clothing. ⁶The letter that he took to the king of Israel read: "With this letter I am sending my servant Naaman to you so that you may cure him of his leprosy."

⁷As soon as the king of Israel read the letter, he tore his robes and said, "Am I God? Can I kill and bring back to life? Why does this fellow send someone to me to be cured of his leprosy? See how he is trying to pick a quarrel with me!"

⁸When Elisha the man of God heard that the king of Israel had torn his robes, he sent him this message: "Why have you torn your robes? Have the man come to me and he will know that there is a prophet in Israel." ⁹So Naaman went with his horses and chariots and stopped at the door of Elisha's house. ¹⁰Elisha sent a messenger to say to him, "Go, wash yourself seven times in the Jordan, and your flesh will be restored and you will be cleansed."

¹¹But Naaman went away angry and said, "I thought that he would surely come out to me and stand and call on the name of the LORD his God, wave his hand over the spot and cure me of my leprosy. ¹²Are not Abana and Pharpar, the rivers of Damascus, better than any of the waters of Israel? Couldn't I wash in them and be cleansed?" So he turned and went off in a rage.

¹³Naaman's servants went to him and said, "My father, if the prophet had told you to do some great thing, would you not have done it? How much more, then, when he tells you, 'Wash and be cleansed'!" ¹⁴So he went down and dipped himself in the Jordan seven times, as the man of God had told him, and his flesh was restored and became clean like that of a young boy.

2 Kings 5:1–14

Second Kings 5:1–14 presents as a model of faith a person laden with multiple layers of obscurity: she is a little girl; she is unnamed; she is a slave; and she is a captive in the land of her enemies. A distinctive Hebrew adjective, *qetannah*, meaning "small" or even "young and trifling," characterizes her.[1] In a crowd, she would be overlooked.[2] Her story, however, upsets traditional formulas and conventions about who is really important. Refreshingly alive and unpredictable, the Bible consistently takes seemingly insignificant people, hampered by difficult and inescapable conditions, and elevates them to positions of prominence and honor. While society may regard this child as a mere onlooker, the text honors her with great significance.

Considering her age, position, and background, this little girl possesses amazing confidence. Undaunted by her circumstances, she renders a bold proclamation of faith that leads to the healing and conversion of her owner.[3] This pint-sized heroine is a plucky leader in what 2 Kings values the most—*faith*. The child's graceful bearing and enduring words provide first Naaman's wife and then Naaman and his household with a model of a new faith. Ultimately this Israelite slave girl, a captive among the Arameans, proves instrumental in showing that God's covenant and power extend beyond the borders of Israel. Although she makes but a cameo appearance in the Hebrew Bible, this anonymous child functions as a key player in the history of God's revelation. Jesus later reminds his hearers of the story of Naaman, the Aramean general healed of leprosy (Luke 4:27).

The Great and the Small

The account of the healing of Naaman, commander of the army of Aram, is one of a series of miracle stories that highlight the ministry of the prophet Elisha (1 Kgs 19–2 Kgs 13). Since Aram, the rough equivalent of modern-day Syria, was traditionally the enemy of Israel, the healing of Naaman quite likely took place during a time of relative peace between the two nations.[4] Second Kings 5 hosts a large cast of characters[5] and presents three main themes:[6] the power of the prophet Elisha to heal, the volatile political relations between Israel and Aram, and the greed and punishment of Elisha's servant Gehazi.

Broadly speaking, 2 Kgs 5 divides into three sections. In the first section, Naaman hears that there is a prophet in Israel who can heal him of leprosy (vv. 1–4). In the second, the unnamed king of Aram grants Naaman permission to go to Samaria, and Naaman receives his healing there (vv.5–19). In the third section, Gehazi, the prophet's servant, exhibits inordinate greed, lies in order to acquire two talents of silver and two sets of clothing, and receives the perpetual punishment of leprosy for his deed (vv.20–27).

There are several important inclusions in this chapter. The presence of leprosy is one of these. What began with the skin affliction of Naaman ends with the skin affliction of Gehazi. As is true in so many biblical stories, the tables turn. Ironically, the one outside the covenant receives healing, and the one within the covenant is afflicted.[7] Another inclusion is the concept of faithfulness. The chapter begins with the faithfulness of an unnamed slave girl and ends with the unfaithfulness of the prophet's servant, Gehazi; the former story brings joy while the latter story carries tragedy.[8] Yet a third inclusion is the idea of youth and youthful skin (vv. 2, 14).

The chapter opens by introducing Naaman. His name is derived from a Ugaritic word meaning "fair and gracious,"[9] and the chapter substantiates these personality traits. He is described as a valiant man, a mighty man, perhaps even a giant in stature, via the Hebrew word *gibbor*.[10] The addition of the Hebrew word *hayil* emphasizes these admirable qualities. A multifaceted word, *hayil* carries with it the ideas of strength, courage, power, command leadership, and the ability to overcome.[11] In contrast with the "small" slave girl, the text presents Naaman as great (Heb. *gadol*) and well-respected (Heb. *nesu' fanim, v. 1*). As commander of the army of Aram, he ranks second only to the king.[12]

The early part of the chapter reveals the home life of this successful military commander. Naaman's wife is described with the same Hebrew root used to describe Naaman himself, *gibbor/gevereth,* which indicates strength and excellence of character. In the feminine, the adjective describes a strong, accomplished, proud, brave, and even queenly woman.[13] By using the same adjective to describe both characters, the narrator indicates the equality and appropriateness of their union: these two are well matched.[14] As a general, Naaman might logically expect and want his home to run as smoothly as his recent military campaign. Apparently it does, for his household has numerous servants (vv. 2–3, 13, 15). The text focuses on a new servant, a little girl from Israel, a child captured by raiding bands from Aram (vv. 2–3). As a new household member, she serves Naaman's wife.

The king of Aram holds Naaman in high regard because Naaman won an unspecified victory for his country.[15] Jewish tradition maintains that as a young nobleman, Naaman shot the random arrow that mortally wounded Ahab, king of Israel (1 Kgs 22:34).[16] The text, however, makes it clear that the Lord (Heb. *Yahweh*) gave this valiant soldier his win. Naaman is a national hero in Aram and stands out in the Hebrew Bible. Rarely do the Scriptures describe a person outside the covenant in such glowing terms.[17]

Naaman, however, is not without flaws. As is so common in biblical texts, the weak point in an otherwise strong character rises to the surface. Leprosy afflicts this valiant soldier.[18] Disclosure of this condition after the narrator's superlative introduction comes as a shock.[19] The reader wonders, Why should someone to whom the Lord has given victory and favor have leprosy? It seems unjust, cruel, ironic.

Although the text provides no direct answer to this question, clues can be found in the structure of the story. Often biblical stories focus on a single problem and allocate a great deal of space to showing how the Lord deals with it. For example, Gen 11:29–30 introduces Abram and Sarai as a childless couple. Much of their recorded story concerns how this problem of barrenness is solved. This couple's point of weakness highlights a principle consistent throughout the Bible: *problems become vehicles for showcasing God's power and glory.*

GREAT FAITH FROM A SMALL SOURCE

The narrator in 2 Kgs 5 moves swiftly from Naaman's greatness to his condition of leprosy, to the healing of his leprosy. Amazingly, the young girl, plucked from her homeland in Israel and described as a "maidservant" (*na'arah,* v. 4), speaks words of faith that start a sequence of events that ultimately lead to the general's healing.

Notice the text's silence about this young girl's background. It spends no time describing Aram's raiding bands or the child's capture. Readers and hearers do not know how she was sold or what horrors, if any, she encountered. And what about her parents? Where are they? The text fails to recount how long the child has been in Naaman's household before she speaks. There are no details about her service and only a few about her life: she is a young girl; she is a captive Israelite; she serves Naaman's wife as a household slave, not as a field worker;[20] and—most importantly—she speaks words of faith, encouragement, hope, and certainty.

But, despite the paucity of information provided in the text, Naaman's national and international standing enables readers to surmise several additional details about the young girl: she is cultured and perhaps beautiful; she knows (or quickly learns) how to serve a great lady; her sweet ways win the lady's trust. Furthermore, the child wants to please; she follows the chain of command; she is kind and observant; she exhibits good manners, knowing when to speak and when to be silent; and she possesses great faith.[21] Judging from the little girl's desire to see her master made well again, it seems likely that Naaman and his wife treat her with kindness. Though this young Israelite girl remains unnamed and serves as a slave, the text bestows high honor on her. Her confident statement of faith gives the chapter its focus: "If only my master would see the prophet who is in Samaria! He would cure him of his leprosy" (2 Kgs 5:3). Through her trusting words, hope dawns for Naaman and his wife. Though the reading of the narrative passes quickly, a significant length of time passes in this story. Yet the young girl's confession and her faith never waver; they stand strong.

At the very least, the young girl's declaration displays remarkable courage and initiative. Her statement rests upon several confident assumptions: first, she knows that God heals;[22] second, she realizes that God's power and presence extend beyond the borders of her homeland—she can serve God just as well in Aram as she can in Israel; third, she understands that God extends compassion to people of other countries who mistakenly serve other gods; fourth, she knows that when a prophet of the God of Israel prays, things happen.[23] She exudes contagious confidence in God and in his prophet.

Whether subconsciously or consciously done, her behavior in following the household chain of command must have impressed the general. Her words acknowledge him with respect. No rebel here! No slave with murder on her mind! Instead, this slave, uprooted from her homeland and probably bereft of parents and friends, desires the well-being of her new household. This slave even brings with her hope for the impossible—healing. This little slave girl instigates a different kind of rebellion: a revolt of hope!

This child's confident, courageous, consistent expression of faith challenges Naaman to the core. He listens. In believing her words, he opens himself up to national and international ridicule and risks his reputation. He stakes his fortune on her faith. Yet is it such a risk? As a warrior, he can smell fear and assess courage. In his years of commanding men and waging war, he knows how to judge truthfulness and character. As a man also under authority, he goes to his master, the king of Aram, and tells him what the Israelite girl has said (2 Kgs 5:1, 4). Trusting the God of Israel makes him vulnerable to scorn and international mockery if the healing fails to materialize. Nevertheless, he seeks permission from his king to go and be healed. Verse 4 records the king's gracious response: "By all means go."

As Naaman begins his journey to Israel for healing, it seems that the young Israelite girl is left behind at home. The servants who accompany Naaman (vv. 13, 15) seem to be adult attendants. Indeed, there would be no reason to involve a young girl in the affairs of state or take her to see the king of Aram (probably Ben-Hadad), the king of Israel, or the prophet. Nevertheless, her influence pervades the chapter.

This story of healing and conversion includes marked contrasts between Naaman and the story's heroine.[24] He is an Aramean, a Gentile who is outside of God's covenant; she is an Israelite, a member of God's covenant community by birth. He is a powerful man; she is a little girl. He has influence and position; she has obscurity and social stigma. He has ready access to kings; she has no protection from any king. He is a commander and slave-owner; she is both captive and slave. He has a dreaded skin disease; she has a child's smooth skin. He has freedom of movement; she has no freedom. He seeks what so far has escaped him—healing; she seeks nothing, not even freedom. He is wealthy beyond imagination, for he carries with him to Israel ten talents of silver, six thousand shekels of gold, and ten sets of clothing (v. 5); she is poor

and has nothing. He causes others to be exiled; she lives in exile. He
encounters the power of the God of Israel; she knows the God of Israel.
He needs a miracle and receives a miracle; she has the faith to believe
in miracles. Differences in characterization such as these make a story
interesting.[25]

A WARRIOR'S CONVERSION

As the story of Naaman's healing and conversion progresses, aspects of Naaman's character develop. It becomes clear that Naaman
expects to be treated as a mighty warrior. After all, he follows the chain
of command, goes through channels, performs (as usual!) beyond expectations, honors the great, pays his way. It is humbling for such a
powerful man to admit a need and come to Israel, a lesser country, for
a solution. As a field marshal, a national hero, a conqueror to be feared,
a warrior of renown, a self-made man of wealth, he deserves respect. As
Iain Provan[26] notes, Naaman prepares well for his healing; he seems
to think he deserves it. His life works like a military drill. He thinks
a prophet can be bought; no doubt he knows many prophets whose
favorable words and potent concoctions are up for sale.

But Elisha refuses to play the game by Naaman's rules. The prophet's
character also emerges in this story. He prefers second-person contacts.
He delegates. He sends messages and messengers to both the king of
Israel and to Naaman (vv. 8, 10). When Naaman arrives at the prophet's house (accompanied by a display of chariots and horses worthy of
his rank as field marshal!), Elisha remains inside. Naaman receives no
personal greeting. Naaman interprets Elisha's public snub as rudeness.
Clearly, it bypasses standards of international hospitality. A messenger
from Elisha conveys the prophet's terse instructions to Naaman: "Go,
wash yourself seven times in the Jordan, and your flesh will be restored
and you will be cleansed" (v. 10).

And the general's reaction? Naaman takes umbrage! He leaves in
a fit of anger that progresses to rage (vv. 11–12). Actually, the prophet's relayed instructions in their simplicity reveal Naaman's arrogance.
The simple instruction to wash in the Jordan seven times shows Naaman's ethnic and regional pride. He angrily tells his attendants that the
Abana and Pharpar are better rivers than the waters of Israel (v. 12)! He

also tells what he expected the prophet and the prophet's God to do: "I thought that he would surely come out to me and stand and call on the name of the Lord his God, wave his hand over the spot and cure me of my leprosy" (v. 11).

But the God of Israel does not meet Naaman's expectations. God does not put on a display of power; he refuses to play Naaman's game or abide by Naaman's rules. Perhaps Naaman's anger stems from keen disappointment and an acknowledgment of the failure of his human efforts to earn immediate healing. Elisha's deliberate, public put-down exposes Naaman's obsession with his own greatness.[27] Perhaps the prophet refuses to see him not because of his infectious skin disease, which makes him ceremonially unclean (Lev 13), but because of the general's pride. Flabbergasted at the dismissal, Naaman pouts. He had expected that a great person like himself would receive a prophet's respect and deference.[28] Truly, the prophet's God should be glad to heal one such as he!

Apparently a man of quick anger, Naaman flares up against the prophet's instructions. Yet the servants accompanying him love him and have studied him for years.[29] They let him blow off steam before approaching him in a rational way. Like their little colleague, the Israelite slave girl, at the very least they want the best for Naaman and his wife.

The servants approach Naaman as a reasonable man and with an argument that appeals to his brilliance as a strategist and field marshal. Strategists themselves, the servants, speaking in unison, call Naaman a father. They cagily allude to his valor and his delight in successfully accomplishing incredibly difficult exploits. Knowing him so well, they know he would have done whatever difficult task the prophet had demanded. So why not, they argue, do this simple little task?

Calmed down, and having come so far, Naaman has a change of heart. Why not do what the prophet's messenger says the prophet says? After all, the prophet and the prophet's God are the ones with something to lose. Naaman will not lose face by obeying the instructions and not being healed.

Thus reassured, Naaman and his entourage head to the Jordan. After washing seven times, "his flesh was restored like the flesh of a little child and he was clean" (v. 14). It is a public miracle, done in a public way, and Naaman and his entourage know there is a prophet—and a God—in Israel!

The importance of the little girl now resurfaces. The narrator makes a point of saying that the newly-healed Naaman has the flesh of a little boy (v. 14). Like the Israelite slave girl, he too has the skin of a child— soft, smooth, supple. The leprosy (or psoriasis) is gone; gone are any battle wounds; gone are wrinkles. As is so common in biblical texts and in life, something outward reflects something inward. Naaman's new flesh reflects his new faith. Like the Israelite slave girl, Naaman's God is now the God of Israel.

Naaman returns to the prophet, and the prophet meets him this time. It is again a meeting of generals. The Israelite slave girl was a general of faith, though pint-sized in stature. The man of God is a general of faith and mature in stature. Naaman, a military general and a man among men, learns from these two generals that the new weapons of faith and obedience lead to winning in a new way.

The narrator supplies no adjective such as *joyful* or exuberant words such as *shouting* and *thanksgiving* to describe the scene at the Jordan, the trip back to the prophet's home, or the meeting with the prophet. Yet imagination readily supplies the details. Naaman must have been patting his flesh, showing off his arms and legs and scalp to all around! All attested to the restoration of his flesh and the absence of leprosy! What wonder and joy there must have been!

True to his name, Naaman is pleasant to all.[30] Naaman's graciousness—even courtliness—smoothes his public meeting with Elisha. As a public figure, he knows how to stand with presence before a crowd. But the two men do not face each other as equal generals, for Naaman chooses to call himself Elisha's servant (v. 17). Naaman's sudden humility is as new as his healed skin. Gone with the leprosy are his arrogance, anger, and command mode. Naaman is new outside and inside!

Naaman and Elisha discourse publicly in front of their servants. They talk immediately of real issues—or rather Naaman talks, for he has already thought through his public duties and how they inherently conflict with his new faith. Naaman knows he cannot avoid his duties as a national hero and counselor to his king. But he reveals to the prophet his new plans for his non-public life. In his private life he will worship the God of Israel. He asks permission to take back the earth of Israel, as much as two mules can carry (v. 17); upon it he will worship the God who healed him. Never again will he offer sacrifices to another god. Leader that he innately is, no doubt Naaman will lead his household in worship of Yahweh. Naaman's bitter arrogance has become a reverent public and private humility.[31] In a distinctly masculine, mature way, he exhibits the same sweet spirit earlier seen by the Israelite slave girl.

IMPORTANT TEXTUAL TWISTS

The preposition *before* links the various scenes of this narrative. Naaman is a great man standing *before* his masters. The Israelite slave girl serves *before* the wife of Naaman; she longs to have Naaman stand *before* the prophet and be healed. Now he stands *before* the prophet, healed. Elisha, who refused to treat Naaman as his superior in rank, now graciously treats him as his equal. Although Naaman dominates the interview with his speech, Elisha acts as the one in charge. Naaman willingly makes himself small and willingly recognizes the authority of the man of God, the prophet Elisha.

Behind all the twists and turns in this story, God is watching. This is an essential principle for a successful reading of biblical narrative. *God's presence and voice may seem absent at times, but that does not mean his sovereign hand falls slack.* Just as God watched and listened to the profession of faith made by the Israelite slave girl, he watches and listens to Naaman's acts of faith.

When Naaman mentions his public duties to the prophet, specifically the demands his king makes upon him when the kings goes to worship, Elisha responds with a blessing and benediction: "Go in peace" (v. 19). The statement recognizes the integrity and courage of Naaman's conversion. Significantly, the prophet offers no prophecy about the future, but instead acknowledges Naaman's newly-found peace. The healing has been bigger than Naaman's outward skin disease. Naaman now enjoys a peace in his spirit. Naaman's change of heart continues, for when Gehazi, Elisha's servant, runs after him and catches up with his caravan, Naaman jumps down from his chariot (v. 21). As J. Robinson aptly notes, this is "a remarkable act of deference for a man of Naaman's rank to a servant."[32] Naaman truly is a humble man.

The story of Naaman's conversion, one of the most detailed and psychologically and sociologically rich in the Hebrew Bible,[33] brings Naaman back into fellowship with human beings and commences a fellowship with the One he now knows as his healer and creator. Naaman's conversion shows what happens when a self-made man, a truly great man in the human sphere, recognizes his sin of pride, humbles himself, and turns to God for many levels of healing. Naaman experiences a conversion of heart and the added grace of bodily healing from a gracious God. Both his heart and skin become little-boy soft.

Elisha (and God) does not expect Naaman to abandon his life. Indeed, Naaman returns to his life as a new person equipped with the promise that rings throughout the Hebrew Scriptures: "Do not be afraid, for I am with you." (Gen 26:24). Naaman's model of faith, remarkably, is the Israelite slave girl. Captured and dragged into a life she did not choose, she nonetheless flourishes. God makes her prosperous in the land of her affliction.

THE BIGGER PICTURE

The story of the Israelite slave girl and Naaman adds to the development of Israel's theology by enlarging the scope of God's power. Independent of national boundaries, God gives military victory to whom he chooses. God looks for faith and finds it in the Israelite slave girl and in Elisha (2 Kgs 5: 3,8). God looks for obedience and finds it in the incredulous Naaman (2 Kgs 5:15). God heals those whom he chooses—even those outside the covenant. The account of Naaman's healing reinforces an important biblical principle: God's grace cannot be bought. God's healing work is not available for a fee. God's grace in the form of healing is beyond price: it is so priceless that it must be accepted as a free gift.

As is common in biblical stories, a miracle ripples out, carrying with it wider theological ramifications. The original need (in this case for healing from leprosy) is met, and something even more wonderful and larger takes place. Naaman, a Gentile, not only receives his physical healing, but also becomes a believer in the God of Israel. Naaman's healing sparks his conversion, or rather, his healing and his conversion appear to occur simultaneously. When he meets the prophet, Naaman expresses his new faith in a personal way: "Now I know that there is no God in all the world except in Israel" (v. 15). He seals his conversion by asking that the prophet allow him to take back earth from Israel so he can worship on it. He switches allegiance from Rimmon, the god of storm and war whose name means "thunder,"[34] to Yahweh, the God of Elisha and Israel.

As a subordinate himself, Naaman respects authority. He understands that the prophet receives his authority from the God of Israel. This God is the only God in all the world. Naaman tells Elisha of his closeness with the king of Aram, a bond so close that the monarch leans on the arm of his general when he bows down to his god, Rimmon. Naaman informs the prophet that he will continue serving his king and asks that the Lord forgive him. The prophet's answer, "Go in peace" (v. 19a), while not condoning service to a foreign god, allows room for the God of Israel to bring about needed character change.

Naaman's affliction leads to his search; his search leads to his healing; his healing leads to his conversion; his conversion leads to his confession. The story of Naaman, a story in which an anonymous Israelite slave girl figures so predominately, further develops the theology of Israel by confirming yet again that the sovereignty and mercy of the God of Israel extend beyond the borders of Israel.[35]

The story of Naaman shares several similarities with themes found in the account of Elijah's sojourn with the widow of Zarephath. Verification of the status of both prophets comes through the mouths of females (1 Kgs 17:24; 2 Kgs 5:3).[36] In both cases, foreign males, born outside the covenant with Israel, are restored to life and health. The agents of covenant faith, Elijah and the Israelite slave girl, both live in the homes of the foreigners who trust them. In both accounts, the hosts are converted to faith in Yahweh, the God of Israel. Both Elijah the prophet and a little girl with a prophet-sized faith share a powerful and effective model of evangelism: *live among a foreign people; as their needs arise proclaim God's provision, and pray for God's miraculous power to meet those needs.*[37]

The faithful words and actions of a diminutive slave girl, marginalized and without rights in a foreign land, set in motion events that bring hope, life, healing, and conversion to a mighty man. Unnamed, probably orphaned and alone, and occupying the lowest position in a hostile, alien society, this child nonetheless makes one of the simplest, purest statements of faith in the Bible. She serves as a model of faith sweetly and confidently expressed during a time of personal crisis. The covenant holds, yes, gloriously holds!

QUESTIONS FOR FURTHER REFLECTION

1. If you were to meet the Israelite slave girl on the street, what do you think she would be like? What personality traits helped her overcome her hardships and multiple obscurities?

2. This narrative, like many biblical stories, brings contrasting characters together in interesting ways. In what ways are the slave girl and her master different? In what ways are they similar?

3. The Israelite slave girl's statement of faith is one of happiest statements of faith in the Bible. What makes her expression of trust so stunning? So endearing? So enduring?

4. Why do you think Naaman believed this young slave girl? What did Naaman risk by taking her at her word?

5. How do you reconcile Naaman's initial willingness to go to Israel for healing with his later anger and reluctance when told to wash in the Jordan River? Describe Naaman's inner struggle as he opened himself up to trust in God.

6. One of the important themes of this account is how God uses immediate needs to address deeper issues in our lives. Can you think of a situation where this has proven true in your life?

9

ATHALIAH
FROM OBSCURITY TO TREACHERY

¹When Athaliah the mother of Ahaziah saw that her son was dead, she proceeded to destroy the whole royal family. ²But Jehosheba, the daughter of King Jehoram and sister of Ahaziah, took Joash son of Ahaziah and stole him away from among the royal princes, who were about to be murdered. She put him and his nurse in a bedroom to hide him from Athaliah; so he was not killed. ³He remained hidden with his nurse at the temple of the LORD for six years while Athaliah ruled the land.

⁴In the seventh year Jehoiada sent for the commanders of units of a hundred, the Carites and the guards and had them brought to him at the temple of the LORD. He made a covenant with them and put them under oath at the temple of the LORD. Then he showed them the king's son. ⁵He commanded them, saying, "This is what you are to do: You who are in the three companies that are going on duty on the Sabbath—a third of you guarding the royal palace, ⁶a third at the Sur Gate, and a third at the gate behind the guard, who take turns guarding the temple—⁷ and you who are in the other two companies that normally go off Sabbath duty are all to guard the temple for the king. ⁸Station yourselves around the king, each man with his weapon in his hand. Anyone who approaches your ranks must be put to death. Stay close to the king wherever he goes."

⁹The commanders of units of a hundred did just as Jehoiada the priest ordered. Each one took his men—those who were going on duty on the Sabbath and those who were going off duty—and came to Jehoiada the priest. ¹⁰Then he gave the commanders the spears and shields that had belonged to King David and that were in the temple of the LORD. ¹¹The guards, each with his weapon in his hand, stationed themselves around

the king—near the altar and the temple, from the south side to the north side of the temple.

¹²Jehoiada brought out the king's son and put the crown on him; he presented him with a copy of the covenant and proclaimed him king. They anointed him, and the people clapped their hands and shouted, "Long live the king!"

¹³When Athaliah heard the noise made by the guards and the people, she went to the people at the temple of the LORD. ¹⁴She looked and there was the king, standing by the pillar, as the custom was. The officers and the trumpeters were beside the king, and all the people of the land were rejoicing and blowing trumpets. Then Athaliah tore her robes and called out, "Treason! Treason!"

¹⁵Jehoiada the priest ordered the commanders of units of a hundred, who were in charge of the troops: "Bring her out between the ranks and put to the sword anyone who follows her." For the priest had said, "She must not be put to death in the temple of the LORD." ¹⁶So they seized her as she reached the place where the horses enter the palace grounds, and there she was put to death.

¹⁷Jehoiada then made a covenant between the LORD and the king and people that they would be the LORD's people. He also made a covenant between the king and the people. ¹⁸All the people of the land went to the temple of Baal and tore it down. They smashed the altars and idols to pieces and killed Mattan the priest of Baal in front of the altars.

Then Jehoiada the priest posted guards at the temple of the LORD. ¹⁹He took with him the commanders of hundreds, the Carites, the guards and all the people of the land, and together they brought the king down from the temple of the LORD and went into the palace, entering by way of the gate of the guards. The king then took his place on the royal throne, ²⁰and all the people of the land rejoiced. And the city was quiet, because Athaliah had been slain with the sword at the palace.

²¹Joash was seven years old when he began to reign.

2 Kings 11:1–21

THE BIBLICAL STORY OF Athaliah, the only reigning queen of either Israel or Judah, is filled with insights into the turbulent political climate of the ninth century B.C.E.[1] Athaliah, born into the house of Omri, was a worshiper of the Canaanite god Baal.[2] Double reference to her story in 2 Kgs 11 and 2 Chr 22:10–23:21 shows its importance to the biblical writers. The largely parallel accounts present insights into the lives of the royals. The emphasis in 2 Kgs is on recounting the historical content, while that of 2 Chr is on presenting the theological validity of those in the Davidic line as the rightful heirs of Judah. In both accounts, daily life in the royal Judean court includes murder, intrigue, harem politics, religious upheaval, coup, and countercoup. How did this seamy state of affairs come about? The narrators' answer, consistent with the voice of the prophets, is apostasy.[3] The two accounts pivot around Athaliah, an obscure woman first named routinely as the mother of Ahaziah in the formulaic succession account (2 Kgs 8:26). Upon her son's death, she murders most of her immediate family and seizes the throne. Suddenly, she is no longer obscure.

Although readers recoil in horror from Athaliah's deed, the narrators of 2 Kgs and 2 Chr present her story quite straightforwardly.[4] The narrators' purpose is not to show that Athaliah is the epitome of evil or that all women in power are evil. Rather, through Athaliah the narrators often set up a series of good and evil contrasts and stress the political and theological vacillation of the people. Among the narrators' aims are to delegitimize Athaliah and to legitimize her successor, the young boy Joash, her grandson and the only survivor of David's line. The bold use of language helps the narrators achieve their aims.

THE FLOW OF HISTORY

Athaliah came to Judah from the northern kingdom. The texts alternately call her the daughter of Omri (2 Chr 22:2)[5] and the daughter

of Ahab (2 Kgs 8:18). Assuming that the latter is the case, and that
Omri was in fact her grandfather, then Jezebel was her mother.[6] Athaliah married Jehoram, son of righteous king Jehoshaphat of Judah,
around 865 B.C.E. Their marriage reflects the influence of Omride Israel over a weaker Davidic Judah.[7] John Bright believes the marriage
alliance was a friendly treaty between equals.[8] Its military and commer-
cial benefits included an attempt to revive overseas trade out of Ezion
Geber (1 Kgs 22:48).

When Jehoram assumed the throne in 849 B.C.E., he put all his
brothers and some princes of Israel to the sword (2 Chr 21:4); significantly, they were loyal Yahwists.[9] Bright acknowledges that the text
has "not a shred of proof for it" but nonetheless wonders if Jehoram's
slaughter of his brothers was not prompted by his wife "because she
felt her own position so insecure."[10] If it does, it foreshadows her subsequent acts of murder and attempted infanticide. Bright's speculation,
therefore, is noteworthy.

Jehoram reigned in Jerusalem for eight years, until 841; he did evil
in the eyes of the Lord and "passed away, to no one's regret," the text
quips (2 Chr 21:6, 20).[11] Ahaziah, the son of Jehoram and Athaliah,
succeeded him and reigned one year (841–840).[12] Ahaziah's ill-timed
visit to his cousins in Israel coincided with Jehu's coup. Jehu killed
Joram, who had succeeded his father, Ahab, as king of Israel. Jehu pursued Ahaziah and wounded him, and Ahaziah died at Megiddo, according to 2 Kgs 9:27. But 2 Chr has a somewhat different version of
his death. It says that Ahaziah fled to Samaria and hid there, but when
he was found and was brought to Jehu, he was killed (presumably at
Jehu's order; 2 Chr 22:9). Nonetheless, the verdict on Ahaziah's reign
resembles that of his father's reign—he too did evil (2 Chr 22:3).[13]

Sometimes scholars attempt to harmonize the accounts in Kings
and Chronicles by claiming that they overlay each other. Generally,
however, the results prove unsatisfactory.[14] For the purposes of this
chapter, Jehu's purge and its subsequent effects on Judah and Israel
serve to show the turbulence of the ninth century.[15] Murder is based
on considerations of blood or alliance and thirst for power.[16] The period seems to have been characterized by lawlessness within the political establishment, similar to an earlier time of lawlessness during the
era of the Judges, "when Israel had no king and everyone did as he saw
fit" (Judg 21:25).

It is interesting to note that the texts of Kings and Chronicles seem to differentiate between segments of the populace, distinguishing "the people of the land" (2 Kgs 11:14) from "the inhabitants of Jerusalem" (2 Chr 22:1). Do these descriptions represent two political groups pitted against each other, or are they merely synonymous? The text is unclear on this issue.

When Athaliah hears of her son Ahaziah's death by Jehu, she seeks to destroy the entire royal family.[17] Perhaps she consciously copies Jehoram's earlier massacre.[18] Her plan fails, however, for one family member escapes. The texts recount the heroic rescue of year-old Joash and his nurse by Jehosheba, the wife of Jehoiada the priest and the older half-sister of Ahaziah. The parallel accounts leave unanswered the natural question of why Athaliah allows Jehosheba to escape slaughter along with others in the royal line. Perhaps Jehosheba escapes because she, too, hides. Perhaps she lives because she's married to Jehoiada. Perhaps she's just lucky. Presumably, Jehosheba is Jehoram's daughter not by Athaliah but by another wife. Jehosheba and Jehoiada, two loyalists and believers in Yahweh, hide the baby and his nurse in the temple.

Six years later Jehoiada orchestrates an elaborate coup involving the Carites, priests, Levites, palace guard, and army. Surrounded by armed protection, Joash, now seven, is led out and loudly proclaimed king. The cheering alerts Athaliah, who comes to see what is happening. She quickly sizes up the situation, tears her garments, and shouts her only recorded words: "Treason! Treason!" (2 Kgs 11:14; 2 Chr 23:13).

Jehoiada orders his soldiers to seize Athaliah. Apparently, she flees. They catch up with her at the gate where the horses enter the palace grounds and put her to death. She, a follower of Baal, is slain outside the temple to save it from being defiled. Next, Jehoiada reestablishes two covenants, the first between the Lord and the people (including the king) and the second between the king and the people. The people then rampage, tearing down the temple of Baal and killing Mattan, the priest of Baal, in front of the altars (2 Chr 23:17; 2 Kgs 11:18).[19]

In marked contrast to many other biblical narratives, both 2 Kgs and 2 Chr abound with parallels of opposites: good and evil, murder and salvation, death and life, injustice and justice. By the end of the chapter, Joash lives and reigns, while Athaliah's kingdom turns away from her and is torn from her just as she tears her own garments. Her career as reigning monarch ends as it began: with death.

The Use of Language

Both the Kings and Chronicles accounts of Athaliah's reign are set within the context of God's faithfulness to his people and his promise that David's line will never lack a male descendant (2 Sam 7:1–17; 1 Chr 17:1–15; 1 Kgs 8:20). Athaliah's story immediately captures the attention of readers and hearers because we know her presence on the throne violates God's promise: she is not a member of David's house. Furthermore, the version in Chronicles continues the chronicler's pattern of presenting a Levitical sermon on God's faithfulness followed by a human example illustrating a person's faithfulness or unfaithfulness.[20] Chronicles see-saws between high points of faith such as Jehoshaphat's response to an upcoming attack from Moab and Ammon (2 Chr 20), and low points of rebellion such as Athaliah's murders.[21]

The first verse in 2 Kgs 11 lends itself to ambiguity because Athaliah's name carries a component of the name of Yahweh. Is she for or against Yahweh? Her very name, which may combine "to grow large" and "to be exalted" with Yahweh, is ironic because, as the reader quickly learns, she has spent her life erecting temples to Baal.[22] Irony appears several other times in both accounts, emphasizing that the narrators assumed their audience knew the historical details of Athaliah's story.

The first clue the narrators give that this story may be a tragedy is with the verb translated *saw:* "When Athaliah the mother of Ahaziah *saw* that her son was dead, she proceeded to destroy the whole royal family" (2 Kgs 11:1, italics added; cf. 2 Chr 22:10).[23] There are several other instances where *seeing* leads to sin, two of which involve women. The first concerns Eve, who *saw* that the fruit was good and then ate the fruit and gave it to her husband (Gen 3:6). When Delilah *saw* that Samson had told her everything, she recounted his words to the Philistines (Judg 16:18).

The importance of verbs in the Kings passage should not be overlooked. Hobbs points out that in 2 Kgs the scepter of leadership passes to Joash via a series of verbs which show the political genius of Jehoiada: he sent, he ordered, he brought out, she saw, he ordered, and she died.[24]

The narrators allow Athaliah only two words, and these are loaded with political, theological, and historical significance. Athaliah shouts, "Treason! Treason!" (2 Kgs 11:14; 2 Chr 23:13). She tries to stop the coup with these words, but the switch to another's leadership has already been made. The repetitive use of *treason* is ironic in that treason has indeed occurred twice: the first time by Athaliah's murderous hands, and the second time—at least from Athaliah's perspective—is happening to her now: Jehoiada is usurping her reign with a coup.[25] Another instance in the Hebrew Bible where the word *treason* is used is in relation to Zimri, who rebelled against Elah, reigned seven days, and died by setting fire to the palace around him (1 Kgs 16:15–20). The ironic connection between Athaliah's story and that of Zimri is further established by the fact that Jezebel, certainly Athaliah's mentor and perhaps even her mother, taunted her assassin Jehu by comparing him with Zimri (2 Kgs 9:31).

The lack of a standard, formulaic introduction to Athaliah's reign in both texts may serve to reinforce the irregularity, illegitimacy, usurpation, and inevitable doom of her tenure. Her reign is not presented as starting in a specific year; her age is not given; the length of her reign (six years) surfaces only because it corresponds to the time her grandson Joash was hidden in the temple; finally and surprisingly, the narrators do not comment on her as one doing evil or good in the eyes of the Lord. The fact that other monarchs accorded such introductions are all males seems secondary to the narrators' view that Athaliah's reign usurps the rightful Davidic line.[26] In contrast to the legitimacy of her predecessor, David, and her successors, Joash and Hezekiah, Athaliah's reign is presented in compressed historical form as an unfortunate interruption in the Davidic dynasty.[27]

THE ELEMENTS OF NARRATIVE

The accounts of Athaliah's reign in both 2 Kgs and 2 Chr utilize contrasts and comparisons as their primary narrative tools. The narrators present absolutes of right and wrong. They portray two distinct courses for the people of Judah to follow: the worship of Baal or the worship of Yahweh. Since the biblical writers unabashedly favor the latter course, the two accounts of Athaliah abound in narrative contrasts to which a reader naturally might assign the value judgments of good and evil. The narrators add a twist to the timeless literary formula of good triumphing over evil by encasing the good in the innocence of a seven-year-old orphan.

The narrators record Athaliah's story in a way similar to many of the terse vignettes presented in Proverbs, which leave no doubt about the moral views of the writer. With broad brush strokes, the narrators pit the Yahwists against the Baalists, the rightful ruler against the usurper, the house of David against the house of Omri, Judah against Israel, monarchy against dictatorship, truth against deception, the passive against the active, the agrarian countryside against the city, life against death, swift justice against outright murder, and the alliance of a courageous woman and her husband against the selfish wiles of a wicked queen. Within these contrasts the narrators utilize silence, one of their favorite devices, as a narrative tool. They divulge no descriptions about life—whether palace, city, or countryside—in those six years, nothing about agriculture, climate, international intrigue, and none of the highlights of Athaliah's reign. Wars, if any were fought, go unmentioned. The dominating silence, like the lack of formal introduction to her reign, may be a technique chosen by the narrators to focus on the illegality of this queen's reign. She is *not* the anointed monarch.

Beside the awkward silences, it is possible that the narrators provide a hint of court intrigue as well. Out of all Ahaziah's unfortunate children, why did Jehosheba choose to rescue Joash? Was it because he was the smallest? Was he the nearest to an escape route and therefore the easiest to snatch and carry to safety? Or may he have been chosen because of his mother? Perhaps baby Joash lived because Jehosheba knew that his mother, Zibiah, hailed from Beersheba, some forty miles south of Jerusalem (2 Kgs 12:2). If this is the case, then Jehosheba, in the instant allowed her to select whom to save, may have wisely reasoned that distance from Jerusalem provided a modicum of safety. In this circumstance, through Jehosheba's split-second choice, the inherent rivalry of co-wives and their offspring in their struggles over succession to the throne may echo the legacy of David.

THE DEVELOPMENT OF CHARACTERS

The narrators of both the 2 Kgs and the 2 Chr accounts carry out their strategy of sharp contrasts by drawing strong characters. Because the characters are polarized in terms of worship of Baal or Yahweh and are pitted against each other politically as representatives with loyalties to Israel or Judah, and to Omri or David, the reader knows instinctively that the upcoming conflict can produce only one survivor. There is no win-win scenario in this chapter: the stakes—political, personal, and theological—are simply too high.

ATHALIAH

Athaliah enjoys one of the longest narrative careers in Scripture. She carries out a complex set of roles, with the texts mentioning her as a daughter, wife, mother, dowager queen, and queen.[28] Her exact identity has sparked scholarly controversy, since she is referred to as the daughter of both Omri and Ahab. Although she is called a daughter of Omri in 2 Kgs 8:26, she is also assumed to be the daughter of Ahab, Omri's son, and Jezebel (2 Kgs 8:18 and 2 Chr 21:6). Some scholars solve this difficulty by following the Septuagint, the Greek translation of the Hebrew Bible, which describes her as the daughter of Omri and the sister of Ahab.[29] The reference to Athaliah as the "daughter of Ahab," is explained as a scribe's later addition.

H. J. Katzenstein believes that Athaliah was born in 881/880 B.C.E., near the time Omri ascended the throne.[30] Omri ruled only until 873/874, so it could be that Ahab was Athaliah's elder sibling by another wife. If Omri died when Athaliah was six or seven years old (ironically the same age as Joash), then she naturally would have lived under the household protection of her older brother. According to Katzenstein, Athaliah was married in 865, when she was fifteen or sixteen years old, and Ahaziah was her first child. Thus, Athaliah is the daughter of Omri, sister of Ahab, and pupil of Jezebel.[31]

Although her genealogy contains discrepancies, what is undisputed in both accounts is that Athaliah's marriage was a political alliance, as royal marriages often were in Israel and Judah. Love is not mentioned in the match between Athaliah of Israel and Jehoram of Judah, son of Jehoshaphat.[32] A notable exception to the rule is Solomon, who combined both love and political alliances, for he "loved many foreign women besides Pharaoh's daughter," married seven hundred wives, and had three hundred concubines (1 Kgs 11:1, 3).

The union of Jehoram and Athaliah evidently eased the tensions between Israel and Judah prevalent since Solomon's time.[33] Scholars speculate that the political payoffs of the brokered marriage included Israel's giving back areas of Benjamin in exchange for Judah's taking a back seat politically to the stronger Israel.[34] If the nobles in Jerusalem negotiated the marriage, then they had too much at stake politically to back out during the turmoil of Jehu's purges and likely supported both Athaliah's coup and her reign. Significantly, the biblical text gives no indication of any moral qualms or questionings on the part of the nobility.

Athalya Brenner assumes that Athaliah's position in Jerusalem for years was not unlike that of any other chief wife: she was consort and mother.[35] The text refrains from commenting much on her life prior to her husband's and son's deaths. During her son's lifetime she, as dowager queen mother, seems to have been a strong figure, one who gave advice and exercised authority.[36] Brenner, however, ignores the narrator's comment that during Ahaziah's reign, Athaliah encouraged her son to do wrong (2 Chr 22:3).[37]

Upon hearing of Ahaziah's death, Athaliah seizes the moment. She consolidates her reign by executing her rivals, almost the entire Davidic line in Judah. Scholars enjoy speculating on her intentions. Josephus wryly credits her with an opportunistic nature, while Lockyer attributes her rise to the throne to envy.[38]

Claudia V. Camp, however, renders a more charitable opinion. Reasoning that Athaliah fears for her life when Ahaziah is killed, Camp believes she then acts in the only way such logic would indicate. Cut off from her family's power base in Israel and from any means of retreat or escape, she preserves herself by murdering others.[39] Camp's view takes into account the unstable political situation in Israel. Jehu likewise clearly took charge through assassination, murder, and terror. N. E. A. Andreasen adds that Athaliah undoubtedly carries out her action with the knowledge and support of the pro-Israelite (i.e., pro-Omri) faction in Jerusalem (2 Kgs 9:16).[40] But H. Schulte believes her murderous rampage ultimately destroys her legitimacy as queen mother. Certainly it sows the seeds of her downfall.[41] Z. Ben-Barak agrees with Camp that Athaliah acts out of self-preservation but emphasizes that her seizure of power was an act of desperation, consistent with her family's history of murder and fratricide. Ben-Barak justifies Athaliah's murders and attempted infanticide by asserting that her action was understandable in light of the annihilation of the royal family in the northern kingdom and the murder of her son and of all the king's brothers.[42]

But Camp, Ben-Barak, and Brenner all fail to note that in biblical texts murder is never justified. While murder may be recounted by a narrator without outward emotion, retribution eventually falls on the one with bloody hands. Cain's murder of Abel gives the scriptural precedent: marked on his forehead, Cain is banished (Gen 4:1–16).

Athaliah fails to remember that Jezebel's murder of Naboth set in motion the prophecy that dogs would devour her by the wall of Jezreel (1 Kgs 21:23; 2 Kgs 9:10, 34–36). And they did.

Yet clearly Athaliah's murder of her family was a political purge that solidified the throne under her for a season.[43] Athaliah—daughter of a king, sister of a king, wife of a king, mother of a king—was now queen in her own right.[44] But did her assassinations carry a theological goal, too? Did she so hate the God of Judah that she wanted to exterminate the Davidic line, the line through which the Messiah would come? The text remains intriguingly silent.[45] But if nothing else, the murders furthered Judah's deterioration both politically and theologically. For evidence of this, the rabbis cite the absence in the days of Athaliah of the greeting, "The Lord bless you," a salutation common in the days of Boaz and Ruth.[46]

The narrators heighten the sense of Athaliah's upcoming doom by recounting in detail the preparations, secrecy, and numbers involved in Jehoiada's plot against her. Athaliah evidently remained ignorant about the maneuvers being instigated by the Yahwist priest. No one told her. No conspirator—and there were quite a few—broke rank. This indicates that she was either too isolated, too confident, or too proud; perhaps power bred arrogance and false security. Athaliah's story shows clearly her failure to learn from Jezebel the importance of having a reliable network of spies and informants.[47]

Athaliah's cries of "Treason! Treason!" suggest that she both saw herself as the rightful heir and immediately perceived the coup's significance. Her exclamations indicate that she believed her own lie—that she was the rightful monarch. The narrators present Athaliah as an isolated character, one duped by her own thoughts of invincibility. Like Job before her, who had complained, "Truly, my fears have come upon me" (Job 3:25), Athaliah's worst fear materialized: another heir emerged.

Brenner suggests that the priests lured Athaliah to the temple, a move assured violently to incite loyal Yahwists against her.[48] Previously she had broken into the temple and taken its cult objects for use in worshiping Baal (2 Chr 24:7). Jehoiada reasoned that in order for the restoration to be complete, Athaliah must die, but cause for her death had to be found. Setting foot in Yahweh's temple when she was a known follower of Baal would provide the needed provocation.[49] Amazingly, she rushes in without her bodyguards. With no one there to protect her, Jehoiada easily orders her capture and death.

JEHOSHEBA

Athaliah and Jehosheba offer sharp contrasts. Athaliah is a murderess, and Jehosheba is a savior. One destroys life, and the other jeopardizes her own life by rescuing a baby and his nurse. Perhaps as she saves Joash, Jehosheba remembers the deeds of the two midwives in Egypt who saved Hebrew babies; the Lord protected them from Pharaoh's wrath and rewarded them with families (Exod 1:15–21).[50] Although he offers no explanation, Josephus believes Jehosheba's rescue takes place after the slaughter rather than before, as the text indicates.[51] First Kings 11 describes Jehosheba in terms of her status: the daughter of King Jehoram and the sister of Ahaziah. But 2 Chr 22 adds a fact crucial for the development of the story: she is the wife of the priest Jehoiada. Both texts stress what she does: she stealthily takes Joash and his nurse, who are about to be murdered, and puts them in a bedroom to hide them from Athaliah. In typical fashion, the biblical writer neither describes her physically, allows her to speak, nor comments on her feelings or motives.

JEHOIADA

The texts move quickly from contrasting Athaliah and Jehosheba to contrasting Athaliah and Jehosheba's husband, the priest Jehoiada.[52] Athaliah's character of extreme evil is balanced by the character of Jehoiada, a man the text portrays as righteous. For instance, Athaliah murders, but Jehoiada preserves life. Athaliah takes power by nefarious means, but Jehoiada restores power to its rightful inheritor. Athaliah dies ignominiously, but Jehoiada lives to the age of one hundred and thirty years and is buried with honor "with the kings in the city of David, because of the good he had done in Israel for God and his temple" (2 Chr 24:16).

While Athaliah has a plan of accession that evidently was concocted quickly and carried out immediately at the news of Jehu's purge and Ahaziah's death, Jehoiada constructs a long-range plan. Their different plans show starkly different natures. They reveal Athaliah as a political novice who thinks only of the moment and Jehoiada as a political savant who keeps the future in view. Athaliah's plan is brutal, spur-of-the-moment, and effective—but negligent regarding a key element: the heir to the throne escapes. By contrast, Jehoiada's meticulous plan of restoration takes in all foreseeable contingencies. Biding his time, he allows himself years to build stable, quiet, and faithful alliances. These alliances lay the groundwork for Joash's reign. Jehoiada's countercoup is more encompassing than Athaliah's, for he plans to reinstate the worship of Yahweh and to leave no survivors of the original coup. According to hints in the text, he covertly organizes his supporters and engages in some quiet networking during the six years the lad stays hidden.[53] The pact or covenant Jehoiada makes with the guards "secured for him a solid power base from which to conduct the coup and virtually guaranteed [its] success."[54]

The texts prove Jehoiada adept at conspiracies.[55] His skills as diplomat, soldier, general, and regent surface in the texts more than his skills as priest.[56] Yet the basis of these skills is his strong religious training.[57] Jehoiada's painstaking actions receive extensive detailing in both texts (2 Kgs 11:4; 2 Chr 23:3).[58] The specific orders are not mentioned in Kings but are briefly outlined in Chronicles as dividing the priests and Levites into thirds and stationing them at the royal palace, the Foundation Gate, and the courtyards (2 Chr 23:5–7). The officers respond favorably and carry out their specific instructions to the letter.[59]

Common to both Kings and Chronicles is the recognition that Jehoiada's plan involves the knowledge of several hundred men. Amazingly, they all keep silent, for Athaliah expresses genuine and tremendous surprise at the coup. One can deduce from the numbers needed to overthrow Athaliah and pronounce Joash as king that there is significant dissatisfaction within the military, although the narrators give no reasons for it. In contrast, the dissatisfaction of the populace seems to ignite spontaneously, fueled by the predictable, pent-up outrage of the Yahwist priests who hate Athaliah for bringing in foreign worship.[60] Athaliah apparently thinks she can count on the support of the nobility and the Baalist priests, but these two contingents prove insufficient.[61]

JOASH

Joash, the middle ground between the Athaliah and Jehosheba/Jehoiada polarity, remains passive throughout the chapter.[62] First he is saved from slaughter; then he is hidden. His childhood is not mentioned. At age six or seven he is paraded about in regal garb by Jehoiada in the palace countercoup and hailed as king.[63]

While no word is given about Joash's six-year confinement, Jewish tradition maintains that he and his nurse were hidden, at least for a

time, in the Holy of Holies of the temple.[64] This is highly likely, for the
Holy of Holies was the only place Athaliah would not have scoured in
her search for survivors of David's line, since the penalty for unauthor-
ized entry into Holy of Holies was death. Hobbs, however, speculates
that Joash was hidden in Jehoiada's bedchamber.[65] Since it is unlikely
that the boy remained in any one location for the full six years, there is
no reason why both could not have been true.

Ironically, in a plot otherwise laden with tensions, Joash seems to
be the only character who remains calm. Throughout the story, he stays
silent, acts as directed, and takes no initiative. He merely stands by a pillar and receives acclaim.[66] Only later does Joash becomes active, at first
in a good direction and later in an evil direction. He repairs the temple,
and allows the people to pay a temple tax, which they joyfully do (2 Chr
24:1–16). However, after Jehoiada, his mentor, dies at age one hundred
and thirty years, Joash begins to drift back to the violence and deviancy
that surrounded him in his childhood. He waffles in his commitment
to Yahweh. He chooses wickedness and even orders the son of Jehoiada,
Zechariah the prophet, to be stoned (2 Chr 24:17–27).

Rabbinic commentary has understandably wrestled with the complex and tragic biblical character of Joash. One legend explains that
when Jehoiada died, the courtiers tempted Joash by telling him that
he must be a god because he had survived living six years in the Holy
of Holies. Rather than rebuking the courtiers, Joash is said to have
taken their message to heart and erected a monument to himself in
the temple. Zechariah, son of Jehoiada, rebuked Joash for this atrocity,
and Joash ordered him killed on the Day of Atonement. Zechariah's
innocent blood is said to have miraculously pulsated for two hundred
and fifty years on the spot where the prophet was slain. In the end, according to the tradition, Joash himself was killed by the Ammonites
and Moabites, descendants of two ungrateful nations.[67]

THE PEOPLE OF THE LAND

In some ways, the biblical narrative about Athaliah resembles the
couplets in Proverbs, with their strong contrasts of good and evil. In
those sayings and in this narrative, one struggles to find middle ground.
Predictably, such middle ground is found in the masses: the people
continually vacillate. Unstable in terms of both their theological and
political allegiances, they wobble between Yahweh and Baal through-

out the broader narratives of Kings and Chronicles. Arguably, the
people hold out to see which side will win before making a decision
about which side—political and theological—to join.

The chapters show three distinct elements in Judean society that
participated in the restoration of the Davidic dynasty: the army, the
priesthood, and the populace.[68] While the priests loyal to Yahweh
clearly opposed Athaliah, no mention is made of protestations by the
army or the populace to her rule. This may be because, despite the violence by which she seized control, no mention is made of any oppression in her rule—unlike the rule of Manasseh, in which the streets of
Jerusalem ran with blood (2 Kgs 21:16). The lack of any immediate
threat to their well-being may have lured the populace into a wait-and-
see attitude. The prophet Elijah had earlier reprimanded the people
for just such an attitude of silence, acquiescence, and unbelief (1 Kgs
18:24, 39).

There are other indicators, however, that the populace of Judah
may not have played such a passive role. Although the priests and
military lead the rebellion against Athaliah, afterwards a spontaneous
purge of the temple of Baal in Jerusalem is led by "the people of the
land" (Heb. 'am ha-'arets, 2 Kgs 11:18). Camp maintains that these
were staunch Yahwists who never forgot the Lord and were appalled
at Athaliah's religious practices.[69] Nelson agrees but adds that these
"people of the land" were the rural gentry who remained faithful to the
Davidic dynasty.[70]

E. W. Nicholson, who examined the more than sixty uses of 'am
ha'arets, concludes that "the people of the land" cannot be identified
with any one particular group. To regard the phrase as a technical term
designating a specific class or group within the population of Judah
is to read too much into its meaning. Rather, the fluid phrase varies
from context to context, as in Exod 5:5, where it refers generally to the
people of Israel in Egypt and in 2 Kgs 26:15, where it designates all the
people giving a particular offering.[71] Unlike those who take the 'am
ha'arets to be a powerful political body within Judah, Nicholson posits
that the coup, organized by Jehoiada and carried out in cooperation
with the army, enjoyed the backing of the nation at large, which had
remained loyal to the Davidic throne.[72]

The texts may further differentiate between the people of the land
(2 Kgs 11:14) and the inhabitants of Jerusalem (2 Chr 22:1). The ambiguity of the texts makes it difficult to determine whether these were

overlapping and mutually supportive groups or whether they represent rival factions. Nevertheless, both groups are important power brokers in Athaliah's story. Either way, Jehoiada calculated—and calculated correctly—that both groups would rally behind young Joash.

Once Athaliah is taken away to be executed, Jehoiada begins his reforms.[73] His immediate take-charge attitude shows he had orchestrated each step of the overthrow. His first reform includes making a covenant between the Lord and the people. He renews the covenant originally made at Sinai, which the people had forgotten and forsaken. Along with the original covenant made with Moses, other covenants, such as the earlier one between Jonathan and David and the later one between Ezra and the people and God, demonstrate the importance of covenant-making events in the minds of the people. The renewal of the most central national covenant represented another brilliant maneuver on the part of Jehoiada. It served to marshal those who may have been marginal supporters of the Davidic line and to make the countercoup a national, Judean event.

The quiet that fell over the city of Jerusalem may reflect several things (2 Kgs 11:20; 2 Chr 23:21). One is peace. The coup that had just taken place involves only the deaths of Athaliah and the priests of Baal; the populace is not put to the sword. To some extent, the quiet may also reflect shock. The people might be stunned and taken by surprise by the day's events. Finally, the quiet may indicate that any remaining followers of Athaliah need time to regroup.

Nelson, however, sees an ominous note in this quiet. He posits that Jerusalem's silence represents indecision on the part of the city's inhabitants and a clear difference between them and the people of the land in terms of their religious and political leanings.[74] Although the texts remain ambiguous, what is clear is that in ninth-century Judah the people expected politics and theology to go hand-in-hand. Political correctness then meant that the royal families openly worshiped and maintained a theological position, and the people, in general, followed the tone set by the royal houses.

An Ominous Comparison

Certainly the adage "Like mother, like daughter" holds for queens as well as for commoners. So it is not surprising that, whatever their precise relationship may have been, the text seems to invite comparisons between Athaliah and Jezebel, the wife of Athaliah's father or brother Ahab and notorious queen of the northern kingdom (1 Kgs 18–21). Their similarities and differences are noteworthy. For one thing, both are foreigners who bring the worship of foreign gods to the people of Yahweh. Jezebel is a foreigner in Israel from Tyre; Athaliah is a foreigner in Judah from Israel. Both led their countries in the worship of Baal. Both fought openly with the followers of Yahweh.

Although the narrators express no overt admiration for either Athaliah or Jezebel, they at least must acknowledge the length of their reigns. If Jezebel and Ahab were married when he began his reign, she reigned with him for approximately twenty-one years (874–853 B.C.E.). While Athaliah's reign is significantly shorter (six years), she must have been politically astute to have survived even that long, especially when other monarchs of the period—men—lasted only a matter of weeks or brief years.[75]

Yet despite Athaliah's tenacity, she lacks Jezebel's street smarts. Jezebel's network of spies kept her informed of Elijah's victory over the prophets of Baal, her son's assassination, and Jehu's immanent arrival at Jezreel. Whereas Jezebel mastered the art of covert dealings, Athaliah isolates herself and becomes a prisoner of her own evil. She does not keep her hand on the pulse of the people or work to enlarge her power base. In her isolation, she inevitably propels her own destruction. Unlike Zedekiah, another ill-fated monarch of Judah who was blinded and led in chains to Babylon, her counselors are not listed.[76] One may presume she had none of merit or, even worse, none at all.

Theologically, Athaliah does not follow in the footsteps of her relative Ahab, who at least initially repented of his wickedness (1 Kgs 21:27). Instead, Athaliah copies Jezebel, who failed to repent and faced death at the hands of those she knew, those who served her (see 1 Kgs 22:29; 2 Kgs 9:30). Yet Athaliah's evil career fails to live up to the standard of her mentor. Athaliah becomes her own prisoner, separated even from the illegitimate base of her power.

Like her exemplar Jezebel, Athaliah suffers an ignominious death among the animals. Jezebel perished by being thrown from her window by turncoat eunuchs and trampled by Jehu's horses. Similarly, Jehoiada orders that Athaliah be executed away from the temple. She dies in a barnyard setting amid animal refuse.[77] Like Jezebel in the moments before her death, Athaliah expresses outrage in defiant and aggressive terms. Like Jezebel, she dies a friendless queen, with no one pitying her or coming to her rescue. Athaliah's death, like Jezebel's, passes without lament; indeed, joy breaks out in Jerusalem at the news of her passing (2 Chr 23:21).

The biblical narrator's recognition of the influence of Athaliah and Jezebel is reflected more broadly in Jewish literature. In the collection of Jewish lore known as the Aggadah, these two are associated with Vashti (the wife of Xerxes and queen of Persia) and Semiramis (the wife of Nimrod and queen of Babylon) as four women who achieved power in the world.[78] These prominent women are remembered more for their misdeeds than for any good they might have accomplished. The biblical texts offer no condemnation of Jezebel and Athaliah because of their gender beyond what their sins of murder and idolatry merit. The Hebrew Bible does not distinctly identify them with the character types of evil, such as the foreign woman who appears in Proverbs (Prov 5, 6:20–7:27) and the prophets (Isa 47:7–8; Zech 5:5–11). However, the New Testament apocalypticist likely carries forward an ancient Jewish tradition when he mentions a false prophetess allegorically or actually named Jezebel (Rev 2:20), who misleads God's servants by encouraging them to practice sexual immorality and to eat food sacrificed to idols.

Understandably, scholars uniformly view Athaliah negatively. According to Brenner, the narrators despise her because she is a woman, a foreigner, a relative or daughter of Jezebel, a Baal worshiper, one who brought Baal worship to Judah, and one who is not of the Davidic line.[79] D. N. Fewell and D. M. Gunn believe the texts hold Athaliah responsible for her husband Jehoram's straying from Yahweh.[80] Lockyer writes, "She personified the evil of her ill-famed parents and transferred the poison of idolatry into Jerusalem's veins." He calls her a revolting figure, licentious, and the personification of despicable arrogance.[81]

The biblical accounts, however, while they recount Athaliah's misdeeds, are more restrained in their reporting than some scholars have been. The only emotive adjective applied to Athaliah is "wicked" (2 Chr 24:7). Biblical writers often handle horrific acts with a degree of detachment, as do modern-day reporters.[82]

More specifically, the biblical narrators do not link Athaliah's misdeeds with her gender. While the writers consistently condemn her sin, their condemnation is consistently gender-neutral. Mary Evans, reflecting more balance than many scholars, argues that while women leaders are rare in the Hebrew Bible, the text gives no indication that women are ineligible for or incapable of leadership and authority.[83] Furthermore, biblical writers give no indication that the leadership of women over men is somehow intrinsically alien to nature. Phyllis Trible, while she maintains that the Hebrew Bible was written in a male-dominated society and that its interpretation has had adverse effects on women, nevertheless believes that "the intentionality of biblical faith . . . is neither to create or perpetuate patriarchy, but rather to function as a solution for both men and women."[84]

Yet despite their restraint, the biblical writers unapologetically define sin, judge it, and record its punishment. Aside from breaking the sixth commandment in attaining the throne by murderous means, Athaliah, when placed in a position of power and influence, violates the principles God laid down for governing his people (see Deut 17:14–20). Failure in her reign is inevitable because she violates key provisions related to rulers in the books of Deuteronomy and Chronicles.[85] She fails to write out for herself a copy of the law (Deut 17:18). She refuses to follow the commands of the Lord to possess the good land and pass it on (1 Chr 28:8–9). She is unwilling to humble herself, pray, and seek the Lord (2 Chr 7:14). She abandons the Lord, and he in turn abandons her (2 Chr 12:5). These failures serve as a checklist that alerts the attentive reader that her reign travels a fast track to ruin.[86]

The narrators of Kings and Chronicles express no sorrow over Athaliah's death. Neither do they promote her story as an explanation of evil or portray her as the embodiment of the principle of evil.[87] Instead, Kings and Chronicles present a consistent picture regarding behavior. Reward and punishment are not overly delayed or deferred. If there is no repentance, sin sets in motion its own judgment. Punishment swiftly follows. Yahweh much earlier established the rules; those who abide by them, be they men or women, live. Rebels such as Athaliah perish, and history archives them into infamous obscurity.

SUMMARY AND CONCLUSION

The story of Athaliah is one of many in the Bible that can be read as an attempt to exterminate the Jews and/or the line of David through which the Messiah will come (Mic 5:2).[88] But in each story,

God's creative ways of salvation—whether of the few or of the many—
dominate. Even in the tragedy of Athaliah's attempt to murder all the
royal line of Judah, God savingly intervenes. Her grandson, Joash, the
rightful heir of Judah's throne in the line of David, represents God's
chosen remnant in fulfilling his purposes.[89]

Athaliah's life and death reinforce the theological principle that
*apostasy and syncretism inevitably produce bloodshed and political
upheaval.* Most tragically, often the results of such upheaval extend
into succeeding generations. Joash, the young prince hidden and ultimately restored to the throne by Jehoiada, forsakes his mentor after
Jehoiada's death and worships Asherah (2 Chr 24:17–18). When rebuked for this by Jehoiada's son Zechariah, Joash orders him stoned
(2 Chr 24:21). It is possible that Joash and Zechariah grew up side by
side as boys and played together in Jehoiada's household. Now, with
his order to kill Zechariah, Joash comes full circle. Like his grandmother Athaliah, he murders out of spite and in a futile attempt to
retain power.

Athaliah's life also has significance within the broader flow of biblical history. The narrators in the parallel accounts of Athaliah's reign
(2 Kgs 11; 2 Chr 22:10–23:21) record her rise as monarch and her
eventual assassination. Her story and character shed light on a tumul-
tuous political and religious era in Judah. Life in Judah teeters between
extremes, as the people vacillate between various political forces and
religious expressions. Various accounts document a general falling away
from the Lord in Judah during this period. Athaliah's story propels this
general plot forward, demonstrating a need for the divine discipline of
Judah on a corporate level. Her story serves to explain and justify the
conquest of Jerusalem by the Babylonians and the subsequent exile of
the Jews to Babylon in 586 B.C.E.

QUESTIONS FOR FURTHER REFLECTION

1. What was Athaliah like? What do you think motivated her to
   do the things she did? Are there any admirable qualities in her?

2. Someone might argue that Athaliah's actions in killing the royal family were in some measure justified in that she was afraid for her life. How would you respond to such an argument?

3. Some interpreters of these narratives link Athaliah's failures and demise with the notion that she is a woman seeking a position and prerogatives that properly belong to men. How does the author of this book respond to this allegation? How do you respond? Can you find biblical examples of women who held political power legitimately?

4. At least one biblical scholar believes that "the people of the land" are culpable in passively allowing the political intrigue to take place in their government. Do you agree? What role should the common people have played in the events surrounding Athaliah's rise to power and ultimate demise?

5. It is likely that Athaliah was following the example of mentors such as Ahab and Jezebel in the ways she sought to gain and retain power. What can we learn from Athaliah's example about how we should interact with the mentors and leaders in our situation today?

6. As you think about your role as a follower of God in a world of interpersonal, corporate, and political power struggles, what lessons have you learned (positively and negatively) from Athaliah?

CONCLUSION
FROM OBSCURITY TO SIGNIFICANCE:
A CONCLUDING TEXTUAL AFFIRMATION

Throughout the writing of this book, I kept in mind a foundational question: *Does the biblical text present women and girls as less important than men?* Broadly speaking, I found that importance is not necessarily measured by the amount of textual space allocated to a character based on his or her social status and gender.

My study included questions highlighting several ways to examine the texts about the seven obscure women and girls—the sister of Moses, Rizpah, the wise woman of Abel Beth Maacah, the wife of Jeroboam, the widow of Zarephath, Athaliah, and the Israelite slave girl. My research ended up making the following affirmations:

1. The interaction of these women and girls with named male characters sheds needed light on the character development of the men.

2. The narrators then use this information in subsequent plot development in which the men figure.

3. The plots of these stories often further the theological and political development of Israel.

4. The passages about each woman and girl, although brief and textually challenging, reveal characteristics about them and allow them to emerge with discernable personalities.

Aside from these four affirmations, my study yielded an insight that I had not anticipated when I began. The stories about these five women and two girls also embellish the biblical portrait of the character of

God. They reveal more of his attributes and show that his actions are consistent with his self-description in Exod 34:6–7a:

> And he passed in front of Moses, proclaiming, "The LORD, the LORD, the compassionate and gracious God, slow to anger, abounding in love and faithfulness, maintaining love to thousands, and forgiving wickedness, rebellion, and sin."

Although the texts sometimes seem to limit God as a participant in the stories in the same way the larger biblical corpus limits the role of women and girls, they nevertheless display God's character in subliminal ways.[1] God's personality and priorities emerge clearly from stories that hardly mention him. God's textual marginalization in the stories often parallels the textual marginalization of the women. Yet as is the case with the women, personality clues and character traits of God emerge from the texts.

My investigation into the lives of these obscure women and girls has shown them to be vital characters in the larger biblical corpus and in the unfolding history of Israel. The stories in which they appear reveal the character strengths and weaknesses of some of the most fascinating men in the Hebrew Bible: an unnamed pharaoh, Naaman, David, Abner, Ish-Bosheth, Joab, Jeroboam, Ahijah, Elijah, and Jehoiada. Furthermore, the narrators then use this information in subsequent stories and plot development surrounding these named men and the unnamed pharaoh. In spite of the terseness of the passages involving each woman and girl, the texts supply enough information about them so that they emerge as personalities in their own right.

THE OLDER SISTER OF MOSES (EXODUS 2)

The story of the deliverance of Moses (Exod 2:1–10) contains four anonymous characters: a Levite, his wife, their daughter, and Pharaoh's daughter. The Levite and his wife remain silent. Their daughter (by tradition Miriam) and Pharaoh's daughter speak. While the words of Pharaoh's daughter predominate and carry the tension in the story,[2] the winsome audacity of a Hebrew slave child makes her the story's beloved little heroine.

To be accurate, the story contains a fifth anonymous character, a baby who is later named as Moses. The narrative starts with a priestly genealogy for this baby and ends with his being given an Egyptian name (verses 1, 10); his dual heritage arguably sets a tone for the rest of the book.[3] In between these verses, the baby cries on cue and creates a crisis.

The story of the deliverance of Moses sparkles with shrewdness, cunning, faith, risk, desperation, adventure, and practicality. Ironically, the Nile that was supposed to be an instrument of death for male Hebrew babies (Exod 1:22) becomes instead the agent of life for one male baby who is drawn out of it (Exod 2:10).

The story tells much about the mother's desperation and her practical preparation to save her beautiful infant. Defying the royal decree, she hides her baby for three months. Then she makes a papyrus ark, seals it with tar and pitch, places the child in it, and sets it among the reeds of the Nile (Exod 2:2–3). When the little ark sets off down the Nile, the baby's protective big sister stands at a distance, watching what will happen (Exod 2:4).

Watching seems to characterize Miriam. Although just a child herself, the text shows she understands cause and effect. If her beautiful baby brother is not rescued soon, he will be killed. So she watches. She sees Pharaoh's daughter and the bathing party. She sees Pharaoh's daughter spot the papyrus basket-boat-ark in the reeds. She hears Pharaoh's daughter send a slave girl to find the child. She sees Pharaoh's daughter open the basket-boat-ark.

And then her baby brother cries.

For three months these cries had signaled danger. Perhaps Miriam for three months had been responsible for hushing those cries immediately. Probably she took her baby brother to their mother for nursing. Consequently, Miriam moves quickly, probably on instinct rather than planning, and politely asks Pharaoh's daughter an obvious question, "Shall I get one of the Hebrew women to nurse the baby for you?" (verse 7).

For Pharaoh's daughter, Miriam offers a way out of an unexpected crisis that occurred on a trip to the Nile to bathe. Probably the princess went regularly with her retinue to walk along the Nile and to have fun bathing in a safe place. Ordering a hungry, helpless baby slaughtered, even if that baby is only Hebrew slave under a death decree, certainly would spoil an otherwise carefree outing. Miriam's actions and words provide an alternative to violence.[4]

Surprisingly, the deliverance of the baby soon to be named Moses is not a hero story about Moses himself. Instead, the story chronicles the surprising, quick bonding of three females—a mother and her daughter on one side and the daughter of Pharaoh on the other. Although they represent different cultures and classes, they join around a common cause—saving a beautiful baby boy from a ridiculous, cruel, and immoral edict.

Like a Russian doll toy, the story of Moses' deliverance is part of a larger story that is part of a still larger story. One of these larger stories concerns the unnamed Pharaoh in chapters 1 and 2. Exodus portrays him as a bumbling buffoon, one whom nature, people, and the God of the Hebrews defy. Chapter 1 shows him as choosing to kill off the means of his dynasty's future workforce, baby male slaves (Exod 1:16, 22). Already in chapter 1, the Hebrew midwives defy him by letting the Hebrew baby boys live (Exod 1:19).

Pharaoh's ineptitude permeates chapters 1 and 2 and presumably his kingdom. Pharaoh cannot stop the Hebrews from having children, he cannot outmaneuver the Hebrew midwives, he cannot change the Nile as a traditional source of life to a sudden source of death, and he cannot control his own daughter.

While Pharaoh promotes a culture of death, his daughter, joined by a little girl and her mother, promotes life. The three females act without any overt direction from God. God is not mentioned as a character or agent in the story, yet clearly God is present below the surface of the story.[5] Cannot the deliverance of one baby from death and slavery signal the deliverance of many? Yes, indeed! Some eighty years later Moses leads his delivered people in song proclaiming the greatness of their warrior God and celebrating the hurling of a subsequent Pharaoh and his chariots into the sea (Exod 15:3–4).

Rizpah (2 Samuel 3)

God as a participating character does not appear in the first story about Rizpah;[6] mention of God comes only in Abner's formula oath of allegiance to David (2 Sam 3:9). Yet the story reveals God's character because it reveals the fulfillment of God's purpose: David indeed will be king (see 1 Sam 16:1–13). The altercation between Ish-Bosheth and Abner over sexual access to Rizpah leads to a fulfillment of God's prophetic word to Samuel. Abner makes good his vow to "transfer the kingdom from the house of Saul and establish David's throne over Israel and Judah from Dan to Beersheba" (2 Sam 3:10).

Thus, this first text about Rizpah paints her as a pawn; it records the dehumanization of a woman in ancient times and carries many modern overtones. Men control Rizpah's body. A kingdom changes hands at the mention of her name. A passive character in this passage, her name and status serve to reveal Ish-Bosheth's and Abner's character traits.

Abner is a bully; Ish-Bosheth is a coward. Ish-Bosheth quails before an irate Abner. The narrator presents this confrontation as a means of justifying the transfer of power from the house of Saul to the house of David. If Ish-Bosheth backs down before a verbal tirade, what will he do in a military attack? Furthermore, if Ish-Bosheth cannot guard sexual access to one of the most important members of his household—his slain father's concubine Rizpah—how can he protect the larger body, the state of Israel, from its foes? Ish-Bosheth's ineptitude reveals him as a spineless leader.

Ish-Bosheth's failure in the verbal contest with Abner advances the plot by hastening his own death. Ironically, Abner's actions regarding Rizpah likewise hasten his death at Joab's hands (2 Sam 3:22–27). 2 Samuel 3 leaves a reader with questions lingering over this named but otherwise obscure figure in Saul's court and household. Who is Rizpah? The biblical text keeps her waiting in the wings for decades before she reenters the stage of Israel's history and delivers a performance forged in suffering.

RIZPAH (2 SAMUEL 21)

After the transfer of the throne to David in 2 Sam 3, the text remains silent for years about Rizpah. A long time spent away from court apparently matures her. Upon her reentry, one is struck by her dignity and courage. In her second appearance in the biblical text, in the story of Rizpah and the Gibeonites, God honors Rizpah's valor by ending the famine. Furthermore, tribal divisions heal somewhat through a public recognition of and mourning for Saul and Jonathan. The country acknowledges the loss of its first king and his noble son. God works in this narrative on a scale larger than the narrow scope of Rizpah's winning a who-blinks-first contest with David. Significantly, the text spends four verses on the recovery of Saul and Jonathan's bones and on their proper burial (2 Sam 21:11–14).

The story is dramatic. Rizpah defiantly beats the scavengers off the bodies of her sons and relatives. Over the years she has lost everything—husband, status, and sons. She faces the equivalent of starvation—a future without a provider. Her circumstances make her unafraid for her own life. She has nothing more to lose. She is a woman alone in the world, one who has outlived her means of support.

Politically, Rizpah's surprising action initially presents a no-win situation for David, for the country surely will side with a grieving mother overseeing the slaughtered remains of her sons. The courage week after week of a defenseless woman creates the modern equivalent of a public relations nightmare for David. Rizpah's vigil over the seven Saulides publicly but silently reprimands established authority—David himself—for his lack of respect toward the dead.

Rizpah's defiant action sheds light on David's character. Again and again in the text David takes a situation like this that comes to him and uses it to his political advantage.[7] As the story of the executions and her defiant vigil progresses, David exhibits political acuity by not ordering her killed. He astutely turns Rizpah's defiance to political good will for his house. Rizpah's action presents David with an opportunity to address a national wound—the loss of a king and a beloved son—and work toward healing on a national level. David acts magnanimously as head of state. A proper burial of Saul and Jonathan quite likely permits a nation to grieve publicly and to make a transition to new leadership under David. Looked at in this way, Rizpah therefore renders the young united nation and its new king a great service.

After their burial, "God heeded the prayers for the land" (2 Sam 21:14). In other words, the normal seasonal cycle of rains resumes; the crops grow; the famine abates; the people eat. The text presents the view that God sends rain not because of the appeasing sacrifice of the Saulides but because of Rizpah's prayerful, defiant, lonely ministry to the exposed bodies.[8]

By appointing herself to watch over the executed Saulides, Rizpah illustrates the theological concept that God honors mercy, courage, and respect for others (see Mic 6:7–8). Even though muted in the text, Rizpah shows that one person acting righteously can wield national influence. Therefore, Rizpah emerges in this second text as a morally courageous fighter and a political savior. As a biblical profile in courage, she illustrates how one person standing alone can inspire a leader and a nation and have a profound impact on the course of history.

The Wise Woman of Abel Beth Maacah (2 Samuel 20)

The story of Joab and the wise woman of Abel Beth Maacah (2 Sam 20) reinforces the biblical principle that wisdom comes from the Lord.[9] Deliverance from a besieging army arrives not via the intervention of another, stronger army, but by the prudent words and actions of two people. In their fast-paced verbal encounter, wisdom and violence square off like boxers in a ring. Surprisingly, violence goes down for the count. Wisdom wins!

Ambiguous, ambitious Joab is a complex character whose life parallels that of David.[10] He lives for and is driven by his position—commander-in-chief of Israel's armed forces. He attains his position as a national hero and serves his king with unquestioned loyalty—until he loses that position. He proves willing to defy his king and even to commit murder to retain his position. Yet there is a good side to Joab's character as well, as shown in his confidence, his ability to command troops, his loyalty to the throne, and his willingness to allow an equal role of leadership to a woman. Keeping his commitment to the wise woman of Abel Beth Maacah, Joab chooses to call off the siege and avoid the unnecessary bloodshed of fellow Israelites. He shares the credit for ending Sheba's rebellion with the wise woman, and in so doing rescues David's throne.

Although the biblical text allows the past history, marital status, and patrimony of this wise woman to remain mysterious, her words and actions prove her wisdom. Following her verbal encounter with Joab, the wise woman shows herself to be an able negotiator who thinks fast on her feet. She upholds the reputation of her city as "a mother in Israel" that brings liberation from oppression; her activities and words ensure the well-being and security of her people. As a result of her encounter with Joab, she emerges as a surprising national leader. More than that, by her example, she contributes significantly to the biblical definition of wisdom. A wise woman achieves her goals by using well-chosen words and employing psychological insights.

The Wife of Jeroboam (1 Kings 14)

In 1 Kgs 14, the prophet Ahijah delivers two harsh words of judgment from God against the house of Jeroboam and the first word of destruction against Israel. God gave Jeroboam a promise of good will through the prophet Ahijah yet later delivered a message of humiliating destruction because of the king's disobedience. The biblical principle in clear: *God's blessing hinges on unswerving obedience to the Lord.*

The wife of Jeroboam is a colorless character muzzled by the text. The chapter does not enlarge upon her role as queen, her physical appearance, any emotions she experiences because of her son's illness, or her reaction to Ahijah's catastrophic prophecy. Because of the way her husband orders her around, the text provides a hint that her marriage is unhappy. Perhaps it is even abusive. She stoically obeys her husband, the prophet, and God. Although a major participant in the chapter and the walking link connecting Jeroboam and Ahijah, the wife of Jeroboam is a flat character.[11]

Yet the character of Jeroboam's wife allows an accurate reflection of the two named men in the story—Jeroboam, king of Israel, and Ahijah, the prophet. Jeroboam's demanding, controlling, and insensitive personality are accentuated by her placidness. Ahijah stands out as one who listens to and obeys God. Though blind, he sees through her disguise and pronounces God's judgment on Jeroboam's disobedient house. The prophetic word propels the plot forward toward household and national destruction.

The biblical story surrounding the wife of Jeroboam illustrates how God often starts a great work in a small way. A prophetic word to an unnamed woman, followed by a boy's unhealed illness and death, foreshadow national death and disaster. Jeroboam's lack of repentance as a leader reflects his nation's unrepentant attitude. His fall from power prefigures a broader judgment to come upon the people of Israel. Although as a character the wife of Jeroboam is bland, she is extremely important as the recipient of the prophetic word concerning God's plan uproot Israel.

THE WIDOW OF ZAREPHATH (1 KINGS 17)

First Kings 17 shows a God who carefully watches over all the activities of his servant, Elijah. God trains his prophet for increasingly arduous duties through the unusual circumstance of living in the household of a foreign woman and her son. By facing the tragedy of the death of the widow's son with prayer to God for the lad's recovery and by handing the child back to his mother alive, Elijah not only is strengthened in his faith but also gains the winning confidence needed to face the prophets of Baal and Asherah. Through Elijah's ministry, God initiates a return to the miraculous and opens up a new phase in which his gracious covenant dramatically extends outside the borders of Israel.

In the course of Elijah's interaction with the widow of Zarephath, insights into both characters emerge. Elijah's sense of humor as well as his proneness to confusion stand out as he and the widow meet the challenges of life together. The widow's predicaments contribute to the text by enlarging Elijah's faith and equipping him with a confident assurance for the greater challenges ahead. Throughout her interactions with the prophet, the character of the widow of Zarephath becomes clear. She is hospitable yet feisty. She is generous, even to the point of sharing her last meal with Elijah. Eventually, she becomes a follower of the God of Israel, and her words serve to validate Elijah's prophetic credentials.

First Kings 17 also emphasizes and expands upon important theological themes laid down by the earlier Deuteronomistic writer in preceding books in the Hebrew Bible. First, the totality and universality of Yahweh's power are reemphasized. Yahweh alone is God; rival deities of the times pale. Second, the text reaffirms the consistency of God's character. God vows to execute justice toward orphans and widows, to love strangers, and to provide food and clothing to the marginal members of society (Deut 10:18). God even desires to bring people outside the nation of Israel into his covenant blessings. Third, God's mercy extends to individuals such as an imperfect prophet and an initially skeptical widow. The power of a lone prophet's intercessory prayer stands out as a vivid reminder that God hears when his people call out in distress.

THE ISRAELITE SLAVE GIRL (2 KINGS 5)

The story of the Israelite slave girl presents a delightful heroine. Depicted as young and physically slight, this pint-sized champion is a leader in training. Simultaneously, her bearing and words guide and train others in faith. Brought as a captive into the home of a successful military commander compromised by a skin disease, she follows the chain of command established in Naaman's household. She serves

Naaman's wife and says to her mistress, "If only my master would see the prophet who is in Samaria! He would cure him of his leprosy" (v. 3).

The Israelite slave girl's faith and boldness captured the valiant Naaman's trust. He risks his reputation on her truthfulness and character. Although willing to pay dearly in gold, silver, and clothing for his healing, Naaman receives no audience with the prophet Elisha. Instead, the prophet sends a servant to Naaman with instructions for his healing. Taken at face value, Elisha's action represents a rebuke—a serious breach of good manners—to this internationally-acclaimed general!

Yet despite his arrogance and anger, Naaman listens. Earlier he listened to his wife who had listened to the Israelite slave girl. Now he listens to the servants who accompanied him to Samaria. They encourage him to obey the prophet's simple instructions, and he complies. Naaman bathes seven times in the Jordan and is cleansed. The Israelite slave girl's words prove true! Naaman receives his healing, and everyone around him sees a spectacular manifestation of the power of Israel's God. With the healthy skin of a young boy in place of his former leprous condition, he boldly confesses faith in the God of Israel. He returns to the prophet humbled and eager to lavish gifts upon him, but Elisha refuses payment.

The miracle of Naaman's healing carries wider theological ramifications. In the broader narrative, the story propels forward the theology of Israel by confirming yet again that the sovereignty of God extends beyond the borders of Israel. Along with this theological confirmation, Elisha grows in standing. The faith and words of a marginalized and enslaved young girl who dared to suggest the impossible confirm Elisha's status as a prophet. The slave girl models a powerful principle of effective evangelism: *courageously live among a foreign people, and as their needs arise, proclaim God's provision and truth, and pray for God's miraculous power to meet those needs.*

Athaliah (2 Kings 11; 2 Chronicles 23)

The narrators in the double stories of Athaliah (2 Kgs 11 and 2 Chr 22:10–23:21) record her rise as monarch and her assassination. Her story and character shed light on the chaotic political and religious times in Judah. Life in Judah during the time of Athaliah teeters between extremes. The people seesaw between various political forces and religious expressions. Athaliah's story comes amid many accounts that provide the textual evidence of a general falling away from the Lord in Judah. Her story propels the plot forward by showing a need for a corporate discipline of Judah. Her story numbers among texts justifying the conquest of Jerusalem by the Babylonians and the subsequent exile of the Jews to Babylon in 586 B.C.E.

The story of Athaliah, a murderous grandmother on the rampage, contains extreme contrasts. Where and when evil flaunts itself, heroism flourishes. What an amazing principle! When Athaliah seizes the throne and murders (she thinks!) all possible rivals, the heroine Jehosheba saves one baby and his nurse from extermination. For six years, Jehosheba and her husband Jehoiada the priest hide the baby-turning-toddler-turning-youngster. Rightful-heir Joash grows up literally under the nose of Athaliah. But she doesn't see it, sense it, or know it. She fails to recognize the threat possibly playing and growing before her that will soon kill her. Truly Jehosheba and Jehoiada can shout with the psalmist, "Both high and low . . . find refuge in the shadow of your wings!" (Ps 36:7). Like her mother or mentor Jezebel, a gifted woman with opportunities for greatness, Athaliah chooses to do evil and to pursue evil. Yet God holds her accountable.

Athaliah's story reinforces the theological principle that apostasy and syncretism inevitably produce bloodshed and political upheaval. A textual irony is that Jehoiada's life is sandwiched between two evil people, Athaliah and Joash. Joash, the young prince whom Jehoiada hides, saves, champions, and restores to his rightful throne, forsakes his mentor after Jehoiada's death and worships Asherah (2 Chr 24:17–18). Jehoiada's son Zechariah rebukes him for his unfaithfulness and Joash orders him stoned (2 Chr 24:21). His action echoes that of his grandmother Athaliah, who committed murder to retain political power. His legacy sadly proves the adage that blood is thicker than water.

THE SIGNIFICANCE OF THE CHARACTER OF GOD IN THE STORIES STUDIED

Consistent with narrative in the Hebrew Bible as a whole, in these stories of obscure women and girls, both the narrator and God are treated as bystanders. The narrator's opinions come through only rarely via isolated adjectives and comments. Likewise, God observes the events that take place, but as a bystander who only occasionally takes center stage. God is often not mentioned or appears behind the scenes with respect to the oversight and control of day-to-day activities.[12]

The first mention of God as a subject in the book of Exodus shows his actions: he was kind to the Hebrew midwives and gave them families of their own (Exod 1:20–21). Arguably, the midwives' choice to fear God and God's choice to be kind to them broadly set the tone for the Exodus narrative. Would it not be logical to expect God's kindness to extend to a specific Hebrew baby in Exod 2? Of course! Throughout the Pentateuch and into Samuel, Kings, and Chronicles, God as a character is mentioned only casually.[13]

Yet God's presence—whether hidden or occasionally manifested—permeates these books and others in the Hebrew Bible. Linguistically speaking, God is not the *direct object* of the stories, as he is in another biblical genre, the praise psalms. Instead, God's character, purposes, presence, and actions are the hidden *subjects* of biblical narrative.[14]

God reveals himself in the stories in less-than-obvious ways as the one who constantly works and the one who remains unquestionably sovereign. Although God occasionally dominates a scene, he nonetheless emerges in the text as the one who looms large in the background. God consistently intervenes, loves, saves, helps, disciplines, and judges his covenant people. In surprising twists, he does the same for those outside the covenant. Consider this as the biblical norm: *God acts creatively, constantly, and consistently on behalf of his creation.*

The stories in biblical narrative reveal a real world of real people who live, on the whole, messy lives. The biblical text routinely focuses on a dysfunctional, hurting, or sinful part of a person's life and only occasionally on a triumphant aspect of that life. Yet the Bible's focus is not negative. Rather, it is liberating, for it often provides a way to showcase God's righteousness, compassion, and miraculous power. Time and again another biblical principle is reiterated: *points of great crisis or trouble often become points of deliverance.*

A third biblical principle begun in the Pentateuch and reinforced in the narratives of Samuel, Kings and Chronicles is that *God,* although consistent in his nature, *works in ways that defy predictable formulas or patterns.* The stories of the five women and two girls studied highlight the theme that although deliverance most surely will come to God's covenant people (and often to those outside the covenant), the ways and means of that deliverance remain creatively open to the sovereign God's choice.

Mention of God and his direct actions appears in the stories studied but does not seem to take center stage as it does in the prophetic texts.[15] This biblical principle about God is as consistent in the texts about the women and girls as it is in the biblical record as a whole. For example, sometimes God gives a surprising prophetic word. This happens to the wife of Jeroboam when she comes to the prophet Ahijah to discover her son's fate. The prophet tells her that her son indeed will die and that her house will be destroyed and that Israel will be uprooted. What a dire word! Yet an earlier prophetic word to Moses followed a similar pattern. The daughters of Zelophehad approach Moses about their inheritance rights (Num 27:1–11). Moses receives an answer from the Lord about their legal rights, but the Lord, according to the textual order and context, tells him at the same time to prepare for his own death (Num 27:12–13).

God also shows consistent concern in the biblical text for foreigners and widows. Elijah is sent directly to a widow in Zarephath and not to any widow in Israel (Luke 4:26–27). Elijah renders her a direct word from the Lord addressing her emotional condition and promising consistent provision for the needs of her household (1 Kgs 17:13–14). Similarly, God's presence is with Naaman, the victorious general of the king of Aram, long before Naaman enters the biblical text (2 Kgs 5). Another foreigner God singles out is Ebed-Melech, a Cushite living in Jerusalem at the time of Jeremiah (see Jer 38:1–13). Ebed-Melech saves the prophet's life (Jer 38:7–12). During the siege of Jerusalem and shortly before its sacking by the Babylonians, the Lord remembers Ebed-Melech's kindness to his prophet and sends Jeremiah to him. Jeremiah prophesies that Ebed-Melech will not be handed over to those he fears and that he will escape with his life (Jer 39:15–18).

The stories of the wife of Jeroboam and the widow of Zarephath in this book bear a fourth biblical principle: *the prophetic message often involves hardship for the messenger.* Prophets are not exempt from the consequences of their prophecies.[16] For instance, the prophetic word of the upcoming uprooting of Israel that Ahijah gave the wife of Jeroboam quite likely meant upcoming hardship for the prophet himself. Likewise, Elijah's prophetic word of an upcoming drought encompassed his life as well as the lives of those in the area. Correspondingly, Huldah's prophetic word of the upcoming destruction of Jerusalem to the messengers from King Josiah addressed her life and the life of her family and neighbors, too (2 Kgs 22).

A final biblical principle shown in multiple stories is that *God is concerned not only on the macro level for nations, but also on the micro level for individuals.* The stories of these five women and two girls— the sister of Moses, Rizpah, the wise woman of Abel Beth Maacah, the wife of Jeroboam, the widow of Zarephath, the Israelite slave girl, and Athaliah—reinforce this biblical principle. Even the challenges of brevity, namelessness, foreign birth, lowly circumstances, silence, and/ or horrific actions that accompany these seven characters mark them surprisingly and significantly as important in each text. They are not overlooked by God. They perform the same functions as other named male characters in the text, although in a more limited way.[17] As stated in the introduction, their entrance flags a text. The narrators use these women and girls to herald the importance of an upcoming event. Consequently, the question Zech 4:10 raises holds true about these five women and two girls: "Who despises the day of small things?" The answer is this: Only one who fails to see the hand of the Lord at work.

ENDNOTES

NOTES TO INTRODUCTION

1. For example, 1 Samuel opens by introducing the family of Elkanah and concentrating immediately on a family problem: the barrenness of his favorite wife, Hannah. When her problem is solved and a son is born, Hannah joyfully sings. Hannah and Elkanah disappear from the text by 1 Sam 2:21. The story next focuses on this long-awaited son, the boy Samuel, who turns out to be prophet, judge, warrior, and king maker. Yet Hannah, in her need, in her prayer, in her tenacity, in her faith, and in her joyful exultation, sets the tone for 1 Samuel.

2. Much modern scholarship concentrates particularly on the contributions of the women in Genesis.

3. My interest in biblical women began in 1989 when I went back to graduate school to pursue an master of arts degree in biblical literature. My thesis, *A Critical Study of Deborah, a Woman of Greatness, Based on Judges 4 and 5* (unpublished, Oral Roberts University, 1991), found that the biblical text succinctly presents Deborah as a woman of incredible importance. She serves Israel as prophetess, judge, general, and songstress. Like David, she exhibits a multifaceted personality. The text presents her, like Joshua, Joseph, and Daniel, with much favor and without any specific character flaws or recounted sins. The text, though containing less about her than about these four men, nonetheless portrays her as one of Israel's greatest leaders.

4. Robin Gallaher Branch, "'Your Humble Servant.' Well, Maybe. Overlooked Onlookers in the Biblical Text," *OTE* 17 (2004): 168–89.

5. See Ruth 1:19; 4:4, 11–12; 4:14–15, 17.

6. See Kathleen Fischer, *Winter Grace: Spirituality and Aging* (Nashville: Upper Room Books, 1998), 118.

7. In this way, I slightly redefined and enlarged but carried on my interest in biblical women that I began exploring in my master's thesis.

8. Robin Gallaher Branch, "The Messianic Dimensions of Kingship in Deuteronomy 17:14–20 as Fulfilled by Jesus in Matthew," *Verbum et Ecclesia* 25 (2004): 378–401.

9. The women and the Israelite slave girl appear as characters only in the texts mentioned and in no other passages. The sister of Moses, by tradition Miriam, appears in other texts (Exod 15:20–21; Num 12; 20:1; Mic 6:4). Tamar, Rahab, and Ruth were foreigners, as was Athaliah.

10. See chapter 5, on the wise woman of Abel Beth Maacah, for a discussion of anonymous characters.

11. Perhaps a reason for little scholarly mention of Athaliah (even though she is the only queen in the biblical text who ruled in her own right in either Judah or Israel) can be attributed to a general revulsion of her because she slaughters her immediate family. Killing one's family or other families in order to secure power for oneself, however, has been practiced by men throughout history and is clearly seen in the biblical text. Two prominent examples are Solomon, who ordered the slaying of his brother Adonijah (2 Kgs 1), and Abimelech, who killed his seventy brothers (Judg 9). In addition, Jehu secured the throne for himself by slaying Ahab's seventy sons (2 Kgs 10).

12. Biblical texts most often define men in terms of the authority they wield as kings, religious leaders, society leaders, or warriors. In contrast, biblical texts most often define women in terms of their family and community relationships. In addition, the biblical definitions of women frequently carry sexual overtones like *concubine* and *wife,* while the details about men frequently concentrate on their functions.

13. In an interesting and no doubt intended slight, this ruler of the known biblical world remains anonymous in Exod 1, although his Hebrew slaves, Shiphrah and Puah, receive the textual honor of being named. For those following the traditional 1446 B.C.E. date for the exodus from Egypt, the king of Egypt who commanded the slaying of male Hebrew babies (Exod 1:15–16) probably was Ahmose I, founder of the eighteenth dynasty (see Kenneth Barker, ed., *New International Version Study Bible* [Grand Rapids: Zondervan, 1995], 84, 88).

14. Among the many expressions of this principle in church history is the *Westminster Confession of Faith,* which states in its opening chapter that "The whole counsel of God . . . is either expressly set down in Scripture, or by good and necessary consequence *may be deduced from Scripture*" (Williamson, G. I. *Westminster Confession of Faith: For Study Classes* [Philadelphia: Presbyterian and Reformed Publishing Co., 1964], 1:6, emphasis added).

15. Brevard S. Childs, *Old Testament Theology in a Canonical Context* (Philadelphia: Fortress, 1985), 6–15. Childs (pp. 11–15) offers several tenets of the canonical approach. First, it allows one to reflect theologically on the text as it has been received and shaped. Second, the final form of canonical literature,

the Bible, reflects a long history and process of development that is marked and shaped by hundreds of unrecorded decisions. Third, the canonical approach sees the discipline of Old Testament theology as combining both descriptive and constructive features. In other words, it affirms the descriptive task of correctly interpreting the part of the text under consideration by acknowledging the text's place in Israel's faith, and it likewise understands that theological investigation also means the modern interpreter must take a stand regarding the text. Fourth, an interpreter taking a canonical approach acknowledges its flexibility. A canonical approach refrains from looking for a "single key" or a "missing link" that works in interpreting all biblical genres. Fifth, a canonical approach acknowledges that the texts have become what we call Scripture within the community of faith. Sixth, the canonical theologian accepts the canon as normative in the life of the Christian community. Finally, the theologian who favors a canonical approach acknowledges his or her need of illumination through the Holy Spirit for both the understanding of a text and its application.

16. J. P. Fokkelman, *Narrative Art in Genesis: Specimens of Stylistic and Structural Analysis* (Amsterdam: Van Gorcum, Assen, 1975), 8.

17. J. Andrew Dearman, a member of my dissertation committee, says that for him, the stories of these women add "depth to the mosaic" of the biblical text.

18. As Esther Raizen, also a member of my dissertation committee, points out, my study emphasizes minutia and looks at the importance of minor women characters in the biblical text.

19. See Robert Alter's *The Art of Biblical Narrative* (New York: Basic Books, 1981), 63–87, for a discussion of the importance of dialogue.

20. For background and help in assessing the stories, see chapter 1, "Hearing the Story."

21. Other national deliverers and political saviors following Moses include the Judges, Joshua, Saul, David, and Esther.

22. B. Margalit, Professor of Hebrew at the University of Haifa, used this phrase about women in Deuteronomistic literature during a tutorial session in spring 1995. Harold Liebowitz agrees, telling me in a private conversation, "Since women generally don't appear [in the text], by contrast, when they appear, it is important."

Notes to Chapter 1

1. Gordon Fee and Douglas Stuart, *How to Read the Bible for All Its Worth* (Grand Rapids: Zondervan, 1993), 78.

2. W. C. Kaiser and M. Silva, *An Introduction to Biblical Hermeneutics: The Search for Meaning* (Grand Rapids: Zondervan, 1994), 68.

3. Ibid., 69.

4. Joe Lostracco and George Wilkerson, in their excellent book, *Analyzing Short Stories* (Dubuque, Iowa: Kendall/Hunt, 1998), devote chapters to each of these headings.

5. Kaiser and Silva, *Introduction to Biblical Hermeneutics,* 71–72.

6. Eugene F. Roop, "Essays," in *Believers Church Bible Commentary: Ruth, Jonah, Esther* (Scottdale, Pa.: Herald, 2002), 271–72.

7. טוֹב, BDB, 373–74.

8. Roop, "Essays," 260–61.

9. Ibid., 260.

10. Robin Gallaher Branch, "Women Who Win with Words: Deliverance via Communication," *IDS* 37 (2003): 299.

11. Ibid., 301. Deborah, the great judge of Israel, also has a prominent speech (Judg 5); she and Barak son of Abinoam sing a song of more than three hundred and fifty words.

12. Alter, *Art of Biblical Narrative,* 182; see also Kaiser and Silva, *Introduction to Biblical Hermeneutics,* 72.

13. Roop, "Essays," 261; Adele Berlin, *Poetics of Biblical Interpretation of Biblical Narrative* (Sheffiled: Almond, 1983), 137.

14. Roop, "Essays," 265.

15. Ibid., 272.

16. Lostracco and Wilkerson, *Analyzing Short Stories,* 35.

17. Consistent with the biblical text as a whole, the narrator lets dialogue and action describe the characters. He validates their words with their deeds (see Alter, *Art of Biblical Narrative,* 63–88). What the narrator chooses not to reveal about Elijah is as important as what is known about him.

18. Fleming James, *Personalities of the Old Testament* (New York: Scribner's, 1939), 173.

19. Uriel Simon, *Reading Prophetic Narratives* (trans. Lenn J. Shramm; Bloomington: Indiana University Press, 1997), 265.

20. Ibid.

21. Ibid., 269. The narrators' job throughout the Hebrew Bible is not to exalt a person, an institution, a situation, or a miracle, but to show examples of adherence to or divergence from the abstract beliefs and concepts central in thought throughout the Bible. Consequently, both major and minor characters rise up in the pages both as models and as warnings; the biblical narrators, however, do not endorse the social order of the day through the plot or any other tools but only endorse the religious and ethical values that are permanent .

22. According to the order of the text, Ahab's sins merit and lead to a national punishment: drought. Similarly, the widow believes the presence of the prophet reveals her sins and leads to her punishment: the death of her son. The biblical text notes the universality of sin (Gen 4:7; Exod 32:32; Num 5:7;

32:23; Deut 24:16; Pss 51:1–6; 119:11, 133; Jer 31:30; Ezek 3:18). It also notes God's ability and willingness to pardon sin (Ps 51:7; Mic 7:18; Zech 3:4).

23. Simon, *Reading Prophetic Narratives,* 263. Most biblical narratives contain a maximum of three characters. Conversation, however, usually is between two.

24. Simon, *Reading Prophetic Narratives,* 268.

25. Jerome T. Walsh, *1 Kings* (Collegeville, Minn.: Liturgical, 1996), 235.

26. See Lostracco and Wilkerson, *Analyzing Short Stories,* 15.

27. X. J. Kennedy and Dana Gioia, *Literature: An Introduction to Fiction, Poetry, and Drama* (6th ed.; New York: HarperCollins: 1995), 68; Lostracco and Wilkerson, *Analyzing Short Stories,* 14.

28. Roop, "Essays," 263.

29. See Lostracco and Wilkerson, *Analyzing Short Stories,* 12.

30. Ibid., 31.

31. Ibid., 58.

32. Ibid., 21.

33. Ibid.,19.

34. Ibid., 25.

35. Ibid., 27.

36. Ibid., 28.

37. Roop, "Essays," 280.

38. Ibid., 262.

NOTES TO CHAPTER 2

1. The text does not specify the slave girl's age. Rabbinic tradition, however, sheds light on the age of Miriam when she is introduced in Exod 2. As usual, the rabbis make their point by telling a story. Their story speculates that Jochebed and Miriam were the two Hebrew midwives, Shiphrah and Puah respectively (Exod 1:15) (see Angelo S. Rappoport, *Ancient Israel: Myths and Legends* [3 vols.; London: Senate, 1995], 2:205; also *Exod. Rab.* 1:17 and *b. Sotah* 11b). The only people named in Exod 1 and 2 are Moses and the midwives, Shiphrah and Puah; the midwives' names mean "beauty" or "fair one" and "splendor" or "splendid one" respectively (J. P. Hyatt, *Exodus* [London: Oliphants, 1971], 60–61). As a young child, most likely about five years old, Miriam assisted her mother in the deliveries of the Hebrew babies and would cry out "puah" when the mothers gave birth, according to the rabbinic story (Athalya Brenner, ed., *Exodus to Deuteronomy* [vol. 5 of *The Feminist Companion to the Bible;* 2nd series; Sheffield: Sheffield Academic, 2000], 107). By the time of the story in Exod 2, a minimum of a year has transpired and Miriam is quite likely about six or seven years old. The rabbis also look at the word describing the slave sister, *'almah.* Traditionally, this word is used for a young woman of marriageable age, as in Isa 7:14 (Hyatt, *Exodus,* 64). *Exodus Rabbah,* however, views *'almah* as a personality trait, a word meaning "to

make haste"—as indeed Miriam does when she runs to get her mother to nurse the baby (H. Freedman and Maurice Simon, eds., *Mishnah Rabbah,* Vol 3: *Exodus Rabbah* [J. Slotki, trans.; 3d ed. New York: Soncino, 1983], 1:30; cf. Brenner, *Exodus to Deuteronomy,* 107). Other scholars also pick up on the winsomeness of this young slave child. For example, J. E. Park endearingly calls her "a watchful little person" ("Exodus," *IB* 1:858).

2. The rabbis list seven prophetesses: Sarah, Deborah, Miriam, Hannah, Abigail, Huldah, and Esther (*Megillah* 14a). Three of these—Deborah, Miriam, and Huldah—are explicitly called prophetesses in the biblical texts. The rabbis also call Sarah, Hannah, Abigail, and Esther prophetesses because their words are prophetic. The Hebrew Bible also lists Noadiah (a false prophetess who tried to terrorize Nehemiah [Neh 6:14]) as a prophetess, but she is not given credit by the rabbis.

3. See *Exod. Rab.* 1:17; *b. Sotah* 12a; *m. Pesah.* 43:4; Brenner, *Exodus to Deuteronomy,* 107–08. The rabbis' interpretation appears to me to be plausible. Where the biblical text is silent, Aggadah literature (Jewish traditions associated with biblical stories) fills in the gaps and solves the problem of the two earlier siblings: in Exod 2, the marriage of a man of the house of Levi and a Levite woman (v. 1) produces a son, a fine child (v. 2). But this child already has a watchful, talkative sister (vv. 4, 7). Later the biblical text mentions another brother who also turns out to be older than this new baby (Exod 3:14; 7:7). The rabbis' explanation of the three births, their legitimacy, and the reasons for what seems to be a re-marriage of the parents (Exod 2:1), fills in the biblical silence and answers questions the text raises.

4. The story of the birth and babyhood deliverance of Moses contains suspense, a battle between good and evil, an element of chance, plenty of irony, a large amount of human initiative, a conflict of seemingly unequal forces, a note of whimsy, and an element of divine guidance. Pharaoh's edict threatening and attempting the annihilation of the Hebrew slaves is only one of many recorded in the Hebrew Bible; see for example Esth 3:8–15.

5. Hyatt, *Exodus,* 63. J. I. Durham, (*Exodus* [Waco, Tex.: Word, 1987], 16) sees this ark not as a cruel means of exposure but as a lovingly-made means of salvation—much like the ark of Noah; furthermore, he sees the actions of the mother and sister as those of keeping careful watch from a distance .

6. T. E. Fretheim (*Exodus* [Louisville: John Knox, 1991], 32) comments that the situation involves an *ethic of defenseless resistance* as well as an action of *creative disobedience.*

7. John Calvin (*Commentaries on the Four Last Books of Moses Arranged in the Form of a Harmony,* vol. 1 [Edinburgh: Calvin Translation Society, 1852], 40–41) believed that the baby's parents were woefully timid, a trait he finds almost inexcusable, for "they almost abandon the child, in order to escape from danger." But Calvin's pastor's heart later becomes visible when he

cautions his readers against judging the parents too harshly, noting that they must have suffered "terrible agonies" and "bitter grief" over the proposed fate of their child.

8. There are at least thirty-two myths and legends from the ancient Near East that can be loosely grouped into a literary motif detailing the adventures of an exposed and abandoned child (Hyatt, *Exodus,* 62).

9. Durham (*Exodus,* 16) goes so far as to argue that the mother and daughter kept watch for some length of time and tended to the baby's needs until deciding on the right time for the launch; he even posits that the ark was relocated for the baby's safety and feeding needs.

10. Perhaps the mother urged Miriam to stand watch over the ark, since as a child Miriam probably would be exempt from danger. Calvin (*Commentaries,* 42–43), while he chastises the parents for their neglect of duty, concedes that their action of having Miriam stand watch proves they retained some hope for the boy's life. B. S. Childs, (*The Book of Exodus: A Critical, Theological Commentary* [Philadelphia: Westminster, 1974], 18) considers the role of the sister in the story as "certainly one of the most delightful features in the narrative."

11. The identities of Pharaoh and his daughter puzzle scholars. As mentioned, Pharaoh was probably Ahmoses I, founder of the eighteenth dynasty; see M. A. Harbin, *The Promise and the Blessing: A Historical Survey of the Old and New Testaments* (Grand Rapids: Zondervan, 2005), 123. The daughter of Pharaoh is traditionally called Tharmuth or Bithia (*Jub.* 47:5; *b. Meg.* 74, 91; *b. Ber.* 41; see Hyatt, *Exodus,* 64). According to rabbinic tradition, Bithia was bathing in the Nile in order to cleanse herself from the impurity of the idolatry so rampant in Egypt (Roth, "Bithia," *EncJud* 2:1059).

12. Durham (*Exodus,* 16), however, argues that there is no textual suggestion that the ark was deliberately placed where a sympathetic princess could find it. On the contrary, he believes that discovery by an Egyptian would put the baby immediately in harm's way because of Pharaoh's order to slay all male Hebrew babies (Exod 1:16, 22).

13. Other examples include Ebed-Melech, who confronted King Zedekiah in public in such a way as to force him to release Jeremiah from the cistern (Jer 38:1–13); Joseph, who knew how to administer a household to please his master; Potiphar (Gen 39:6); Harbona, a eunuch who attended Xerxes/Ahasuerus, the king of Persia, and told the king of Haman's plot to hang Mordecai (Esth 7:9); and the Israelite slave girl who belonged to Naaman and his wife, who knew that Elisha could cure her master of leprosy (2 Kgs 5:3).

14. Another person in the Hebrew Bible who knew the habits of a regent was Hegai, the eunuch in charge of the harem of Xerxes. Hegai noticed Esther immediately, provided her with beauty treatments, special food, seven maids

to wait on her, and moved her into the best section of the palace (Esth 2:8–9). The text indicates that by this special notice he considered Esther the best candidate among the young virgins competing to be the next queen. Hegai clearly wanted her to win the beauty contest and to wear the crown. Why? Probably because he thought it would be better for him.

15. The same word used to describe the baby Moses—good (Heb. *tov*)—is used to described God's various actions in creation (Fretheim, *Exodus,* 38).

16. G. A. Chadwick describes her reaction as one of embarrassment (*The Book of Exodus* [vol. 2 of *The Expositor's Bible,* ed. W. R. Nicoll; New York: George H. Doran, 1898], 129).

17. A repetitious word may also signal the reader to pay attention; see Alter, *Art of Biblical Narrative,* 95.

18. See R. Eales-White (*The Power of Persuasion: Improving Your Performance and Leadership Skills* [London: Kogan Page, 1997], 41–45) for a thorough discussion of incentives and empathy.

19. For an excellent discussion on the role of character in narration, see Kaiser and Silva, *An Introduction to Biblical Hermeneutics,* 67–84.

20. Eales-White, *Power of Persuasion,* 42.

21. Ibid.

22. Ibid., 43.

23. Ibid. Other questions or statements in this approach could include the following: I trust your judgment. How do you feel about this? I understand your position; now let me explain mine. I agree. My goodness; that must have been a terrible disappointment for you. Please give me your opinion on this. I'd like to hear your ideas.

24. Ibid.

25. According to Jewish tradition, Bithia, Moses' foster mother, was still alive when Moses returned to Egypt (cf. Exod 4–5) and they were reunited. Moses interceded with God for her, and she alone of all the Egyptians was spared the plagues, including the plague upon firstborn children (*Exodus R,* 18:3). She became a proselyte to the Hebrews' God and married Caleb. God honored Bithia, Jewish tradition continues, by allowing her to enter Paradise in her lifetime (Midr. Prov. 31:15). She, like the wise woman of Abel Beth Maacah, is numbered among twenty-two women of valor in the Hebrew Scriptures (Roth, "Bithia," *EncJud* 2:1059–60).

26. The princess later continues the God-given role of bestowing a name (see Gen 1; 2:19; 3:20). While the name *Moses* may have a Hebrew etymology meaning "to draw out," it could also be a form of "to be born." There are similarities with the names of pharaohs like Thut-mose, which means "The god Thut is born" (Hyatt, *Exodus,* 65).

27. The text is silent about the housing arrangements the princess and the wet nurse/birth mother make. Hyatt (*Exodus,* 64) speculates that the Mesopotamian practice was followed, namely, that the wet nurse took the child to her own home, received wages for her services, and then delivered the child, once weaned, to her employer, who then adopted the child.

Notes to Chapter 3

1. "Succession narrative" is a scholarly, literary term that refers to the stories about who is king of Israel and who will be king. These stories, often sordid, seamy, and gory, involve nations, houses, families, men, wives, children, and siblings. In the broadest sense, the succession narrative dominates the books of Samuel and continues into Kings; in the narrowest sense, it focuses on David and his house.

2. Rizpah may have had non-Israelite blood, for *Aiah* is a Hurrian name that means "falcon" (Anderson, *2 Samuel* [WBC; Waco, Tex.: Word, 1989], 56; J. Blenkinsopp, *Gibeon and Israel: The Role of Gibeon and the Gibeonites in the Political and Religious History of Early Israel* [New York: Cambridge University Press, 1972], 60). In ancient Hebrew, *Rizpah* means "hot stone" or "coal" ("רִצְפָּה," BDB, 954), while in modern Hebrew it means "floor."

3. Abner and Ish-Bosheth probably viewed David's ascent to the throne at Hebron as an act of treason (2 Sam 2). David's bizarre behavior throughout the succession struggle, and especially his finding respite in Gath with Israel's sworn enemy, the Philistine king Achish, raised legitimate questions not only about his loyalty to Israel but also about his sanity (1 Sam 21:10–15). See F. C. Fensham, "The Battle Between the Men of Joab and Abner as a Possible Ordeal by Battle? (2 Sam. 2:12ff.)," *VT* 20 (1970): 357.

4. Walter Brueggemann, *First and Second Samuel* (Louisville: Westminster John Knox, 1990), 221. Yehezkel Kaufmann (*The Religion of Israel* [Jerusalem: Musad Bialik, 1947], 641) adds the interesting note not found in the biblical text that Abner crowned Ish-Bosheth king in a valley.

5. Lostracco and Wilkerson, *Analyzing Short Stories,* 28.

6. Eugene H. Peterson, *First and Second Samuel* (Louisville: Westminster John Knox, 1999), 150.

7. Michelle Ellis Taylor, "Dog," in *EDB,* 352.

8. Ken Stone, *Sex, Honor and Power in the Deuteronomistic History* (JSOTSup 234; Sheffield: Sheffield Academic, 1996), 86. Briefly tracing the story through the end of the chapter is helpful in understanding this six-verse passage. True to his vehement threat, Abner immediately initiates negotiations with David's camp. David responds by demanding that Ish-Bosheth release

David's first wife, Michal (2 Sam 3:12–17). Joab, David's general and Abner's rival for the position of commander-in-chief of the army of Israel, is angry that David let Abner go in peace. Joab pursues and kills Abner, thereby avenging the slaying of his brother, Asahel. The deed is done deceitfully during a private and presumably safe conversation between Joab and Abner (2 Sam 2:22–27). David rebukes Joab and orders an elaborate funeral and mourning for Abner. The text stresses David's innocence in Abner's death (2 Sam 3:28–39).

9. Phyllis Trible, *Texts of Terror: Literary-Feminist Readings of Biblical Narratives* (Philadelphia: Fortress, 1984), 66.

10. C. Rabin, "Origin of the Hebrew Word *Pileges*," *JJS* 25 (1974): 353, 361.

11. The biblical text says that David had ten concubines (2 Sam 15:16) and eight wives (Michal, Ahinoam, Abigail, Maacah, Haggith, Abital, Eglah, and Bathsheba). The rabbis say he had eighteen wives, the maximum allotted (I. Epstein, ed., *Babylonian Talmud,* Part 4, vol. 4: *Sanhedrin* 1 [Jerusalem: Soncino, 1961], 939:22a).

12. Use of the words *concubine* and *wife* for Bilhah and Zilpah (Jacob's concubines or wives), and Keturah (Abraham's concubine or wife) points as well to some fluidity of roles between wife and concubine in biblical times. Because the word *pilegesh* seems to be used interchangeably at times with *wife* and is not accompanied by moral comments, it appears at times that the biblical text views concubines somewhat neutrally. Yet at other times a concubine like Bilhah is called a slave (Gen 29:29; 30:3). Similarly, Gideon's unnamed concubine (Judg 8:31) is also called his slave (Judg 9:18). Sons of concubines were allotted paternal land at their father's discretion. Bilhah's and Zilpah's four sons—Dan, Naphtali, Gad, and Asher—received a blessing with their half-brothers from their father Jacob (Gen 49:16–21) and land in Canaan (Josh 13:24–28; 19:24–48). But while the Hebrew Scriptures recount selected instances of family relationships involving concubines, it would be incorrect to assume that concubines were standard members of Israelite families. Their inclusion was the exception and not the rule. More commonly, concubines in Israel (and throughout the ancient Near East) were the political tools and goods of the powerful (see Peggy Day, "Concubine," *EBD,* 273).

13. Ancient literature contains stories about concubines. In Greek literature, Phoenix, the son of the Great King, sleeps with his father's concubine. Angered, the Great King curses him with childlessness. Phoenix responds by wanting to kill his father. The other gods put Phoenix under house arrest.

14. M. Tsevat, "Marriage and Monarchical Legitimacy in Ugarit and Israel," *JSS* 3 (1958): 241.

15. See J. P. Brown, "The Role of Women and the Treaty in the Ancient World," *BZ* 25 (1981): 12.

16. Ibid., 13.

17. This explanation of the status of concubines in the ancient world sheds light on two other biblical passages: Reuben's sleeping with Bilhah, his father Jacob's concubine or wife, and Absalom's doing the same in public view during his bid for kingship. The text gives no reason for Reuben's action; perhaps it was lust or an attempt to displace his father and take over the family's leadership. But his deed prompted his father, in everlasting enmity, to forego giving him the place and status of the firstborn (Gen 35:22; 49:3–4). Absalom, David's son, pitched a tent in full view of all Jerusalem, "and he lay with his father's concubines in the sight of all Israel" (2 Sam 16:22). This well-planned part of his rebellion attempted to legitimize his kingship. Absalom's bid for kingship, however, ended with his death.

18. Stone, *Sex, Honor and Power,* 85.

19. Lostracco and Wilkerson, *Analyzing Short Stories,* 21.

20. The triangular story of Rizpah/Ish-Bosheth/Abner parallels other such relationships in Scripture (Bathsheba/Uriah/David, Tamar/Amnon/Absalom, Solomon/Abishag/Adonijah, and Joseph/Potiphar's wife/Potiphar (2 Sam 11, 13; 1 Kgs 1; Gen 39).

21. Abner, a major player in Israelite politics for more than a generation, is a fascinating character, most likely a legend in his own time. According to Jewish tradition, Abner was the son of the witch at Endor (1 Sam 28) (see Ginzberg, *Legends of the Jews* [Philadelphia: Jewish Publication Society, 1909–1938], 6:70). Abner's name means "father of light." Rabbinic tradition claims that he was the head (father) of the Sanhedrin and that he loved the Torah (ibid., 6:240). The most important man in Saul's court and kingdom, Abner was a man of extraordinary size and strength. According to one legend, once when David chanced to steal a pitcher placed near the sleeping Abner's feet, Abner moved, pinning David between his legs. Propitiously, a wasp stung Abner, and his reflex action freed David (ibid., 6:73, 90–91).

22. Lostracco and Wilkerson, *Analyzing Short Stories,* 35.

23. Ibid., 37.

24. Stone, *Sex, Honor and Power,* 87.

25. S. D. Goldfarb, "Sex and Violence in the Bible," *Dor le Dor* (1975): 130.

26. Anderson, *2 Samuel,* 56. The *Encylopedia Biblica* (Jerusalem: Bialik Institute, 1966), 7:435, summarizes Abner's actions this way: Abner had sexual relations with her, and then, because of Ish-Bosheth's accusation, he abandoned Ish-Bosheth and sided with David.

27. Anderson, *2 Samuel,* 56.

28. This technique—a narrative statement followed by an affirmation in a direct quotation—appears throughout the Bible. A New Testament example is

the annunciation, the visit of the angel Gabriel to Mary. The writer of the Gospel of Luke says she is a virgin and soon she says so herself (Luke 1:27, 34).

29. J. C. Vanderkam, "Davidic Complicity in the Deaths of Abner and Eshbaal: A Historical and Redactional Study," *JBL* 99 (1980): 531.

30. Lostracco and Wilkerson, *Analyzing Short Stories,* 49–50.

31. Part of the genius of the biblical text is that it refuses to add details that encumber its purpose. Focused and terse, the text streamlines its selections—thereby leaving much to both (godly) imagination and (scholarly) speculation.

32. Stone, *Sex, Honor and Power,* 87.

33. The story of Abner and Ish-Bosheth ends with an ironic twist: David orders Ish-Bosheth's assassins killed and Ish-Bosheth's head buried in Abner's tomb at Hebron (2 Sam 4:12).

34. Stone, *Sex, Honor and Power,* 87.

35. Anderson, *2 Samuel,* 56.

36. Goliath, the Philistine giant, presents an interesting parallel to this passage. Upon meeting the youthful David, Goliath bellows, "Am I a dog that you come at me with sticks?" (1 Sam 17:43). Both Goliath and Abner, men who refered to themselves as dogs, meet violent ends. David kills Goliath (1 Sam 17:51) and Joab guts Abner (2 Sam 3:27).

37. Anderson, *2 Samuel,* 57.

38. Jewish legend continues to shed information on Abner's place in Israel's history by elaborating on the final struggle between Abner and Joab. Once Joab struck him fatally in the belly with his sword, Abner almost killed Joab with the sword in return. What prevented him was the people's cry that if Joab also died, they would be orphaned and left to the will of the Philistines (Ginzberg, *LJ* 4:73). Thus Abner refrained from killing Joab and died both a martyr and a hero.

39. Stone, *Sex, Honor and Power,* 90.

40. Likewise, Judah's honor depended on Tamar's chastity (Gen 38).

41. The rabbis posit an interesting explanation for Abner's switch of allegiance: timing. Abner backed Ish-Bosheth for two and a half years because of a Benjaminite tradition that Israel had to have two kings from Benjamin (Ginzberg, *LJ* 4:74). Ish-Bosheth's accusation signaled the end of that season.

42. The incident involving Rizpah serves the general well, for Abner, the power broker, seems to be itching to cut a deal with David. Vanderkam believes that Abner held the post of *sar saba,* the same position held by Joab in David's army; see Vanderkam, "Davidic Complicity," 531. In modern terms, Abner longs to be chairman of the Joint Chiefs of Staff on the winning side. David remains silent about Abner's offer. "The king must have calculated that Abner and Joab could not coexist in one camp," Vanderkam (ibid., 532) writes. This judgment is supported by the fact that David, Joab, and Abner go back a

long time. Earlier, outlaw David had insulted Abner's status and pride while Joab and both armies listened nearby. David "publicly castigated Abner for dereliction of duty" regarding the general's lack of protection of Saul in 1 Sam 26:14–16; see Frederick H. Cryer, "David's Rise to Power and the Death of Abner: Analysis of 1 Sam. 26:14–16 and Its Retaliation and Critical Implications," *VT* 35 (1985): 386–87.

43. Stone, *Sex, Honor and Power*, 93.

44. Trible, *Texts of Terror*, 68.

45. Ibid.

46. "בָּאַשׁ," BDB, 93.

47. An interesting legend about Saul's Ahinoam has her encouraging Saul in their courtship. Citing her as one of the dancing maidens sought as wives for the Benjaminites (Judg 21:21), the legend explains that she spotted the shy, tall Saul and took the initiative by suggesting that Saul capture her (Ginzberg, *LJ* 6:232).

48. Another irony regarding family names that is particularly significant in the later narrative concerning Rizpah in 2 Sam 21 is that both her and Jonathan's sons were named Mephibosheth. One escapes death, and one does not.

49. Vanderkam, "Davidic Complicity," 527–28.

50. From my own study of David as a political savant, I believe it is entirely possible that he took Saul's wife Ahinoam before Saul died, an action that blatantly laid claim to the throne of Israel. For more on David as a politician see my article "David and Joab: United by Ambition," *BRev* 19 (2003): 14–23, 62–63.

NOTES TO CHAPTER 4

1. Scholars question the order and placement of 2 Sam 21–24, the addendum chapters of 2 Samuel that lack chronological order. Second Samuel 21 and 24 chronicle two of David's deeds involving deaths: the execution of the descendants of Saul and the census of his fighting men. The Lord punishes David for the census by sending a plague in which seventy thousand people from Dan to Beersheba die (2 Sam 24:25). In between these two chapters are a list of his heroes and their exploits, David's long psalm of praise, a recounting of the Lord's promise to David, and yet another list of heroes and their exploits. Walter Brueggemann (*First and Second Samuel*, 336) explains the odd addition and arrangement of these four chapters as a deliberate attempt by the narrator, writing with a considerable degree of irony, to show a very different side of David from that presented in earlier chapters. The incident with Bathsheba (2 Sam 11, 12), however, may already have prepared the reader to see the flaws in David's character.

2. M. Ben-Yasher ("A Study of the Case of Rizpah Daughter of Aiah," *Beth Mikra* 27 [1966]: 41) believes the incident took place in the thirty-third year of David's reign.

3. The story, which took place immediately after Saul was chosen king (1 Sam 10:9–27), cemented Saul's valor as a military leader and endeared him to the people of Jabesh Gilead. The story from 1 Sam 11 bears repeating. The besieged people of Jabesh Gilead seek a treaty with the Ammonites. Nahash the Ammonite arrogantly agrees, saying "I will make a treaty with you only on the condition that I gouge out the right eye of every one of you and so bring disgrace on all Israel" (1 Sam 11:2). Undoubtedly terrified and horrified, the elders of Jabesh Gilead send messengers throughout Israel asking for help. Saul and Samuel respond with three hundred thousand men from Israel and thirty thousand from Judah (1 Sam 11:8). Saul breaks his army into three divisions, invades the camp of the Ammonites during the last watch of the night, and slaughters them until the heat of the day (1 Sam 11:11). Public favor rests upon Saul, and Samuel leads the people in worship and in reaffirming Saul's kingship (1 Sam 12:12–15).

4. Scholars traditionally group the two sons of Rizpah, Armoni and Mephibosheth, and the five sons of Saul's daughter Merab (2 Sam 21:8) under the heading *Saulides*.

5. Gibeon, which figures strongly in the second story about Rizpah, emerges early on as an unsettling force in David's reign. After David's anointing at Hebron, the Israelites under Abner and Ish-Bosheth regroup at Mahanaim but confront Joab and his leaders at Gibeon in Benjamin. Surprisingly, Gibeon is expected to side with David, even though the confrontation takes place in the land of Saul's tribe; see Fensham, "Battle Between the Men of Joab," 357. In 2 Sam 21, the reason Gibeon sides with David is understood: the Gibeonites, a people who exchanged their freedom for their lives during the conquest, became slaves of the Israelites and hated Saul because of an alleged but unrecorded incident in which their blood was shed. Kaufmann (*Religion of Israel*, 638) argues that Saul sought to kill the Gibeonites and others in the land of Canaan throughout his reign.

6. R. D. Bergen, *1, 2 Samuel* (NAC 7; Nashville: Broadman and Holman, 1996), 444.

7. Ibid., 445.

8. Ibid., 446. Rizpah's sons may have been doomed to die in part because of their inferior status as sons of a concubine and not of a legal wife. As such, they could never ascend the throne.

9. Brueggemann, *First and Second Samuel*, 336.

10. Questioning of David's motives continues by scholars writing about 1 and 2 Kgs. For example, see Iain W. Provan's excellent discussion of David's

last actions as king (1 Kgs 1–2) in *1 and 2 Kings,* (NIBCOT 7; Peabody, Mass.: Hendrickson, 1995), 23–28, 31–34.

11. Ibid., 337.

12. V. P. Hamilton, *Handbook on the Historical Books: Joshua, Judges, Ruth, Samuel, Kings, Chronicles* (Grand Rapids: Baker, 2001), 360.

13. Vanderkam, "Davidic Complicity," 537–38. Consequently, some scholars argue that 2 Sam 21:1–14 belongs before 2 Sam 9:1 (p. 538). The final editor of 2 Sam, they contend, did not want to identify any of the people David sought to show kindness to in 2 Sam 9:1 (p. 539). Perhaps after the slaughter of two sons and five grandsons of Saul, only Mephibosheth, the crippled son of Jonathan, remained. Shimei, David's accuser and a member of Saul's clan, shamed David publicly for killing Saul's sons and grandsons (2 Sam 16:5–8; 2 Sam 21), and David admitted having done so (p. 539).

14. Jewish tradition notes ten famines that accosted the biblical world. This one in David's time, the sixth in the list of ten and lasting three years, is the only one given a time frame. Other famines happened during the lives of Adam, Abraham, Isaac, Jacob, Elimelech, Elijah, and Elisha. The ninth famine is described by the rabbis as "piecemeal from time to time" and the tenth and worst as coming before the Messiah, "when the famine will be for the word of the Lord" (Ginzberg, *LJ* 1:220–21).

15. Ibid., 4:72.

16. Ibid., 6:269.

17. Brueggemann. *First and Second Samuel,* 337.

18. Henri Cazelles, "David's Monarchy and the Gibeonite Claim," *PEQ* 87 (May–Oct 1955): 170.

19. Anderson, *2 Samuel,* 249. One rabbinic tradition credits David with offering to give the Gibeonites silver and gold as compensation for the loss of seven members of their clan. They refuse. David then cries out to the Lord for three gifts to Israel: compassion, chastity, and graciousness of service to their fellow men. David quickly perceives the Gibeonites' lack of compassion and consequently excludes them from further communion with Israel (see Ginzberg, *LJ* 4:110–11).

20. The number seven here may be a symbolic representation of the number of Gibeonites slain by Saul, or it may be the actual number.

21. Cazelles, "David's Monarchy," 173. Saul's sons by Rizpah his concubine could not legally ascend the throne; however, in story after story from the ancient Near East, the political ambitions of second sons and so-called lesser sons by concubines are recognized as realities. Cazelles offers another suggestion as well. He notes that a royal concubine had a special relationship to the sacral character of the king in the eyes of the common people.

22. Anderson, *2 Samuel,* 250.

23. Cazelles, "David's Monarchy," 167.

24. Blenkinsopp, *Gibeon and Israel,* 93.

25. Ibid. The biblical narrative of the deaths of Saul's relatives has elements found in other, earlier tales from Ugarit and the Hittites. In the Baal and Anat cycle, Mot is killed by Anat between the harvest and the autumn rains. Furthermore, the use of the rare verb *yaqa'* is consistent with the dismembering and exposing of the body of Mot in Ugaritic texts. The verb means "to sever, to impale, to allow pieces to drop by rotting" (J. Strong, *Strong's Exhaustive Concordance of the Bible.* Peabody, Mass.: Hendrickson, 2007, 1511). An earlier Hittite story is also similar to the story of Rizpah. Evidently a plague broke out during the reign of the Hittite king Murshili (1340–1310 B.C.E.). Murshili sought the oracle and learned that the plague was because of the treaty his father Shuppiluliuma signed with the Egyptians. This treaty angered the Hattian storm god. Both national disasters—the famine in David's time and the plague in Murshili's—were the result of actions by previous kings (A. Malamat, "Doctrines of Causality in Hittite and Biblical Historiography: A Parallel," *VT* 5 [1955]: 9).

26. Anderson, *2 Samuel,* 249. Anderson supports crucifixion (249). Cazelles believes the bodies were dismembered ("David's Monarchy," 167–68). The rabbis support hanging because they say Esther argued for hanging Haman's sons and because Saul's sons were left hanging for half a year (Ginzberg, *LJ* 4:444). Yet according to Cazelles, *talah,* "to hang," demands an explicit correlation in the text that is not supplied ("David's Monarchy," 167–68).

27. Lostracco and Wilkerson, *Analyzing Short Stories,* 25.

28. "Rizpah," *EncBib* 7:435.

29. See 2 Sam 16:5–9. Shimei the Benjamite curses David, and Abishai son of Zeruiah wants to cut off his head.

30. H. Freedman and Maurice Simon, eds. *Mishnah Rabbah,* vols. 5 & 6: *Numbers Rabbah* (trans. J. Slotki; 3rd ed.; New York: Soncino, 1983), 1:221–22.

31. Ibid., 1:221.

32. Significantly, all Israel mourned the death of Abijah, the son of Jeroboam, as well (1 Kgs 11:18). To be mourned by "all Israel" represents a singular national honor.

33. *Numbers Rabbah* 1:221.

34. Ibid., 1:222–23, 223.

35. See Branch, "Women Who Win with Words," 299–305.

36. See Branch, "David and Joab," 16.

37. The biblical text enumerates his holdings: "A certain man in Maon, who had property there at Carmel was very wealthy. He had a thousand goats and three thousand sheep" (1 Sam 25:2).

38. Branch, "Women Who Win with Words," 301.

39. She says that when David is leader over Israel, "my master will not have on his conscience the staggering burden of needless bloodshed" (1 Sam 25:31).

40. The rabbis say there are seven prophetesses: Sarah, Deborah, Miriam, Hannah, Abigail, Huldah, and Esther (I. Epstein, ed., *Babylonian Talmud*, part 2, vol. 4: *Megillah* 14a [Jerusalem: Soncino, 1961], 193).

41. The adjective or title "wise" may indicate an office or that the woman is clever or shrewd; see B. B. Birch, "1 & 2 Samuel," *NIB* 2:1313.

42. Ibid., 1314.

43. Bergen, *1, 2 Samuel*, 392.

44. Alter, *The Art of Biblical Narrative*, 126.

45. Brueggemann (*First and Second Samuel*, 337) argues that the biblical narrator uses irony to show David as a ruthless opportunist who was presented, by the famine and the Gibeonites' demands, with a way to eliminate the Saulide threat. David cloaks his deed of political expediency with religious justifications and jargon. This is consistent with an earlier argument that Shimei, a relative of Saul, saw David's spin doctoring and cursed him for it (2 Sam 16:8). Although one can argue that the accusations Shimei hurls at David refer to this episode specifically, Anderson contends that the text endeavors to show David as just and loyal to Jonathan's memory and to Yahweh (Anderson, *2 Samuel*, 251). Nevertheless, Anderson holds that the chapter remains a clever political chronicle of David's ridding the land of potential usurpers of his throne while at the same time appearing to be doing God's will (p. 251). R. H. Pfeiffer argues that the deaths of Saul's descendants seem to present an opportunity for David to rid himself of serious rivals "under the guise of piety" (*Introduction to the Old Testament* [New York: Harper and Brothers, 1948], 353). Cazelles, however, sees the incident as showing that David is loyal to Saul and Jonathan because he acts with justice and pity: justice toward the Gibeonites and pity toward Mephibosheth, Jonathan's son ("David's Monarchy," 74).

46. Brueggemann, *First and Second Samuel*, 336.

47. Ibid.

48. See Alter, *Art of Biblical Narrative*, 117–25.

49. David's action regarding the executions of Saul's sons and grandsons receives no praise or condemnation in the biblical text. In contrast, a somewhat similar action under Alexander Jannaeus, ruler of Judah from 102 B.C.E.–76 B.C.E., receives condemnation by the rabbis. They call him the "lion of wrath" while they themselves are the "seekers of smooth things" (J. M. Baumgarten, "Hanging and Treason in Qumran and Roman Law," *ErIsr* 16 [1982]: 7). The story goes like this: It seems Alexander Jannaeus ordered the crucifixion of eight hundred rebels captured in a civil war. For this action, the rabbis called him the man who hangs men alive (ibid.). This incident, while

outside the biblical text, nonetheless sheds light on how differently the public may have regarded the executions ordered by David, while the writers of biblical history recorded it without moral comment.

50. Ginzberg, *LJ* 4:110–11.

51. God's gracious assessment forgives and ignores or forgets David's adultery with Bathsheba; his murder of her husband, Uriah; his failure to discipline his sons; his implication in the murders of Abner and Ish-Bosheth; the execution of Saul's two sons and five grandsons; and his motive of pride in the census. The biblical principle is this: *repentance brings forgiveness, but the consequences of one's sinful actions remain.*

52. The executions or sacrifices have fulfilled their purpose (Ben-Yasher, "A Study of the Case of Rizpah," 41).

53. Cazelles, "David's Monarchy," 167.

54. Another view is that the executions caused God to stop the drought and bring the rains. ("Rizpah," *EncBib* 7: 435).

55. Bergen, *1,2 Samuel,* 446.

56. Ginzberg, *LJ* 6:273.

NOTES TO CHAPTER 5

1. Other women the Hebrew Scriptures treat as political saviors include the Hebrew midwives Shiphrah and Puah, who defied Pharaoh's order to slay the male Hebrew babies (Exod 1:15–22); the older sister of Moses, traditionally known as Miriam (Exod 2:1–10); Rahab, the woman in Jericho who hid the Israelite spies (Josh 2); Deborah, the prophetess, songster, and judge who co-led a rag-tag Israelite army against a seasoned Canaanite army fully equipped with nine hundred iron chariots (Judg 4–5); Jael, the Kenite woman who put a tent peg through the temple of Sisera, the Canaanite general who oppressed Israel (Judg 5:24–27); Abigail, whom David credits with saving him from unnecessary bloodshed (1 Sam 25:32–33); Jehosheba, daughter of King Jehoram, who saved Joash from being slain by Athaliah (2 Kgs 11:2); and Queen Esther, who saved her people from annihilation.

2. C. F. Keil and F. Delitzsch (*The Books of Samuel* [Edinburgh: T&T Clark, 1872], 455), note that in the late 1800s Abel Beth Maacah had become a large Christian village called Abil-el-Kamh. Located on the northwest side of Lake Hulah and on the eastern side of the river Derdara, the village enjoyed a reputation for growing excellent wheat.

3. For an excellent discussion of Serah, see Leila Leah Bronner, "Serah and the Exodus: A Midrashic Miracle," in Brenner, *Exodus to Deuteronomy*, 187–98.

4. Gen 46:17; Num 26:46; 1 Chr 7:30.

5. Ginzberg, *LJ* 2:39. Others who did not die include Enoch, Elijah, and Ahijah; the Hebrew Scriptures substantiate the continued life (or at least the escape from death) of Enoch and Elijah, and Jewish tradition claims the same for the prophet Ahijah. According to another Jewish legend, when Joseph's brothers returned from Egypt and had to tell their father that Joseph was alive, they asked Serah, by now a beautiful maiden, to play on the harp and to sing the news to the elderly Jacob. She sang, "Joseph, my uncle, liveth; he ruleth over the whole of Egypt; he is not dead!" (ibid., 2:115). Jewish tradition says that as she played, Jacob believed, and the spirit of prophecy, which never visits except when a seer is in a state of joy, again visited him. Jacob rewarded her with these words, "My daughter, may death never have power over thee, for thou didst revive my spirit!" (ibid., 2:116). Jewish tradition maintains Serah escaped death, served her people as the wise woman of Abel Beth Maacah, and entered paradise alive (ibid., 2:116).

6. The weight of textual evidence about Joab indicates that he, like David, had become a legend in his own time; see Branch, "David and Joab," 62.

7. Walter Brueggemann views Absalom's rebellion as the dramatic center of what he aptly calls "the pathos filled narrative of David and his family" (*First and Second Samuel*, 300).

8. Perhaps Joab thought that eliminating this threat to the throne would please David, but Absalom's death broke David's heart; see Patricia M. Mc-Donald, *God and Violence: Biblical Resources for Living in a Small World* (Scottdale, Penn.: Herald, 2004), 207.

9. Such recorded rebukes of biblical heroes are rare. David received an earlier rebuke from the prophet Nathan regarding his adultery with Bathsheba and the murder of her husband, Uriah (2 Sam 12), which he arranged. Earlier still, Abram's deception regarding Sarai his half sister/wife brought Pharaoh's rebuke (Gen 12:18–19), and years later a similar rebuke from Abimelech (Gen 20:9–10). See Robin Gallaher Branch, "Genesis 20: A Literary Template for the Prophetic Tradition," *IDS* 38 (2004): 218.

10. Branch, "David and Joab," 23.

11. Amasa is the son of David's sister Abigail. Joab, Asahel, and Abishai are the sons of David's sister Zeruiah. David included all four nephews in his inner circle of military men but made Joab commander-in-chief of his army (2 Sam 8:16); see V. Voinov, "Old Testament Kinship Relations and Terminology," *BT* 55 (2004): 117. David's judgment in replacing Joab with Amasa, who led Absalom's revolt against David (2 Sam 18:24), seems questionable and extraordinary (p. 117). Perhaps revenge for Absalom's death at Joab's hands motivated David. Since Joab had taken from David what David loved most—his son Absalom—perhaps David took from Joab what Joab loved most—his position as commander-in-chief of Israel's army.

12. Jane Cahill, "Jerusalem in David and Solomon's Time: It Really Was a Major City in the Tenth Century B.C.E.," *BAR* 30 (2004): 20, 63.

13. Joshua A. Berman (*Narrative Analogy in the Hebrew Bible: Battle Stories and Their Equivalent Non-Battle Narratives* [Leiden: E. J. Brill, 2004], 175), notes the way the Hebrew links two verbs together to imply a sharp instrument (see also 2 Sam 1:15; 3:27).

14. Barker, *NIV Study Bible,* 450.

15. Abruptness is a frequent characteristic of biblical narrative. Name, tribe, husband's name, age, occupation, physical description, description of clothing, and children's names are among the details about the wise woman of Abel Beth Maacah the text lacks. Nonetheless, the text presents this lone woman as the city's chosen representative. Similarly, Elijah erupts onto the biblical stage without introductory remarks about his tribe and father and it is only later in the cycle of stories about him that he is given the appositive "prophet" (1 Kgs 17:1; 18:22, 36).

16. The narrator does the same thing in 1 Sam 25. He introduces Abigail as an intelligent and beautiful woman and her husband, Nabal, as a man who is surly and mean in his dealings. After making this editorial statement about them, the narrator backs up his assessment with the story of their dealings with David, at that time an outlaw on the run from Saul. Abigail's intelligence is demonstrated in her quick decision to prepare a picnic to waylay David's forces and thereby forestall his impending sword against her household. Furthermore, the text seems to substantiate her beauty, because when Nabal conveniently dies, David sends his servants to her and asks her to become his wife. The rabbis go even further; they say Abigail ranks with Sarah, Rahab, and Esther as one of four women of surpassing beauty in the Hebrew Scriptures (Branch, "Women Who Win with Words," 299). See the discussion of Abigail in ch. 4.

17. R. Eales-White describes four approaches to persuasive communication: logic, incentives, empathy, and group. Of the four, the wise woman's strategy is most consistent with the logical approach. For more about the insights in this paragraph, see R. Eales-White, *The Power of Persuasion,* 5, 34–35.

18. Lostracco and Wilkerson, *Analyzing Short Stories,* 31.

19. "The introduction of direct discourse, a new character, the change of perspective from besiegers to besieged all signal the beginning of a new event," writes M. L. Geyer. "The effect of the woman's cry on the attackers is to check their frenzied advance, to make them stop and listen," she adds ("Stopping the Juggernaut: A Close Reading of 2 Samuel 20:13–22," *USQR* 41 [1987]: 36).

20. The *Shema,* probably the most well-known creed in Israel, starts with the same verb, שְׁמַע (Deut 6:4).

21. The many textual references to Joab paint a complex portrait of Israel's most famous general over David's forty-year reign. They point to a man who is a brilliant military strategist and never loses a battle, a courageous war-

rior, a legend in his own time, a nephew loyal to David and David's house, a military giant who never casts a covetous eye on David's throne, and a statesman who is probably more politically astute than his king (Branch, "David and Joab," 20, 62).

22. The descriptions of and insights about communication are from Eales-White, *Power of Persuasion,* 35, 36, 37.

23. Ibid., 39, 42–43; see also Branch, "Women Who Win with Words," 291.

24. Although Sheba sounds a call to national rebellion and separation from David, Jesse's son (2 Sam 20:1), the narrator gives him no further voice in the chapter. Readers and hearers do not know, for example, if he sought political sanctuary at Abel Beth Maacah. Pamela Barmesh ("The Narrative Quandary: Cases of Law in Literature," *VT* 44 [2004]: 15, 13) points out that formal legal texts assume that asylum is legitimate solely for those who had slain another human being, but narrative texts (for example, 2 Sam 14, in which the king intervenes in a sanctuary dispute) show that asylum applied to political offenders as well.

25. Anderson notes that the wise woman's speech has a poetic quality. The essence of the wise woman's argument seems to be that the people of Abel Beth Maacah are people of good sense. In contrast, the besiegers appear foolish because they bypassed negotiations in favor of battering (Anderson, *2 Samuel,* 241).

26. See JoAnn Davidson, "Genesis Matriarchs Engage Feminism," *AUSS* 40 (2002): 171. The wise woman of Abel Beth Maacah comes from a tradition of biblical women who make decisions about their futures and the futures of others, whose prayers are heard, and whose spiritual insights are acknowledged (177).

27. The wise woman of Abel Beth Maacah follows a tradition in Israel of women who publicly recognize a man's expertise. For example, Ruth, in bowing before Boaz with her face to the ground (Ruth 2:10), honored him in front of his workers. Similarly, Abigail's action of hastily dismounting from her donkey and bowing down before David with her face to the ground honored David in front of his men (1 Sam 25:23); see Branch, "Women Who Win with Words," 300, 303.

28. Ken Mulzac, "Hannah, the Giver and Receiver of a Great Gift," *AUSS* 40 [2002]: 213.

29. Kathleen Robertson Farmer, "Ruth," *NIB* 2:928.

30. Richard Schultz, "שִׁפְחָה" *NIDOTTE* 4:211–13.

31. See Philip R. Drey, "The Role of Hagar in Genesis 16," *AUSS* 40 (2002): 185.

32. This is because of an earlier exchange with the wise woman of Tekoa (see 2 Sam 14).

33. Farmer, "Ruth," 2:928.

34. The woman speaks a proverb that the text appears to recount only partially; see Hans Willem Hertzberg, *I and II Samuel: A Commentary* (Philadelphia: Westminster, 1964), 373.

35. Geyer ("Stopping the Juggernaut," 37) sees a history of judicial proceedings at Abel Beth Maacah. She believes the city may have been a seat for second trials, where verdicts were re-examined under a change of venue. Clearly the city was known for its administration of justice, for its expert verification of testimony, and for its ability to settle disputes (37).

36. Robert P. Gordon, *I and II Samuel* (Grand Rapids: Zondervan, 1986), 296.

37. The geographic location of Abel Beth Maacah should be noted here. The fact that it is in the outer reaches of the kingdom suggests Sheba's exhaustion, his loss of hope of successfully escaping Joab's pursuit and rallying Israel against David, and his last opportunity to seek refuge.

38. Edith Dean, *All the Women of the Bible* (Edison, N.J.: Castle Books, 1955), 361.

39. Gordon, *I and II Samuel*, 296. The wise woman calls her city a *mother* city; as such, it potentially has daughter cities, satellite cities. Biblically, literal mothers are honored equally with fathers in the instruction of sons (Prov 1:8). They are viewed as protectors; Ps 57:1 speaks of a hen protecting her chicks, and Ps 61:4 speaks of the shelter that wings provide. In the early traditions of the Hebrews, a mother city was a tribal designation (Gen 25:16; Num 25:15); a metropolis in Phoenicia; a kinship term in Ugaritic; and a military unit in old Babylon (P. K. McCarter, Jr., *I and II Samuel: A New Translation with Introduction, Notes, and Commentary* [Garden City, N.Y.: Doubleday, 1984], 430).

40. The obscure term has few commentators. See J. Cheryl Exum's article on mothers in Israel who built up the house of Israel through their own resourcefulness and the fame of their sons: "The Mothers of Israel: The Patriarchal Narratives from a Feminist Perspective," *BRev* 2 (1986): 60–67.

41. Keil and Delitzsch (*Books of Samuel*, 456) view the phrase "mother in Israel" as jargon for the capital of an area. They believe Abel Beth Maacah is celebrated and widely known for the wisdom of its inhabitants (p. 455). They also note that the woman speaks in the name of the city (p. 455). They pick up on her concern for the city's heritage as a recognized place of wisdom and on her concern for the city's inhabitants (pp. 455–56).

42. Exum, "Mothers in Israel," 85.

43. If the wise woman indeed refers to herself, she purposefully equates herself to a judge in Israel; she talks of herself as a woman carrying on the tradition of Deborah, the great judge. This raises the interesting possibility of a tradition of female judges in Israel up through the monarchy of David.

44. Canaanite oppression for twenty years had forced the Israelites to abandon their villages and scatter. Deborah and Barak and the tribes they led rout the Canaanites in an amazing victory. They destroy Sisera's army and his nine hundred chariots. No wonder Deborah breaks into song! Deborah sings that village life "ceased, ceased until I, Deborah, arose, arose a mother in Israel!" (Judg 5:7).

45. The key phrase, "swallow up the heritage of the Lord," may mean that the people of Abel Beth Maacah held an inalienable title to their land, an action in accord with the tradition of Yahweh's allocations to the tribes during the settlement period (see Lev 25:23, 28; Num 27:1–11; 36:7–9; 1 Kgs 21:3–4; see Gordon, *I and II Samuel*, 296).

46. "Deuteronomistic" is a scholarly term reflecting a unity in literary style, language, and content among the books of Deutreronomy, Joshua, Judges, Samuel, and Kings (Gary N. Knoppers, "Deuteronomistic History," *EDB*, 341).

47. Other instances where the word *inheritance* is used include God's giving the land of Israel to the tribes as their inheritance (see Josh 19) and David's comment that Saul had cut him out of his inheritance, the fellowship of his kindred Israelites (1 Sam 26:19). See also Ps 78:71, where all Israel is the inheritance of God.

48. Abigail used a similar argument with David (see 1 Sam 25). Just as she prevented David with her wise counsel from slaying innocent blood in her compound, the wise woman of Abel Beth Maacah prevents Joab from slaying innocent blood with her argument.

49. Thomas W. Gillespie, "A Question of Authority," *PSB* 24 (2003): 3.

50. As in many somber situations in the Hebrew Bible, the story being told in 2 Sam 20 contains some humor. For example, the woman's words wryly remind Joab that his methods of battering ram and siege ramp are not the usual ways one seeks counsel at Abel Beth Maacah. Is it not more reasonable to ask first than to batter first?

51. Perhaps for this reason, Hertzberg (*I and II Samuel*, 373) describes Joab's encounter with the woman as delightful.

52. Geyer, "Stopping the Juggernaut," 38.

53. See 2 Sam 3:28–32.

54. From Heb. חֵרֶם, a "consecrated possession," a thing devoted to God for utter destruction ("חֵרֶם", BDB, 742). See Deut 3 for a list of cities where *herem* is imposed.

55. Dean sympathizes with the inhabitants of Abel Beth Maacah. "The people," she writes (*All the Women of the Bible*, 361), "were in such a plight, the innocent victims of one man who had sought refuge inside their walls and had brought an avenging army knocking at their gates."

56. Baruch A. Levine ("Vows, Oaths, and Binding Agreements: The Section on Vows in Light of Aramaic Inscriptions," *ErIsr* 26 [1999]: 84)

discusses Num 30:2–17, a section on voluntary oaths. He finds that voluntary vows were traditional practice among the Israelites. He notes that it becomes clear in the Hebrew Scriptures that men and women make voluntary vows during events in their lives so that they can remember them during upcoming circumstances and do them. Although Levine's article covers only Num 30, it suggests a tradition in Israel that endured beyond the time in the wilderness. Joab's voluntary oath to the woman of Abel Beth Maacah binds him to taking only Sheba. By not destroying the city, Joab keeps his oath.

57. The phrase "Far be it from me" (2 Sam 20:20) and its slight variations occurs six times in First and Second Samuel and once in Job (1 Sam 2:30; 20:9; 22:15; 2 Sam 20:20 [twice]; 23:17; Job 34:10). Joab speaks it twice in this verse alone. Elsewhere, four times it is spoken by a man, once by God, and never by a woman. Part of its significance may be that it is an oath spoken only by men; women in Deuteronomistic literature employ a milder oath. For example, Ruth says to Naomi, "May the Lord deal ever so severely with me" (Ruth 1:17).

The apparently milder oath—"May the Lord deal with me, be it ever so severely"—seems to be a phrase used by both women and men. For example, the priest Eli uses it when asking the boy Samuel for the Lord's word (1 Sam 3:17). Saul condemns his son Jonathan to death with it (1 Sam 14:44). Jonathan swears to let David know about Saul's attitude toward David with it (1 Sam 20:13). David, apparently talking to himself, uses it in his vow to kill all the males in Nabal's household because of Nabal's slight to David and his men (1 Sam 25:22). After Absalom's rebellion, David swears with this oath to Amasa, Absalom's general, that Amasa now is the commander-in-chief of the army in place of Joab (2 Sam 19:13). Solomon, when confronted with his brother Adonijah's request for Abishag, his father David's beautiful caretaker, swears to his mother Bathsheba with this oath that Adonijah will pay for his request with his life (1 Kgs 2:23). Jezebel makes a vow with this oath to kill Elijah within a day (I Kgs 19:2). Ben-Hadad, king of Aram, attacks Samaria and boasts with this oath that he will level it (1 Kgs 20:10). During a famine, Joram the king of Israel vows with this oath to sever Elisha's head from his body within a day (2 Kgs 6:31). The milder oath also conveys strong feelings and involves times of crisis. The primary difference between it and the stronger "Far be it from me" seems to be that it is more often employed by the stronger to the weaker in society, to children, by women, and between friends or kinfolk.

58. Cryer ("David's Rise to Power," 389) believes that Joab graciously accedes to the woman's request that he withdraw. Furthermore, Cryer believes the text presents a favorable picture of Joab.

59. This is similar to an earlier battle Israel faced, when credit for quelling the Canaanites went to Deborah and Jael rather than to the commanding general, Barak (Judg 4–5).

60. Gillespie, "A Question of Authority," 4.

61. That Sheba sought, without much success, to overthrow the kingdom undoubtedly added to the strength of the woman's argument. The narrator calls him a worthless fellow, a troublemaker, a fool (2 Sam 20:1). He is clearly presented as an unattractive character, one without much charisma (unlike David and Joab), one who could not muster enough forces for a rebellion against the king. Sheba presents an interesting contrast to Joab. When Joab commands, men obey; later he sounds a trumpet (2 Sam 20:22) and men disband, heeding the order to disperse, go home, and shed no more blood.

62. Geyer, "Stopping the Juggernaut," 38.

63. Branch, "David and Joab," 20.

64. The named characters he slays are Abner, Absalom, and Amasa; he obeys David's order to pull back and let Uriah be slain by the Ammonites.

65. Branch, "David and Joab," 62.

66. Ibid.

67. In this, Joab resembles Barak, an earlier military leader from the tribe of Naphtali. Deborah, the judge and prophetess, prophesies that Barak will share a decisive victory over the Canaanites with a woman, who turns out to be Jael, the Kenite (see Judg 4–5).

68. Branch, "David and Joab," 23. In contrast to his treatment of Joab and the wise woman of Tekoa (2 Sam 14), David honors and thanks Barzillai the Gileadite for his kindness to him during Absalom's rebellion (2 Sam 19:31–38).

69. See Prov 3:13, 19; 4:5–9.

70. For a fine, brief summary on the significance of the wise woman of Abel Beth Maacah, see Athalya Brenner, *The Israelite Woman: Social Role and Literary Type in Biblical Narrative* (Sheffield: JSOT, 1985), 35–37. Brenner adds that Joab may have been ready to talk with her because her garments identified her as a professional woman skilled in a specific occupation (p. 37). Perhaps that occupation was mediation.

71. First Samuel 17 illustrates this principle in the story of David and Goliath. Evidently, it was the solitary preparation of tending sheep, a low-status job in the household, that ultimately prepared David to meet the giant. The hours David spent overseeing the sheep were also spent learning skills with a rock and sling. He protected his sheep against the deadly onslaught of both lion and bear. This skill brought a boastful giant down and brought the youthful giant killer fame throughout all Israel. Undoubtedly, David also began composing his songs to the Lord with a herd of sheep as his first audience. When Israel heard his psalms, the people gave David the beloved and enduring title of "sweet psalmist of Israel" (2 Sam 23:1).

Notes to Chapter 6

1. Herbert Lockyer, *All the Miracles of the Bible* (Grand Rapids: Zondervan, 1965), 108.

2. This threefold theme of devastation is the heart of the passage; see Lostracco and Wilkerson, *Analyzing Short Stories,* 1.

3. Her obscurity, anonymity, and silence carry over into Jewish literature. Combing through rabbinic and Aggadah literature, I could find no mention of her name, birthplace, or parents.

4. D. W. Gooding, "Septuagint's Rival Versions of Jeroboam's Rise to Power (1 Kings 11–12)," *VT* 17 (1967): 187–88; M. Auerbach and L. Smolar, "Aaron, Jeroboam, and the Golden Calves (Ex 32; 1 Kgs 12:28ff.)," *JBL* 86 (1967): 72. See also M. Auerbach, "Jeroboam's Rise to Power (1 Kings 12)," *JBL* 88 (1969): 69–72.

5. Other biblical characters referred to possessing *hayil* (Heb. חַיִל) are Boaz (Ruth 2:1), Ruth (Ruth 3:11), Naaman (2 Kgs 5:1), and the virtuous woman described in Prov 31. Each is a person of exemplary and noble character.

6. R. L. Cohn, "Literary Technique in the Jeroboam Narrative," *ZAW* 97 (1985): 26.

7. J. Holder, "The Presuppositions, Accusations, and Threats of 1 Kings 14:1–18," *JBL* 107 (1988): 197.

8. B. Halpern, "Levitic Participation in the Reform Cult of Jeroboam I," *JBL* 95 (1976): 31; D. W. Van Winkle ("1 Kings xii 25–xiii 34: Jeroboam's Cultic Innovations and the Man of God from Judah," *VT* 46 [1996], 109), however, disagrees, contending that Jeroboam's paranoia—namely his fear of losing the kingdom—surfaces early in his reign, with these fortifications and his cultic reforms.

9. W. I. Toews (*Monarchy and Religious Institution in Israel under Jeroboam I* [Atlanta: Scholars Press, 1993], 149) makes the intriguing observation that the biblical text gives no record of Ahijah, Elisha, or Amos, the prophets of the day, voicing objections to Jeroboam's calves.

10. The term "man of God" is one of the ways a prophet is described in Deuteronomistic History (Thomas Overholt, "Prophet, Prophecy," *EDB,* 1086).

11. Intercession represents the first if not the primary job of a prophet. See Gen 20, the story of Abraham and Sarah and Abimelech; note v. 7.

12. The Septuagint (Greek) version of this narrative contains more information. For example, details of the boy's illness are given; Ahijah the prophet has a servant, and the queen has maidservants. The careful wordplay on the sound of the queen's footsteps, however, is omitted. For a fuller discussion of the differences, see H. N. Wallace, "Oracles Against the Israelite Dynasties in 1 and 2 Kings," *Bib* 67 (1986): 26.

13. Alter (*Art of Biblical Narrative*, 65) notes that narration usually serves as a bridge between larger units of direct speech.

14. Cohn, "Literary Technique in the Jeroboam Narrative," 23.

15. Lostracco and Wilkerson, *Analyzing Short Stories*, 19–21.

16. Holder, "Presuppositions, Accusations, and Threats," 27–28.

17. Alter, *Art of Biblical Narrative*, 80.

18. Ibid., 60. Alter notes that biblical writers seldom reveal the thoughts of a person. Instead they prefer to let direct speech reveal character and the varied relationships between people.

19. Simon DeVries, *1 Kings* (WBC 12; Waco, Tex.: Word, 1985), 177.

20. Alter, *Art of Biblical Narrative*, 72.

21. The rabbis (I. Epstein, ed., *Babylonian Talmud*, Part 4, vol. 4: *Baba Bathra* [London: Soncino, 1961], 121b) record three traditions regarding Ahijah. First, they claim he was one of seven men whose lives spanned the world's history. According to the rabbis, Methuselah saw Adam; Shem saw Methuselah; Jacob saw Shem; Amram saw Jacob; Ahijah the Shilonite saw Amram; and Elijah, who still lives, saw Ahijah. Second, Ahijah's eyes were dim because he raised up a wicked disciple, Jeroboam. Third, the rabbis credit the prophet's dim eyesight to sin. Citing Isaac's similar problem, the rabbis say "his eyes dimmed from seeing the evil of that wicked man, his son Esau." (H. Freedman and Maurice Simon, eds., *Mishnah Rabbah*, vol. 2: *Genesis Rabbah* [H. Freedman, trans.; 3d ed.; New York: Soncino, 1983], 585).

S. Frolov ("Days of Shiloh in the Kingdom of Israel," *Bib* 76 [1995]: 216) speculates that since no priestly duties are mentioned for him, Ahijah probably was not a priest and did not belong to Eli's lineage. Ahijah, however, is singularly referred to as *the* prophet.

22. By using the verb *nakar*, the text indicates that the wife of Jeroboam comes to Ahijah disguised as a foreigner ("נָכַר," BDB, 648; see *TWOT* 2:580).

23. He literally says to her, "I am sent to you with hard (words)" (1 Kgs 14:6).

24. "שָׁלַח," BDB, 1019–20.

25. DeVries, *1 Kings*, 179. According to Lostracco and Wilkerson (*Analyzing Short Stories*, 37, 49–50), this tone of utter loathing is conveyed by a skillful use of language. A vivid choice of words like this appeals to the imagination and the senses.

26. "בָּעַר," BDB, 128–29.

27. Pritchard, J. B., ed. *The Ancient Near East, Volume 2: An Anthology of Texts and Pictures* (2 vols.; Princeton, Princeton University Press, 1975), 69.

28. Throughout the biblical text, God's judgments come in response to willful sin and disobedience. The flood, for example, came after the prolonged, persistent, and unrepentant wickedness and violence of the human

race (Gen 6:5, 11). Gen 6:6 gives some of Scripture's saddest words: "The Lord was grieved that he had made man on the earth and his heart was filled with pain."

29. The lad Abijah must have been a darling child, clearly the favorite of his father Jeroboam and the delight of all Israel. I make this assumption because of the repeated emphasis on "all Israel" as mourning for him (1 Kgs 14:13, 18). The mourning of "all Israel" represents a singular honor: the hoary prophet Samuel, kingmaker and judge of Israel, received it, too (1 Sam 25:1).

30. A. Reinhartz, "Anonymous Women and the Collapse of the Monarchy: A Study in the Narrative Technique," in *A Feminist Companion to Samuel and Kings* (ed. A. Brenner; Sheffield: Sheffield Academic, 1994), 45.

31. Ibid., 63–64.

32. Disobedience is another stunning parallel between Jeroboam and Saul. Jeroboam tried to seize the man of God, arguably to do him bodily harm (1 Kgs 13: 4). Earlier, Saul grasped Samuel's robe only to tear it, a prophetic sign of God's decision to rend the kingdom from Israel's first king. The Jeroboam cycle further shows that only when something occurs that Jeroboam cannot control—like his shriveled hand or his son's illness—does Jeroboam admit his need and seek God. Just as he asked the man of God to intercede with God regarding his shriveled hand, so he sends out his wife to seek the prophet regarding their son.

33. Jeroboam's action indicates he has no concept of an all-seeing God such as Hagar's (Gen 16:13), or of an omnipresent God such as David's (1 Sam 17: 45–47). Jeroboam lacks belief in the God of his fathers; he tries to control and deceive the prophetic word; he succeeds at neither.

34. The rabbis (*Babylonian Talmud, Ta'anita,* 20a) claim that the curse of Ahijah the Shilonite is better than the blessing of Balaam the wicked. The rabbis posit that Ahijah cursed Israel and compared Israel with a reed shaken in water. A reed grows by water and has many roots and can grow new shoots. But Balaam's prophecy contains a reference to a cedar beside the waters (Num 24: 6), a fact, the rabbis point out, that cannot be true. Cedars do not grow beside water; their stock does not grow new shoots and their roots are not many. Therefore Ahijah's prophecy of Israel's downfall is better because a pen can be made from a reed and used for the writing of the Law, the Prophets, and the Hagiographa (*Babylonian Talmud, Ta'anita,* 20a–20b).

35. Holder, "Presuppositions, Accusations, and Threats," 27.

36. Ibid., 27–28. Holder maintains that the Jeroboam cycle rests on several premises dear to the Deuteronomistic narrator, namely that the Davidic dynasty is the single legitimate dynasty in Israel, Yahweh's presence manifests itself only in the ark in Jerusalem, and Jerusalem is the only legitimate place where Yahweh is found. However, by so asserting, Holder denies the legitimacy of the prophetic word to both Jeroboam and Rehoboam, and later to

Elijah, whose prophetic work presumes God's presence in the northern kingdom of Israel. Holder discredits the prophetic word and its ability to legitimize what it so chooses. Furthermore, Holder fails to see that Jeroboam's fear
of losing the kingdom and his lack of belief in God's ability to protect Israel
caused him to sin.

37. See the excellent article by David Instone-Brewer, "What God Has
Joined," *Christianity Today*, October 2007, 26–29. See also the classic work
by Lenore Walker, *The Battered Woman* (New York: Harper & Row, 1979).
Malachi 2:16 recounts that God hates divorce and a man's violence against
the wife of his youth.

38. Actually, no one in Israel was to be abused. The Ten Commandments
(Exod 20:1–17) span both the individual and the community. The first three
deal with how the covenant community and covenant individuals should
worship God. The fourth prohibits work on the Sabbath. The fifth stipulates
honoring one's parents. The sixth through the tenth broadly outline right conduct within the community. Members of the covenant community were not
to murder, commit adultery, steal, lie about each other, or covet the people or
possessions in another's household. Arguably, the most intimate of all the communities within the covenant community was the marriage between a man and
a woman. Hence, the Ten Commandments provide the basic legal framework
for asserting that no one in the covenant community was to be abused.

39. Margi Laird McCue, *Domestic Violence: A Reference Book* (Santa Barbara, Calif.: ABC-CLIO, 1995), 108–9.

40. Opportunities for repentance include his encounter with the man
of God (1 Kgs 13) and hearing the prophetic word from Ahijah that was delivered by his wife upon her return (1 Kgs 14:17). One would think that the
death of his son would have humbled him and brought him to repentance,
as it did David (2 Sam 12:15–25), but it did not. One would think that the
judgment against his house and Israel would have brought him to repentance,
as it did Ahab years later (2 Kgs 21: 25–28), but it did not.

41. James Alsdurf and Phyllis Alsdurf, *Battered into Submission: The Tragedy of Wife Abuse in the Christian Home* (Downers Grove, Ill.: InterVarsity,
1989), 67. One study found that more highly educated batterers inflict more
serious injuries than do less educated abusers (see Jeffrey A. Fagen, Douglas K.
Steward, and Karen V. Hansen, "Violent Men or Violent Husbands?" in *The
Dark Side of Families* [ed. David Finkelhor et al.; Beverly Hills, Calif.: Sage
Publications, 1983], 57).

42. Ibid., 42–43. In an abusive, dysfunctional marriage like that of Jeroboam and his wife, the first step toward healing is to recognize abuse as sin.
Jeroboam does not do this. Another step is for a husband with a propensity
toward control to direct his ability to control toward controlling his own im-
pulses. A husband needs to take responsibility for his actions and experience

the natural consequences of his behavior. Jeroboam's cowardice in sending his wife in his place to Ahijah shows his perpetual avoidance of taking responsibility for his actions.

43. See Tom L. Eisenman, *Temptations Men Face: Straightforward Talk on Power, Money, Affairs, Perfectionism, Insensitivity* . . . (Downers Grove, Ill.: InterVarsity, 1990), 115–16.

44. Abusive men are frequently irrationally jealous about their wives and the activities of their wives. Consequently, they monitor their wives' use of space and time and question all contact with other men; see Donald G. Dutton, *The Abusive Personality: Violence and Control in Intimate Relationships* (New York: Guilford, 1998), 44.

45. Ibid., 49.

46. Gary Hankins, *Prescription for Anger: Coping with Angry Feelings and Angry People* (with Carol Hankins; New York: Warner Books. 1993), 15.

47. Research shows that the more frequently the woman is verbally abused, the less capable she is of seeing her relationship as positive (see Barbara Wexler, *Violent Relationships: Battering and Abuse Among Adults* [Information Plus Reference Series; Detroit: Thomson Gale. 2003], 48).

48. Dutton, *Abusive Personality,* 45.

49. See Charles L. Allen, *When a Marriage Ends* (Old Tappan, N.J.: Fleming H. Revell, 1986), 15.

50. Ibid., 13.

51. See 1 Kgs 17, 19 and 2 Kgs 11.

52. See Robert Hemfelt, Frank Minirth, and Paul Meier, *Love is a Choice: Recovery for Codependent Relationships* (Nashville: Thomas Nelson, 1989), 159–62.

53. McCue (*Domestic Violence,* 84) cautions against looking for the causes of male violence in women, which may be another way of blaming the victim.

54. Alsdurf and Alsdurf, *Battered into Submission,* 68.

55. McCue, *Domestic Violence,* 84.

56. See Alsdurf and Alsdurf, *Battered into Submission* (57, 59). Violence is a sign of the batterer's choice to allow such corruption to take root and become evil. The New Testament offers many insights on violence. Peter changed from a man of the sword (John 18:10) to a man who loudly told the Sanhedrin he and the other believers in Jesus would continue speaking what they had seen and heard (Acts 4:20). Saul/Paul changed from one condoning the deaths of believers (Acts 8:1; 9:1, 2) to a man ruled by the peace and grace of Jesus. Paul described himself this way: "Even though I was once a blasphemer and a persecutor and a *violent* man, I was shown mercy because I acted in ignorance and unbelief" (italics added).

57. Wexler, *Violent Relationships,* 33.

58. Ibid., 33–34.

59. Alsdurf and Alsdurf, *Battered into Submission,* 53–62.

60. Ibid., 56.

61. McCue, *Domestic Violence,* 95.

62. Alsdurf and Alsdurf, *Battered into Submission,* 62. Studies show that violence against women cuts across all racial and economic classes. For example, at a given time in Montgomery County, Maryland, there were as many calls reporting domestic disturbances as there were in downtown Washington, D.C. Some studies, however, show that there is more domestic violence among the poor and working class (cf. McCue, *Domestic Violence,* 85).

63. In the 1920s it was believed that women of low intelligence tended to stay in abusive relationships. In the 1930s and 1940s, it was believed that battered women were masochistic. From the 1970s on, it has been believed that battered women are isolated and have fewer educational and social resources as backups (McCue, *Domestic Violence,* 112–16).

64. Ibid., 113–14.

65. Alsdurf and Alsdurf, *Battered into Submission,* 74.

66. Wexler, *Violent Relationships,* 46.

67. Ibid., 49.

68. Ibid., 48.

69. Alsdurf and Alsdurf, *Battered into Submission,* 76.

70. Wexler, *Violent Relationships,* 47. Women living in the cycle of abuse are constantly on guard and become so insecure that they further isolate themselves. A woman who is imprisoned in her home with no individual freedom does not seek help because she has been physically and psychologically locked into her situation. Isolation becomes a habit, a mode of survival.

71. Perhaps the wife of Jeroboam is passive for good reason. First, repeated battering, like electrical shocks, diminishes a woman's motivation to respond. She becomes passive. Second, her cognitive ability to perceive success is changed. She does not believe her response will result in a favorable outcome, whether or not it might. Third, having generalized her helplessness, the battered woman does not believe anything she does will alter any outcome. Fourth, her sense of emotional well-being becomes precarious (Alsdurf and Alsdurf, *Battered into Submission,* 73–74).

72. Biblical texts do sometimes provide such background information about women. The names of the mothers of Rehoboam and Abijah, kings of Judah (1 Kgs 14: 21; 15:1–2), for example, are provided. However, the 1 Kgs text about Jeroboam's successor, his son Nadab, contains no mention of Nadab's mother (1 Kgs 15: 25).

73. McCue, *Domestic Violence,* 84.

74. Ibid., 85.

75. Ibid., 90. A modern woman living in an abusive situation fears losing face in the community. To report a condition of domestic violence may

isolate or cut a woman off from her community as well as from her family. In addition, an older woman who was brought up to keep her family problems private is much less able to reach out for help.

76. Ibid., 86.
77. Ibid., 113–14.
78. Ibid., 115
79. Ibid.
80. Ibid., 114.
81. Wexler, *Violent Relationships,* 46.
82. Coping skills include denial, minimalization, anger, shock, nightmares, and dissociation (McCue, *Domestic Violence,* 100).
83. Ibid. In an actual battering event, shock and dissociation can numb the woman's mind and body while the assault takes place.
84. Ibid.
85. Ibid., 109.
86. Dutton, *Abusive Personality,* 42.
87. McCue, *Domestic Violence,* 100.
88. Ibid., 99.
89. Nancy Leigh DeMoss, *Lies Women Believe and the Truth That Sets Them* Free (Chicago: Moody, 2001), 66
90. Ibid., 70–71.
91. Lostracco and Wilkerson, *Analyzing Short Stories,* 11.
92. Perhaps the harsh prophetic word of household destruction, the death of the boy, and the upcoming judgment upon Israel could have been averted with repentance. See also Pss 16:10; 30:2–3; and 56:13; and Deut 32:2; Job 33:28, 30; Exod 15:26.
93. See Barker, *NIV Study Bible,* 496.

NOTES TO CHAPTER 7

1. For the purpose of this study, the *Elijah cycle* is defined primarily as the set of stories, traditions, and anecdotes that have been woven with great skill into one continuous narrative in 1 Kgs 17–19; see Simon, *Reading Prophetic Narratives,* 155. Elijah's influence and deeds, however, continue throughout the days of Ahab, king of Israel, and in the days of Ahaziah his son and heir ("Elijah," *EncBib* 1:337). Perhaps at the root of the stories about Elijah is God's concern for humankind; see A. J. Heschel, *The Prophets* (New York: Harper & Row, 1955; repr., Peabody, Mass.: Hendrickson, 2007), 483.

2. Most encyclopedias introduce Elijah immediately with the title "prophet in Israel" (cf. "Elijah," *EncBib* 1:337). However, in contrast to Abraham (Gen 20:7),

Moses (Exod 3–4), and Jeremiah (Jer 1:5), the biblical text refers to Elijah as a prophet for the first time later, after a series of impressive miracles (1 Kgs 18:36). Neither is the appositive *prophet* routinely connected with Elijah's name as it is with Miriam (Exod 15:20), Deborah (Judg 4:4), and Ahijah (1 Kgs 11:29).

3. Scholars traditionally see the widow as a Gentile, one outside of the covenant God made with Israel. This becomes apparent as she recognizes the deity worshiped by another people, the Israelites, when she speaks to Elijah. In Luke's gospel, Jesus refers to her and Naaman the Syrian in a context that indicates that both were outside the covenant (Luke 4:28–30; see Donald G. Miller, *Luke* [Richmond: John Knox, 1966], 57–59). Put another way, "Jesus pointed out that when the prophet Elijah needed a place to hide from the Israelite king who sought his life, he hid with a Phoenician woman, not an Israelite" (Michael E. Williams, ed., *The Storyteller's Companion to the Bible*, vol. 3: *Judges-Kings* [Nashville: Abingdon, 1992], 158).

4. I do not use the terms *resurrection* and *resuscitation* in connection with the boy for several reasons. First, resurrection, which seems to be only a slowly developing concept in the Hebrew Scriptures, primarily refers to God's power over death and to a national restoration; see Deut 32:39; 1 Sam 2:6; Isa 25:7; and Isa 26:19; Ezek 37:13–14; and Hos 6:1–2 respectively (David Rolph Seely, "Resurrection" in *EDB*, 1120–121). The widow's son was raised to life but died again at a later, unspecified time. Resuscitation carries with it the idea of restoring to consciousness, vigor or life, but may not imply a restoration from death. Resurrection is a more developed concept in the New Testament. The Gospels tell of Jesus' actions of restoring life to several dead people, including Lazarus (John 11), the son of the widow of Nain (Luke 7:11–16), and Jairus' daughter (Luke 8:40–56). But again, these three died later. In the full New Testament sense, Jesus is the first one to be resurrected from the dead. His resurrected body could come through walls and could ascend into heaven (John 20:26; Acts 1:9).

5. DeVries, *1 Kings*, 216.

6. Kaufmann, *Religion of Israel*, 248.

7. Richard D. Nelson, *First and Second Kings* (Atlanta: John Knox, 1987), 109.

8. The other women cited include Noah's wife, Sarah, Rebekah, Leah, Rachel, Bithia (the foster mother of Moses), Jochebed (Moses' mother), Miriam, Hannah, Jael, Naomi, Rahab, Bathsheba, Michal, Hazlepinith (Samson's mother), Elisheba (Aaron's wife), Serah (Asher's daughter, identified by Jewish tradition as the wise woman of Abel Beth Maacah as discussed in ch. 4), the wife of the prophet Obadiah, the Shunammite, Ruth, and Esther (see Ginzberg, *LJ* 5:258).

9. The rabbis deal with the roughness of the transition between 1 Kgs 16 and 17 with a story that connects Moses, Joshua, and Elijah (*Babylonian Talmud*,

Sanhedrin 113a–113b, 780–81). They write that Ahab, upon hearing that his good friend Hiel had lost his sons Abiram and Segub, journeys to comfort Hiel. Hiel is described as "that wicked man" (*Babylonian Talmud, Sanhedrin,* 113a, 780). Ahab asks Elijah to accompany him. While in the house of mourning, Ahab asks Elijah if Moses' proclamation still holds true. If Israel turns aside from God and worships idols, will God shut up the heavens (Deut 11:16ff.)? In this passage, Ahab draws a connection between Joshua and Moses. Elijah proclaims the prophecy's efficacy "straightway" (*Babylonian Talmud, Sanhedrin,* 113a, 780) and pronounces that the land will have no dew or rain.

10. The giving or withholding of rain is generally viewed as a sign of God's favor or disfavor (see Jer 3:3; Hos 6:30; Joel 2:23; Job 29:23); Frank S. Frick, "Rain," *ABD,* 5:612). In the ancient Near East rain means life, literally and figuratively. The implicit challenge of no rain in 1 Kgs 17 becomes an explicit challenge to Baal in 1 Kgs 18. When rain does come, the Lord and only the Lord is the one who sends it (Nelson, *First and Second Kings,* 109).

11. Other patterns in the chapter include thirteen commands, ten examples of obedience, four miracles, four accusations or complaints, three statements taken as fact, and one prayer. In the broader context, however, 1 Kgs 16:29–18:2 begins and ends with promises from God.

12. The Bible portrays Joshua as a man who combines the qualities of military leader and prophet ("Joshua," *EncJud* 10:265). As the anointed successor of Moses, the one on whom Moses laid hands, Joshua is filled with the spirit of wisdom (Num 27:18–20; Deut 34:9). In common with Moses, the Bible refers to him with the appositive "servant of the Lord" (Josh 24:29); see also Josh 1:2, where the Lord says, "My servant Moses is dead." The text establishes Joshua as the successor of Moses also by the fact that the Lord speaks to him (Josh 1:1–9). The Bible attributes to him "the character of a prophet-legislator in the style of Moses" ("Joshua," *EncJud* 10:265).

13. For an excellent study of the word נָבִיא (prophet), see John Huehnegard, "The Etymology and Meaning of the Hebrew 'Nabi,'" *ErIsr* 26 (1999): 88–93. Elijah's prophetic ministry takes place during the time of the divided kingdom. He apparently succeeds Ahijah, a prophet during the time of Solomon and Jeroboam.

14. The traditional argument presents Elijah as the Moses of his generation (see Simon, *Reading Prophetic Narratives,* 168).

15. Nelson, *First and Second Kings,* 103. Ahab comes under the curse of Joshua in this section (John Gray, *I and II Kings: A Commentary* [2nd ed.; Philadelphia: Westminster, 1970], 369). Yet structurally, in terms of shared words, there is no transition from 1 Kgs 16:34 to 1 Kgs 17:1. Instead, the narrative's abruptness and unexpected turn disrupt the text. Truly 1 Kgs 17:1, the opening verse of the Elijah cycle, defies classification and has no parallels in prophetic literature (DeVries, *1 Kings,* 215).

16. Walsh, *1 Kings,* 225–26.

17. Gaalyahu Cornfeld, ed., "Elijah," in *Pictorial Bible Encyclopedia: A Visual Guide to the Old and New Testaments* (Tel Aviv: Hamikra Baolam,1964), 273. Whatever the original meaning, the story's first hearers knew something about the word that is lost to modern ears. However, scholarly opinion in general agrees that Elijah was from Tishbe in Gilead ("Elijah," *EncBib* 1: 337).

18. Although the location remains unnamed, the confrontation with Ahab probably occurs in Samaria. Specific reasons for the confrontation are not given. The narrator is silent with respect to Ahab's reaction, if he had any. In 1 Kgs 17, drought and death punish a wayward, idolatrous king.

19. For instance, Elijah's decree offers two possibilities. First, perhaps in an earlier, unrecorded episode of his life he stood before the Lord and received personal instructions as did Isaiah (Isa 6). Or perhaps the words are his own, indicating audacity, confidence, and presumption in his zeal for the living Lord. The text is unclear (see Claudia V. Camp, "1 and 2 Kings," in *The Women's Bible Commentary* [eds. Carol A. Newsome and Sharon H. Ringe; Louisville: Westminster/John Knox, 1992], 96–105).

20. Ginzberg, *LJ* 1:50–51.

21. I. W. Slotki, *Kings: Hebrew Text & English Translation with an Introduction and Commentary* (London: Soncino, 1950, 124.

22. The psalmists frequently command God because of the urgency of their needs. See Pss 4:1; 5:1; 10:1;12:1; 13:1; 17:1; 22:1; 26:1; 28:1; 35:1; 43:1; 54:1; 57:1; 61:1; 64:1; 69:1; 70:1; 86:1; and 119:145.

23. First Kings 21:25–26 continues the vilification, citing him as one "who sold himself to do evil in the eyes of the Lord urged on by Jezebel his wife. He behaved in the vilest manner by going after idols like the Ammonites the Lord drove out before Israel."

24. The Hebrew Scriptures earlier present God and Pharaoh as a duo in conflict. As in the earlier contest in Egypt, the contest now in Israel concerns exactly who God is, how far his territory extends, and over whom he rules. Furthermore, a stated purpose emphasized repeatedly is that Moses is being sent to Pharaoh as God's spokesman (Exod 3:10; 5:1; 6:10; 8:1; 9:1). The events of Exod 2–13 can be seen as God's attempt to bring repentance to Pharaoh's hard heart; likewise, the drought can be seen as God's attempt to bring Ahab to repentance. Pharaoh in Exodus and Ahab in 1 Kgs 17 choose not to repent.

25. Elijah and Ahab view Ahab's conduct differently. Ahab does not see his promulgation of Baal as incompatible with his forefathers' worship of Yahweh (John Day, "Baal," *ABD*, 1:547). Elijah does. Although Ahab gives his sons Hebrew names with a God component, his son Ahaziah (the Lord has sustained) worships Baal. After Ahab's death, Ahaziah consults Baal-zebah when he is ill, an action which insults and angers Elijah (2 Kgs 1:2–16).

26. Cornfeld, "Elijah," 274.

27. Angelo S. Rappoport, *Ancient Israel: Myths and Legends,* 3:240. In this test, according to tradition, Ahab and the people prayed to Baal to end the famine, and nothing happened. Elijah then prayed to the God of Israel, rain fell, and the earth produced herb and corn. But the people soon returned to their idol worship (ibid.).

28. Stuart Lasine ("Matters of Life and Death: The Story of Elijah and the Widow's Son in Comparative Perspective," *BibInt* 12 [2004]: 119) wonders if the text's silence about the boy reflects Elijah's lack of interest in the child. To me it seems that the narrator's purpose focuses instead on validating Elijah as a prophet.

29. Jewish tradition maintains the boy grew up to become the prophet Jonah (Ginzberg, *LJ* 4:196–97).

30. Domination does not equal veneration, however. Nowhere in the Hebrew Scriptures is a prophet or prophetess put on a pedestal. Instead, their lives are used to point toward the God they serve, the one who deserves worship. Elijah identifies himself as an intimate counselor and obedient minister, as one who stands before Yahweh the God of Israel (1 Kgs 17:1; see DeVries, *1 Kings,* 218).

31. Scholars define pre-classical prophets like Elijah and Elisha as "non-writing prophets" and classical prophets like Isaiah and Jeremiah as "writing prophets." However, Elijah briefly served as a writing prophet if the letter to Jehoram king of Judah truly is his (2 Chr 21:12–15).

32. Because the text reveals so little about Elijah and his life, tales and legends about him grew in rabbinic literature. Some believed Phinehas and Elijah were the same man; others that Elijah was not human at all but was always an angel. Elijah was believed to have gone to the same cave where Moses encountered God. Because he did not die, legends have it that Elijah can traverse the world with four flaps of his wings, and hence that no spot on earth is too far removed from his help. In the future, Elijah will be one of the Messiah's key lieutenants, one who will lead Israel in repentance and solve the nation's legal problems; he will serve as one of the eight princes in the cabinet of the Messiah. In short, what Moses is to the Torah, Elijah is to the Kabbalah. See Ginzberg, *LJ* 1:283, 351; 3:114, 307; 4:201–04, 210–11, 229, 233–35.

33. Cornfeld, "Elijah," 273.

34. "Elijah," *EncJud* 6:632.

35. The emotional breadth depicted within the cycle portrays Elijah as an authentic human being (Alexander Rofé, "Classes in the Prophetical Stories: Didactic Legend and Parable," in *Studies in Prophecy: A Collection of Twelve Papers* [ed. G. W. Anderson; VTSup 26; Leiden: Brill, 1974], 143–64). The narrative reveals his orthodoxy, his zeal, his anger, his compassion, and his sense of not really knowing what to do other than to pray when confronted

with death. Nevertheless, he and his deeds are undeniably so extraordinary that he becomes the subject of legends.

36. James (*Personalities in the Old Testament,* 183) asserts that to Elijah, God was everything and man was nothing. But here James misses a crucial point: Elijah, for all his gruffness, cares deeply for Ahab because he chastises the king's waywardness; and he cares deeply for the widow and her son because he cries out to the Lord for them in their distress and need.

37. Rofé, "Classes in the Prophetical Stories," 143.

38. Cornfeld, "Elijah," 273. In some ways, Elijah's sudden appearances and disappearances follow the biblical pattern established by angels. They resemble the comings and goings of angels in the earlier stories of Gideon and Manoah and his wife (see Judg 6, 13). Elijah, the man of God, pops in and out of the text like a *Deus ex machina,* strengthening the impression of mystery and other-worldliness (Rofé, "Classes in the Prophetical Stories,"160). The suddenness of Elijah's appearances serve to show that the messenger belonged to God. But Elijah is no "angel" in the sense of being an easy person to be around; the text clearly records his anger, his exhaustion, his uncertainty, and his need for food, water, and security.

39. Compare Elijah in 1 Kgs 17 to the pattern seen in other prophets. Isaiah calls himself a man of unclean lips who lives among a people of the same (Isa 6:5). Amos appeals to his simple profession as a shepherd and tender of sycamore-fig trees before the Lord commanded him to prophesy to Israel (Amos 7:15). Jeremiah despairs, moaning the ridicule he faces when he delivers his prophetic message and even curses the day he was born, wishing instead that his mother's womb had been his tomb (Jer 20:7, 14–18).

40. Although Jewish tradition and modern scholars do not credit him with the authorship of 1 Kgs, Elijah apparently did briefly serve as a writing prophet. Yet scholars differ as to the historicity of this letter. Some posit it was written by Elijah himself before his death; others argue it was written by the Chronicler based on his knowledge of Elijah (Raymond B. Dillard, *2 Chronicles* [WBC 15; Waco, Tex.: 1987], 167). A third view is that the Chronicler may well have wanted his readers to understand that Elijah's letter came from heaven (J. Gordon McConville, *I and II Chronicles* [Philadelphia: Westminster, 1984], 199).

41. Cornfeld, "Elijah," 273.

42. According to Jewish tradition, Elijah descended from the tribe of Gad (Ginzberg, *LJ* 1:365). According to one derivation, Gad's name means "cutter." Elijah reflects his heritage in that he cuts down unbelievers. According to Jewish tradition, a psalm written by Moses foretells that the Gadite Elijah would wreak the vengeance of the Lord upon unbelievers: "O Lord, Thou God to whom vengeance belongeth, for the tribe of Gad" (Ginsburg, *LJ* 3:462).

43. His primary purpose is to root out impotent idolatry from Israel (Cornfield, "Elijah," 340).

44. Although Elijah fought against Baal worship all his life and with all his might, he was unable to defeat it (Simon, *Reading Prophetic Narratives,* 155).

45. See 1 Kgs 19:27–29 for how he taunted his rival prophets.

46. Elijah, a stranger, acts presumptuously. But his presumption follows a biblical principle: *God tells people what he wants them to do.* God already had commanded the widow to feed him (1 Kgs 17:9). She knew she had to risk her last supplies because God had already spoken to her. In 1 Kgs 13 the same principle holds: God commanded the man of God not to eat bread or drink water or to go home by the way he came (1 Kgs 13:9); the man of God disobeyed because another prophet deceived him. As punishment for not obeying God's word, the other prophet prophesies that the man of God will not be buried with his fathers (1 Kgs 13:22). True enough, the man of God dies en route home when a lion mauls him (1 Kgs 13:24).

47. A strong indication that Elijah serves as God's spokesman is his command to the woman, "Do not be afraid." Elijah's words to her represent a theophany, an expression of God's presence and watchcare (DeVries, *1 Kings,* 217). "Do not be afraid" is a common prelude to a saving action of God (Nelson, *First and Second Kings,* 110). Throughout the Hebrew Scriptures, a prophet represents God's presence among his people and the prophet's words are spoken and heard as God's words. The text presents the lack of rain as the first indication that Elijah truly is a prophet. It presents the admonition, "Do not be afraid," as the second confirmation. "Do not be afraid" is a common command of both prophets and God when they are about to bless. For example, God speaks the command to Abram (Gen 15:1); to Hagar (Gen 21:17); to Isaac (Gen 26:24). Joseph says it to his brothers (Gen 50:19); Moses says it to Israel (Exod 20:20); God says it to Joshua (Josh 8:1); Joshua says it to his soldiers (Josh 10:25).

48. Perhaps Elijah also speaks to himself when he says, "Do not be afraid." Later readers and hearers get a glimpse of Elijah's fear in his reaction to Jezebel when he says that all the prophets except him have been slaughtered, and now he is about to die too (1 Kgs 19:10).

49. Elijah does not talk about her sin. Yes, she is a sinner, although a catalogue of her sins is (graciously) absent from the text. Yet the universality of sin clearly remains a fundamental biblical principle (see Gen 3:6; Deut 29:17–18; Ps 51:5; Prov 5:22; 10:9; 20:9; Isa 64:5; Hos 6:7). His silence allows God to lead her to repentance and faith.

50. According to DeVries, the widow's theology of divine judgment is so erroneous that Elijah does not spend time refuting it (DeVries, *1 Kings,* 221).

51. Contrast his reaction here with his response to Ahab in the next chapter. When the woman blames him for the death of her son, Elijah does not answer. But when Ahab blames him for the woes in Israel, Elijah reverses the criticism (1 Kgs 18:16–18).

52. Camp, "1 and 2 Kings," 106.

53. She speaks unbelief on the ground floor of her house; she is in Baal's territory. Elijah takes her son to a territory where the God of Israel reigns, and the God of Israel reigns where Elijah is, in the upper room.

54. The boy's illness and death represent a larger struggle that occurs frequently in the Hebrew Scriptures, namely the struggle between two territorial and opposing deities. For example, the God of the Hebrew slaves opposes the gods of Egypt (Exod 7–11) and wins. The God of Samson takes umbrage when the Philistines worship Dagon and enables Samson to slay them (Judg 16:23–31). And the God of Elijah waits while the 450 prophets of Baal (and possibly the 400 prophets of Asherah, v. 19) supplicate their gods to send fire upon a sacrifice; standing alone, Elijah commands the God of Israel to answer him "so that these people will know that you, O Lord, are God, and that you are turning their hearts back again" (1 Kgs 18:37). These examples show that the God of Israel is stronger than territorial gods, and in the case of the widow's son, stronger than death.

55. According to Walsh (*1 Kings*, 232), the prophet stretches himself out over the boy as a sign or act symbolic of committing the prophet's will into the boy.

56. By not mentioning magic, the text reduces to a minimum any connotation of human skills or arts in connection with the child's restoration to life. In place of magic, the story insists upon Elijah's role as one who prays (Rofé, "Classes in the Prophetical Stories," 149).

57. The miracle of life illustrates Elijah's swift thinking, his ability to pray effectually, and his intimate relationship with Yahweh (R. L. Cohn, "The Literary Logic of 1 Kings 17–19," *JBL* 101 [1982]: 336).

58. Robin Gallaher Branch, "Evangelism Via Power and Lifestyle: Elijah's Method in 1 Kings 17," *Missionalia* 31 (2003): 299.

59. DeVries, *1 Kings*, 222.

60. Ibid.

61. Other sons in the Scriptures die and remain dead: both Jezebel's son Joram and Athaliah's son Ahaziah die, and a prophet is not sent to restore life to them (2 Kgs 9:24; 11:1). Earlier, David's prayers for the healing of his first son by Bathsheba receive a negative answer, and the unnamed baby dies (2 Sam 12:18).

62. God's job description for a prophet includes intercession (see Gen 20:7, 17). See Branch, "Genesis 20," 225.

63. The text indicates he brings the son up to his chamber and then brings him down to his mother, a literary parallelism helpful in mentally tracing the event.

64. Cohn, "The Literary Logic of 1 Kings 17–19," 337.

65. James, *Personalities of the Old Testament*, 180.

66. God also commands Elijah throughout the cycle beginning with four verbs: leave, turn, hide, and drink (1 Kgs 17:3–4). In verse 9 and in 18:1, God commands Elijah to go to Zarephath and then to go and present himself to Ahab. Yet an aspect of God that is both interesting and perplexing, humbling and wonderful is that in this chapter and throughout the Hebrew Scriptures he permits others to command him and he obeys. The psalms and this passage present prayer as supplication, confusion, entreaty, and, yes, command. Prayer is fundamentally a conversation between friends. Elijah and God are used to dialoguing; each knows the other's voice. The prayer of desperation that is Elijah's when he is faced with the death of the widow's son drops formalities and bypasses niceties. The supplicant cuts to the chase. The beseecher *commands*.

67. "Widow," *EncJud* 16:477–88. Widows in the Hebrew Scriptures include Tamar (Gen 38) and Ruth, Orpah, and Naomi (book of Ruth). The Scriptures recognize their pressing needs for provision, husbands, sons, and status in society. Although Abigail became a widow at Nabal's death, presumably she had ample means of financial support because Nabal had been a wealthy Judean (1 Sam 25). The Scriptures acknowledge the prominence of some widows' sons: Huram and Jeroboam I (1 Kgs 7:14; 11:26, the king of Tyre and the king of Israel respectively).

68. Jopie Siebert-Hommes, "The Widow of Zarephath and the Great Woman of Shunem: A Comparative Analysis of Two Stories," in *On Reading Prophetic Texts: Gender-Specific and Related Studies of Fokkelein Van Dijk-Hemmes* (ed. Bob Beeking and Meindert Dijkstra; Leiden: E. J. Brill, 1996), 236.

69. Jyrki Keinanen (*Traditions in Collision: A Literary and Redaction-Critical Study of the Elijah Narratives 1 Kings 17–19* [Gottingen: The Finnish Exegetical Society in Helsinki, 2001], 25, 31) notes that 1 Kgs 17:7–16 and 17–24 differ; she cites literary inconsistencies and thematic differences and says the story may be about two different women. I find the evidence for a second women unconvincing.

70. Quite likely Elijah enjoyed a high degree of physical fitness because he ran before the chariot of Ahab after decreeing the advent of rain (see Kaufmann, *Religion of Israel,* 513).

71. In 2 Kgs 1:8, Elijah's garment seems sufficiently unusual to merit narrational pause.

72. Margaret Sangster, *The Women of the Bible: A Portrait Gallery* (New York: Christian Herald, 1911), 169.

73. Nelson, *First and Second Kings,* 110.

74. Sangster, *Women of the Bible,* 167.

75. Ibid., 169.

76. Ibid., 170.

77. The text often associates people and cultures with other gods by naming location only. The text does not belabor the point of other religions but leaves

readers and hearers with the mental equation that the Philistines, for example, equal those who serve other gods, namely Dagon; Jezebel from Tyre equals one who serves Baal; and the Ninevites equal those who serve still another god.

78. "As the Lord lives" is a formulaic oath that appears twice in the passage, sworn first by Elijah and then echoed by the widow (vv. 1, 12). Elijah and the widow seem to know—or at least their formulaic oaths declare—that the drought is a struggle between the God of Israel and another god, Baal, and between life and death. They speak a common phrase in Scripture, recurring more than forty times in the Hebrew Bible. It appears as a kind of oath in Deut 5:24; Judg 8:19; Ruth 3:13; 1 Sam 1:26; 14:39, 45; 19:6; 20:21; 25:26; 26:16; 28:10; 1 Kgs 1:29; Dan 4:34.

79. Walsh, *1 Kings*, 229.

80. Letty M. Russell, "Practicing Hospitality in a World of Difference and Danger," *PSB* 24 (2003): 208.

81. Perhaps his request is really a challenge for her to put her trust in the God of Israel and in his prophet. Elijah blesses her with a salvation oracle (1 Kgs 17:14) that promises a wondrous renewal of oil and flour (DeVries, *1 Kings*, 217).

82. In rabbinic tradition, a male relative supports a widow as long as she is in his house (*m. Ketub.*12:147). But 1 Kgs 17 overlooks kinship; presumably the widow has no close male relative with whom she and her son can take shelter. One of the role reversals in this story is that the widow offers Elijah shelter and food; another is that God miraculously supplies the provision.

83. Rofé, "Classes in the Prophetical Stories," 149.

84. Unlike Rahab, she is not referred to as an innkeeper, and no tradition of prostitution grew up around her name.

85. Camp (*1 and 2 Kings*, 106) speculates that the widow's starvation predicament and the death of the widow's son represent two different widows, for in the second story she seems to be wealthier because she has a two-story house. But Camp fails to back this up with a reference in the text. She merely concludes that being a widow implies poverty and that having a two-story house implies wealth. She gives no credence to the possibility that the narrator at first withholds the details of the house simply because they are not needed. In the later account of the raising of the widow's son, these details may have been introduced to show a sense of physical separation between the unbelief represented by the widow and the belief represented by Elijah. Her domain of unbelief is located on the lower level; his chamber of prayer and faith is on the upper level.

86. Russell, "Practicing Hospitality," 215.

87. Sangster, *Women of the Bible*, 174.

88. Similar declarations of faith in the Hebrew Bible from those who were outside the covenant come from Rahab, Ruth, Naaman, and Nebuchadnezzar (Josh 2:9–13; Ruth 1:16–17; 2 Kgs 5:15; Dan 4:37).

89. Compare Num 12:6–8 (God's praise of Moses), for example, or Jer 1:9 (God's assurance that he puts his words in Jeremiah's mouth), or 1 Sam 3:19–20 (Israel's recognition of Samuel as a prophet).

90. The majority of biblical texts indeed deal with concerns that threaten to engulf human beings. But it presents intriguing exceptions as well. A notable group consisting of foreigners presents an exception to the text's general rule of talking about large groups of people. The widow of Zarephath, Rahab (Josh 2, 6), Ruth (Ruth), Ebed-Melech (Jer 38; 39:15–18), Naaman the Syrian (2 Kgs 5), and the Ninevites (Jon 1, 3, 4) show how God consistently reaches out to those outside the covenant with offers of forgiveness, mercy, healing, and safety.

91. This seems somewhat irregular to modern readers. Modern introductions follow three basic rules: a man is introduced to a woman, a young person is introduced to an older person, and a person of lesser importance is always introduced to the more important person (Elizabeth L. Post, *Emily Post's Etiquette* [15th ed.; New York: HarperCollinsPublishers, 1992], 6–7).

92. Thomas W. Overholt, "Feeding the Widow, Raising the Dead. What Counts as Cultural Exegesis?" in *Text and Experience: Towards a Cultural Exegesis of the Bible* (ed. David Smith-Christopher; Sheffield: Sheffield Academic, 1995), 117.

93. A *wadi* is a stream that flows in a rainy season. Humor is evident in the name of the wadi, Kerith. Its root means "to cut." Walsh, *1 Kings*, 228, appreciating the humor, calls it "Cut Off Creek."

94. According to Jewish tradition, the ravens brought Elijah food from the larder of pious king Jehoshaphat (Ginzberg, *LJ* 4:196). Elijah's feasting on meat shows God's abundant, even flamboyant, care for his prophet in a time of famine, drought, and want. Meat was a delicacy in ancient Palestine (Nelson, *First and Second Kings*, 109).

95. Zarephath is seven miles south of Sidon on the Mediterranean (DeVries, *1 Kings*, 217).

96. Common biblical themes include the care of widows and orphans and the mandate not to take advantage of those who are traditionally the weakest in society (Exod 22:22; Deut 10:18). But in this text, a major reversal occurs: the widow provides for Elijah. Or rather, God provides for all—widow, Elijah, and her son—by replenishing the oil and flour.

97. Later, the prophet Jeremiah writes about the Lord's ability to change hearts and to write his covenant on hearts as a new sign (Jer 31:33). This change happens to the widow upon her conversion when she acknowledges Elijah's god as God.

98. This rich Hebrew word *hesed* is traditionally translated "loving-kindness"; see Katharine Doob Sakenfeld, *The Meaning of Hesed* (Missoula, Mont.: Scholars Press, 1978), 12, 168.

99. A subplot in the chapter and cycle is that through Elijah, Yahweh, the God of Israel, struggles with Baal, the Canaanite storm god (Day, "Baal,"

545). Yahweh challenges Baal on his own terrain as the so-called god of the rain and god of the mountain. Yahweh, the God of Israel, working through Elijah, vanquishes Baal on both accounts. The biblical writers show great disdain for Baal. His name becomes synonymous with *bosheth* (shame), and "shame" is substituted for his name in several places (see Jer 3:24; 11:13; Hos 9:10). The Baal of Ahab and Jezebel probably was the Baal Melqart of Tyre, because by the second century B.C.E. Baal is referred to as Melqart (Frick, "Rain," 548). The Baal cult was associated with the "high places" (*bamoth*) and with "pillars" (*matsevoth*), symbols of a male deity (Day, "Baal," 548). Social prostitution was part of the fertility cult that formed part of the Baal religion (ibid.). Hosea 4:14 parallels prostitutes with holy ones, for example. Baal also figures as a war god. In a stele at Ugarit, he appears standing on a mountain or in the clouds waving a club in his right hand and brandishing a lance in his left (ibid., 545). Baal's consort is Anath; in Ugaritic texts, Anath searches for Baal in the underworld and fights Mot with him (ibid.). Baal's Greek and Roman counterparts, Hercules and Zeus, surface in various Mediterranean sects (ibid.).

100. Commentators offer various insights into the story's miraculous aspects. Sangster (*Women of the Bible*, 172–73) believes the message inherent in the miracle of provisions is that if the widow of Zarephath becomes one who serves the God of Israel, she need not fear. James (*Personalities of the Old Testament*, 180) groups Elijah and Elisha together. He believes the two men lived so completely with God that for them the impossible did not exist; miracles were part of their lives.

101. Reading canonically, Gen 18:14 states, "Is anything too hard for the Lord?" and Luke 1:37 states, "For nothing is impossible with God."

102. Multiplication stories proliferate in the Hebrew Bible. God sends quail and manna in the wilderness (Num 4); Elisha helps another widow pay off her debts with oil (2 Kgs 4:1–7). Furthermore, the multiplication miracle in the Elijah cycle is consistent with another pattern previously established in the Moses cycle. An instrument through which many miracles are performed is something quite normal; for example, Moses' staff is thrown down and becomes a snake that later eats up other snakes (Exod 4:3). In 1 Kgs 17, flour and oil keep multiplying in the jars of the widow's home.

103. Evangelism represents one way to extend God's love for Israel outside the boundaries of Israel (Branch, "Genesis 20," 217). Elijah expresses no hatred toward the Sidonians ("Elijah," *EncBib* 337).

104. And where God is, there is bounty, wealth, and abundance. David caught this vision. Psalm 16:11 states: "In thy presence is the fullness of joy, in thy right hand, pleasures forevermore." Blessings likewise came to Obed-Edom (2 Sam 6:11). While the ark of the covenant remained at his house, the Lord blessed Obed-Edom. The same principle applies: where God or his representative lodges, blessing and abundance follow.

105. Rofé, "Classes in the Prophetical Stories," 151–52.

106. Branch, "Evangelism," 301.

107. Slotki, *Kings,* 127.

108. Similarly in the story of Jonah, the sailors, the great fish, the storm, the Ninevites, the Ninevite king, the vine, the worm, and the scorching east wind all obey God. Jonah alone disobeys.

109. Deut 28:1–14 lists the blessings that come with obeying God and following all his commands, while 15–68 lists the curses that will overtake those who choose not to follow God. First Sam 15:22 states the biblical principle succinctly: *Obedience is better than sacrifice.*

110. DeVries, *1 Kings,* 216.

111. The fact that Elijah immediately obeys God's direct word to go to the Wadi Kerith argues for Elijah's obedience to an earlier (and unrecorded) word of the Lord to impose a drought.

112. The care of Yahweh, the God of Israel, for his prophet throughout 1 Kgs 17 is "almost farcical," Walsh says (*1 Kings,* 233). God surely pampers Elijah. The ravens and then the widow take care of him at God's command. Ravens and widows, incidentally, fall into a category of those singled out for merciful kindness from the Lord (Ps 147:9; Job 38:41). There is nothing sinister about ravens in the Elijah cycle; however, in Isa 34:11 and Prov 30:17, they are referred to as birds of prey.

113. Rofé, "Classes in the Prophetical Stories," 149.

114. When God made a covenant with Abram, he said that through Abram all peoples of the earth will be blessed (see Gen 12:1–3).

115. Quite likely the first conversion was Rahab's (see Josh 2).

116. Branch, "Evangelism," 302.

117. Simon, *Reading Prophetic Narratives,* 224–25.

118. God begins slowly his re-conversion of Israel and his plans for Israel to bless the whole world by starting with a foreign widow, one outside the covenant.

119. Kaufmann, *Religion of Israel,* 278.

120. Camp, "1 and 2 Kings," 106.

121. Siebert-Hommes, "The Widow of Zarephath," 237.

122. Nelson, *First and Second Kings,* 111.

123. Proselytes are uncommon in Israelite history. Yet when they do appear, they are significant. The first proselytes are the riffraff who came with the Hebrews out of Egypt in the exodus. They become integrated into tribal society. Rahab the innkeeper at Jericho becomes a proselyte (Josh 2, 6). In Hebrew tradition she marries Joshua; the Christian tradition says she marries Salmon and is in the line of Jesus (Matt 1:5). Ruth the Moabitess marries Boaz and becomes the grandmother of David (Ruth 4:22). David gathers many non-Israelites around him, and they become mighty men of valor (1 Chr 11:26–47). An unnamed

widow in Zarephath cares for Elijah (1 Kgs 17:7–24). Naaman, a Syrian general, comes to Elisha for healing from leprosy and returns home a believer in the God of Elisha (2 Kgs 5:15). The Ninevites, at least briefly, turn to the Lord (Jonah 3, 4).

124. Cohn, "The Literary Logic of 1 Kings 17–19," 336.

125. Sally A. Brown, "Overturned: Jonah 3:1–4:3," *PSB* 24 (2003): 182.

126. Ibid., 183.

127. The text leaves unrecorded any examples of how Elijah reached the point where he had enough faith to declare a drought. Presumably the success of the drought led him to declare as the Lord's word the multiplication miracle of the oil and flour. The verses involving the widow, therefore, give the needed evidence for how he develops sufficient faith to call upon God to raise the dead.

128. On another level, the stories deal directly with death. The widow swears she and her son will die. In an ironic twist, God apparently honors the woman's words: she predicts her son's death, and he dies. But God has the last word, and he lives!

NOTES TO CHAPTER 8

1. M. Daniel Carroll R. (Rodas), "קָטֹן," *NIDOTTE,* 3: 910.

2. This chapter elaborates on a portion of my published article about the significance of servants in Hebrew Bible narrative entitled "'Your humble servant.' Well, maybe. Overlooked onlookers in Deuteronomistic History," *OTE* 17 (2004): 168–89.

3. Significantly, the impetus of kidnapping, being sold as a slave, and ownership of human beings are not considered at all in this text.

4. T. R. Hobbs, *2 Kings* (WBC 3; Waco, Tex.: Word, 1985), 62.

5. The characters are Naaman, his wife, her Israelite slave girl, the king of Aram, the king of Israel, Elisha, Gehazi, Naaman's servants, and Elisha's unnamed messenger.

6. Hobbs, *2 Kings,* 61.

7. Choon Leong Seow, "The First and Second Books of Kings: Introduction, Commentary, and Reflections," *NIB* 3:192.

8. Ibid.

9. Ibid., 62.

10. J. Strong, *Strong's Exhaustive Concordance of the Bible* (Peabody, Mass.: Hendrickson, 2007), 1481.

11. Robin Wakely, "חַיִל," *NIDOTTE,* 2:116.

12. The king of Aram is probably Ben Hadad II (Barker, *NIV Study Bible,* 526n). The unnamed "J. king of Israel" (2 Kgs 5:7) may have been Joram (849–842 B.C.E.), Jehu (842–815 B.C.E.), Jehoahaz (815–802 B.C.E.), or Jehoash (802–776 B.C.E.); see T. R. Hobbs, *2 Kings,* 63.

13. See Robin Wakely, "גִּבּוֹר" *NIDOTTE* 1:806; *TWOT* 1:148.

14. Biblical texts occasionally give a few indications of a narrator's view on aspects of the story being told. The narrator here seems to comment on the happiness and suitability of Naaman's marriage by his word choice; he uses compatible words, *gibbor/geberet,* to describe Naaman and his wife. Similarly, the narrator of Ruth arguably favors the marriage of Boaz and Ruth because he uses the same word, *hayil,* to describe both of them (Ruth 2:1; 3:11). Note as well the mismatching of Abigail and Nabal; Abigail is described as intelligent and beautiful while her husband is described as a Cabelite, surly and mean in his dealings (1 Sam 25:3).

15. The victory in question may have been against the Assyrians in the aftermath of the battle of Qarqar in 853 B.C.E. However, this victory is not otherwise recorded in any detail in the Hebrew Bible (Barker, *NIV Study Bible,* 526n).

16. Flavius Josephus, *Ant* 15:5.

17. The Bible also praises Melchizedek (Gen 14:18–20) and Job (Job 1:1–8; 42:7–8).

18. Scholars doubt that Naaman had Hansen's disease, the modern name for leprosy; *tsara'ath,* the Hebrew word for leprosy (Lev 13–14), is a generic name indicating a variety of skin disorders known for their chronic discoloration of the skin and the formation of mold or mildew on the walls of houses. See H. Avalos, "Leprosy," *EDB,* 801. The symptoms of Hansen's disease include pain, widespread infection of the joints, horrible disfigurement, eventual loss of limbs or extremities, and, paradoxically, no sense of feeling in the extremities (see Hobbs, *2 Kings,* 63). However, the text gives no indication that Naaman lived in quarantine, so it is unlikely that he had Hansen's disease. In addition, the text gives no indication that he was ritually unclean, even though the regulations applying to those who are ritually unclean (see Lev 13) would not apply to him, a person outside the covenant. Leithart speculates he had psoriasis (Peter J. Leithart, *Brazos Theological Commentary on the Bible: 1 & 2 Kings* [Grand Rapids: Brazos, 2006], 193).

19. R. D. Nelson, *First and Second Kings,*177.

20. *Na'arah* generally indicates a household servant; see Victor Hamilton, "נַעַר," *NIDOTTE* 3:124–27.

21. Characters reveal themselves in a variety of ways, including their dress, distinctive features, unusual or individualistic mannerisms, friends, enemies, gestures, actions, desires, or words; see B. Hochman, *Character in Literature* (Ithaca, N.Y.: Cornell University Press, 1985), 38. The Israelite slave girl and Naaman reveal themselves in many of these ways.

22. God's healing power is attested to in numerous places in the Hebrew Bible. Consider these: Gen 20:17; Exod 15:26; Lev 14:3.

23. Earlier biblical stories attest to this principle. The first prophet, Abraham, prays for healing for Abimelech and his household, and it happens (Gen

20). Elijah prays for life to return to the widow of Zarephath's son, and the boy is revived (1 Kgs 17). Elisha prays for provision for a prophet's widow and her two sons, and provision comes (2 Kgs 4:1–7). Elisha prays for life to return to the Shunammite's son, and it does (2 Kgs 4:8–37).

24. This comparison was inspired by a much shorter comparison given by P. R. House, *1, 2 Kings* (Nashville: Broadman and Holman, 1995), 271–72.

25. S. Sorenson, *How to Write Short Stories* (New York: Macmillan, 1994), 13.

26. Iain Provan, *1 & 2 Kings,* 192.

27. Rick Dale Moore, *God Saves: Lessons from the Elisha Stories* (Sheffield: JSOT, 1990), 76.

28. Donald J. Wiseman, *The Tyndale Old Testament Commentaries: 1 and 2 Kings* (Leicester: InterVarsity, 1993), 207.

29. Branch, "Your humble servant," 185.

30. Moore, *God Saves,* 71.

31. Robert Cohn, *Berit Olam: Studies in Hebrew Narration and Poetry: 2 Kings* (Collegeville, Minn.: Liturgical, 2000), 38.

32. J. Robinson, *The Second Book of Kings* (Cambridge: Cambridge University Press, 1976), 55.

33. Leithert, *Brazos Theological Commentary,* 193.

34. Barker, *NIV Study Bible,* 527n.

35. Branch, "Evangelism," 301.

36. Ibid., 300.

37. Ibid., 303.

Notes to Chapter 9

1. Athaliah is the only reigning female monarch recorded in Scripture; no other Israelite or Judean woman managed to become queen again until the Second Temple era, when Salome Alexandra reigned (76–67 B.C.E.). Salome Alexandra ascended the throne after the death of her second husband, Yannai. She earlier had been the wife of his brother, Aristobulus I. Since that union ended without a son and heir, she was required to marry Yannai in accordance with the laws of levirate marriage. She merits comparison with Athaliah in a number of ways: 1) Salome strictly observed Jewish religious traditions while Athaliah did not. 2) Salome won the affection of the Judean populace by influencing Yannai to end his persecution of the Pharisees, a prominent religious sect, while Athaliah had no close working or spiritual relationship with the Yahwist priests of her day. Throughout her reign Salome maintained a close relationship with the Pharisees yet did not punish their rival sect, the Sadducees, when she had the opportunity. 3) Salome had two sons by Yannai, Hyrcanus

and Aristobulus; the former was incompetent and the latter gathered a large mercenary force and usurped his older brother's throne. Athaliah had one known son, Ahaziah, and other unnamed sons (2 Chr 24:7). 4) While the rabbis condemn the reign of Athaliah, they praise Salome's nine-year reign as a time of piety, peace, and prosperity, a time when wheat, oats, and lentils grew to extraordinary sizes ("Salome Alexandra," *EncJud* 14:691–93).

2. Perhaps because she followed Baal, she is omitted from the genealogy of Jesus in Matt 1:1–17. The genealogy mentions five women: Tamar, Rahab, Ruth, the wife of Uriah, and Mary. Tamar, Rahab, and Ruth are non-Israelites who contribute significantly to the biblical text and the life of two faith communities: the Jews and the Christians.

3. The prophets repeatedly chastise Judah for forsaking Yahweh; early references are 1 Kgs 3:2 and 22:43.

4. Kaufmann (*Religion of Israel,* 1947], 485) calls her a murderer and usurper of the throne.

5. Omri is of interest to biblical scholars because his influence extends beyond his reign (c. 876–869 B.C.E.). For a fascinating article on an ongoing excavation at Tel Jezreel, site of an outpost of the house of Omri, see David Ussishkin's "The Fortified Enclosure of the Kings of the House of Omri at Jezreel," *ErIsr* 25 (1996): 1–14. Ussishkin writes that in the tel and its descent were found rock utensils from the Neolithic Period and many potsherds from the Late Bronze Age (1).

6. "Athaliah," *EncJud* 3:814.

7. Dillard, *2 Chronicles,* 174.

8. John Bright, *A History of Israel* (Philadelphia: Westminster, 1981), 242. Herbert Lockyer (*The Women of the Bible* [Grand Rapids: Zondervan, 1967], 32) disagrees, saying Jehoshaphat's giving of his son Jehoram to Athaliah in marriage was "a blot on his otherwise good memory."

9. Solomon set a historical precedent for this fratricide at the beginning of his reign by ordering the death of his half-brother Adonijah. Solomon interpreted Adonijah's request for Abishag, their father David's concubine, as a bid for the throne (see 1 Kgs 2:13–25). Fratricide, however, has a long biblical tradition. Cain killed Abel, and Joseph's brothers hated him so much that they almost killed him (see Gen 4; 37:20).

10. Bright, *History of Israel,* 252. See also "Athaliah," *EncJud* 3:814.

11. During Jehoram's reign, Edom rebelled against Judah and set up its own king. The Philistines also rose against Jehoram and carried away his palace treasure, his wives, and his sons, all except for Ahaziah, the youngest. Elijah wrote Jehoram a letter accusing him of doing evil and causing the people to prostitute themselves as the house of Ahab had done. Elijah told Jehoram he was about to be struck with an incurable bowel disease. This happened, and Jehoram died. These events and Jehoram's punishment help explain the

narrator's quip, a one-of-a-kind in Scripture, that he died "to nobody's regret" (2 Chr 21:20).

12. With Athaliah as a mother, Ahaziah never had the chance to develop any finer qualities of character (Lockyer, *The Women of the Bible*, 32–33). Brenner (*The Israelite Woman*, 31), however, admires her for the various roles she played throughout her life as king's daughter, king's wife, king's mother, intimate adviser to her son Ahaziah, and regent after his death.

13. The differences regarding the events surrounding the death of Ahaziah are among the most difficult textual questions in the Old Testament. Among the differences are the following points: 1) in 2 Kgs, the slaughter of the princes and officers of Judah is reported after the murder of Ahaziah but before it in 2 Chr; 2) the place of death is listed as Megiddo in 2 Kgs and somewhere in Samaria (at the hand of Jehu) in 2 Chr; 3) in 2 Kgs, he is buried in the city of David, while in 2 Chr no specific place is mentioned. Dillard explains the differences by saying that 2 Chr was written after the exile from the vantage point of postexilic Judah (*2 Chronicles*, 172). This explanation, however, fails to account for the factual differences between the texts.

14. Ibid., 173.

15. Bloody conditions prevailed, as Jehu's maneuvers against the house of Omri indicate. For instance, Jehu cleverly had others (the officials of Jezreel) execute his potential rivals and contenders for the throne—the seventy sons of Ahab who were being reared in Jezreel. He then killed all those who remained loyal to the house of Ahab along with Ahab's chief advisors, close friends, and priests, "leaving him no survivors" (2 Kgs 10:1–11).

16. Yet Jehu was commanded by Yahweh and anointed by Elijah to obliterate the house of Ahab (1 Kgs 19:16–17). Later, he was commended for carrying out God's instructions against Ahab (2 Kgs 10:30). Athaliah, meanwhile, received no commission to exterminate her house and no divine praise for doing so.

17. The rabbis add that these violent deaths serve as punishment for David's having kept himself in safety while his army fought against Absalom; see Ginzberg, *LJ* 4:268.

18. Bright, *History of Israel*, 252.

19. The more detailed account in 2 Chr adds several theological insights. God brought Ahaziah's downfall and there was no one strong enough to retain the kingdom after him (2 Chr 22:7, 9b). Into this political vacuum walks Athaliah, who takes over, but only for six years until "Jehoiada showed his strength" (2 Chr 23:1). Jehoiada's well-planned takeover involves numerous members of the army and gains added legitimacy by the use of David's shields and spears (23:9–10).

20. J. Blenkinsopp, "Wisdom in the Chronicler's Work," in *In Search of Wisdom: Essays in Memory of John G. Gammie* (Leo G. Perdue et al., eds.; Louisville: Westminster/John Knox, 1993), 29–30.

21. Gerhard von Rad, "The Levitical Sermon in I and II Chronicles" (*The Problem of the Hexateuch and Other Essays* [New York: McGraw-Hill, 1966], 267), posits that the writer of Chronicles used extreme examples to encourage subsequent generations to remain loyal to Yahweh.

22. Hobbs, *2 Kings,* 138. Added to the puzzle surrounding her name is the light it sheds on her father Ahab's spiritual condition. Ahab gave three of his children names compounded with Yahweh—Athaliah, Ahaziah, and Jehoram (James, *Personalities of the Old Testament,* 172). Earlier texts present Ahab ambiguously as one who repents (1 Kgs 21:27–29) and yet one who is judged as doing more evil in the eyes of the Lord than any king before him (1 Kgs 16:30). Athaliah's name, however, has no Hebrew root. Scholars think it may be derived from an Akkadian phrase meaning "Yahweh has manifested his glory"; likewise, it may have an Arabic derivation meaning "bulky" or "robust" (W. Thiel, "Athaliah," *ABD,* 1:511). It could mean "Taken away from the Lord" or "Yahweh has afflicted" (Lockyer, *Women of the Bible,* 32). Yet scholars agree that there is no other biblical woman's name with a theophoric component of Yahweh in it (Thiel, *ABD* 1:511).

23. Syntactically, Athaliah's story in 2 Kgs begins with an arrangement typical of the book: the *waw* is followed by a subject and the perfect tense (see also 2 Kgs 11:1; 3:1; 4:1, 38, 42; 5:1; 6:8; 8:1 and 9:1; Hobbs, *2 Kings,* 136). A check of these references indicates that they cannot be signs heralding only evil or good; they are merely narrative forms of introducing a new topic and not narrative clues signifying a momentous event for blessing or for ill. Hobbs (*2 Kings,* 136) breaks 2 Kgs 11 down to two large sections. Verses 4–12 reflect a priestly account of the fall of Athaliah, while the people's perspective is presented in verses 13–18. Nelson, however, argues that verses 1–12 are the climax of the narrative and verses 13–20 show the results (*First and Second Kings,* 209–10).

24. Hobbs, *2 Kings,* 137.

25. See Alter, *Art of Biblical Narrative,* for a more detailed account of the use of repetition throughout the Hebrew Bible (88–113).

26. For examples of such formulaic introductions, see 1 Kgs 16:1; 17:1; 18:1; 21:1; 2 Chr 25:1; 26:1; 27:1; 28:1.

27. Hobbs, *2 Kings,* 138.

28. As such, she can be compared with Miriam, the sister of Moses, and Aaron, whose life is recorded as a child, prophetess, and co-deliverer with her brothers of the Israelites from Egypt (Exod 2:1–10; 15:20; Num 12; Mic 6:4).

29. Theil, *ABD,* 1:511.

30. H. J. Katzenstein, "Who Were the Parents of Athaliah?" *IEJ* 5 (1955): 197.

31. Ibid.

32. In contrast, the text says King Solomon loved many foreign women (1 Kgs 11:1).

33. Kaufmann (*Religion of Israel*, 233) writes that in the days of the kingdom of Judah, there was Baal worship in the royal family for many years, a situation that would facilitate the union of representatives of two different religions.

34. Thiel, *ABD*, 1:512.

35. Brenner, *Israelite Woman*, 29.

36. Ibid.

37. The Hebrew verb *ya'ats* ("to give counsel"), translated "encouraged" by the NIV, may indicate that Athaliah flaunted evil and made it attractive to Ahaziah, who then bought into its lifestyle.

38. Josephus, *Jewish Antiquities* 9.7.141, in *Complete Works* (trans. W. Whiston; Grand Rapids: Kregel, 1981); Lockyer, *Women of the Bible*, 33. Jewish tradition equates Athaliah's purge with Saul's slaughter of the priests of Nob (1 Sam 22:6–23). The rabbis say that Athaliah's reign of terror was how God exacted payment from the house of David for his transgression in connection with the extermination of the priests at Nob (Ginzberg, *LJ* 4:257–58). Even as Abiathar alone survived the sword of Saul (1 Sam 22:20), Joash alone survived his grandmother's bloodbath.

39. Camp, "1 and 2 Kings," 104.

40. Andreason, "The Role of the Queen Mother in Israelite Society," *CBQ* 45 (1983): 190.

41. H. Schulte, "The End of the Omride Dynasty: Social-Ethical Observations on the Subject of Power and Violence," *Semeia* 66 (1994): 136.

42. Z. Ben-Barak, "The Status and Right of the *Gebira*," in Brenner, *A Feminist Companion to Samuel and Kings*, 177.

43. Kaufmann (*Religion of Israel*, 268) compares Athaliah's purge with the days of Manasseh, son of Hezekiah, when the blood flowed down the streets, the blood of prophets and sons of prophets and even perhaps that of Jeremiah.

44. Athaliah comes from a distinguished line of queen mothers in Israel and Judah. Both countries enjoyed a tradition of powerful women. The influence of the queen mother in both seemed to follow the pattern of the Hittite and Ugaritic cultures and other Near Eastern cultures (Andreasen, "The Role of Queen Mother," 182). In general, a queen mother's power was independent of that of either her husband or her son as kings. If her husband predeceased her, she served as regent. If the king was absent, she acted in his stead. Throughout, she had a preeminent role in religious matters (ibid.).

Possibly, a queen mother assumed a natural role of advisor and grand woman once her childbearing years ended. The story of Bathsheba's later years indicates this. Once she left David's bed and Abishag crept in it, there is evidence of a shift in Bathsheba's role to that of distinguished stateswoman. Bathsheba was not banished when her role and function changed but continued to enjoy easy access to both David and Solomon, as well as to command influence over both father and son (see 1 Kgs 1–2). Significantly, both David and Solomon listened to her and accorded her much respect. A queen mother, in line with the tradition begun with Bathsheba, held a definite position and great political power throughout the era of the monarchy (Dillard, *2 Chronicles,* 174).

A queen mother is called *gevirah* in the Hebrew Bible. Significantly, Athaliah is not addressed by this title. Ben-Barak ("Status and Right of *Gebira,*" 185) suggests that an extraordinary woman called *gevirah* was able to secure the royal succession for her son and thereby put herself in a position of power in the realm. *Gevirah* as a title of respect designates a political station—that of chief counselor, second to that of the king. It occurs mainly in Judah and is a title surviving from the matriarchal period (ibid., 171). The Hebrew phrase *bene hammeleh* (lit., "sons of the king") may mean the royal family and *bene hagevirah* ("sons of the queen mother") may mean the actual sons of the king and queen mother (ibid., 176).

A queen mother is mentioned with the ascent of each new king of Judah. Maacah, the grandmother of Asa and first significant queen mother after Bathsheba, was deposed from her position as queen mother, the text says, because she had made a replica of the Asherah pole (1 Kgs 15:18). Nehushta, the daughter of Elnathan in 2 Kgs 24:8, wore a *tara* (a crown), with her son Jehoiachin (Jer 13:18), and so great was her power that the enemy regarded her as dangerous to the point of meriting banishment with the sovereign (ibid., 174; also Andreasen, "Role of Queen Mother," 180).

For Athaliah to have been Ahaziah's counselor was the normal role for a queen mother in the ancient Near East and in Israel (ibid., 188–89). Ben-Barak sees Athaliah's seizure of the throne as evidence showing that considerable power had accrued to the station of queen mother ("Status and Right of *Gebira,*" 175).

45. Other attempts throughout the ages to exterminate the Jews also failed. Pharaoh's order to kill all the male Hebrew babies (Exod 1:15–16) and Haman's determination to destroy the Jews (Esth 3:8–9) are among them.

46. Ginzberg, *LJ* 6:191; H. Freedman and Maurice Simon, eds., *Mishnah Rabbah,* Vol. 8: *Ruth Rabbah* [L. Rabinowitz, trans.; New York: Soncino, 1983]), 4.4.

47. For texts that show Jezebel's political acumen, see 1 Kgs 19:1; 21:8, 15.

48. Brenner, *Israelite Woman,* 30.

49. Slotki (*Kings,* 231) writes that levitically unclean persons were not allowed to enter the temple.

50. Although the texts present Jehosheba as a rescuer, a latter-day Pharaoh's daughter, she is not portrayed as a winner; the winners in the story, according to D. N. Fewell and D. M. Gunn (*Gender, Power, and Promise: The Subject of the Bible's First Story* [Nashville: Abingdon, 1993], 167), are two males—a priest and a little boy.

51. Josephus, *Ant.* 9.7.1.

52. Jehoiada appears in Scripture without prior distinction or mention, much as Elijah arrives suddenly in 1 Kgs 17. The narrators use the tool of unexpected introduction in both cases. Both Elijah and Jehoiada live in the real world and engage is its politics. They move freely among monarchs and armies. Elijah proclaims a drought because of sin, and Jehoiada clearly chooses to save life and restore the Davidic line to the throne of Judah. Both men as Yahwists are foes of the house of Omri and the line of Ahab.

53. Six is an important number in Scripture, one associated with completion and blessing. For example, the Lord completed the heavens and the earth in six days (Gen 2:1). Noah was six hundred years old when the flood came (Gen 7:6). Leah had six sons (Gen 35:23). A field can be sown for six years before it rests (Lev 25:3). The narrators combine the number six with the tool of silence. They jump from the royals' slaughter to the countercoup six years later.

54. Hobbs, *2 Kings*, 139.

55. Kaufmann (*Religion of Israel*, 485) notes that Jehoiada appears as a rebellious priest but returns the legal government to its place.

56. Yet for most of his life he served as a priest. In a discussion about offerings, the rabbis offer a clarifying contribution by Jehoiada the high priest. "This is the general rule: what is offered for an act of sin or guilt . . . must be bought there with burnt-offerings, the flesh for God and the hides for the priests" (I. Epstein, ed., *Babylonian Talmud*, Part 2, vol. 4: *Shekalim* [Jerusalem: Soncino, 1961], 6:256).

57. In 2 Chr 23:1, for instance, he makes a covenant with the military commanders.

58. A reconstruction of the coup is as follows: A company of the Carites guarded the palace. It came on duty on the Sabbath. A second company stood guard at the gate called Sur. A third company stood guard at the palace and city entrances. Two platoons protected the king; their members did not come on duty on the Sabbath (Hobbs, *2 Kings*, 140).

59. Ibid., 137.

60. Bright (*History of Israel*, 252), however, believes Athaliah's cult of Baal Meqart had little following in Judah and was merely a court fad. Furthermore, Athaliah almost certainly had no real following; she was an outsider, a non-Davidic ruler, a woman, and one who seized the throne by an act universally regarded as criminal.

61. The narrators show that Jehoiada does not want to go back to a theocracy, a time when God ruled through human judges like Samuel and Deborah, a pre-Davidic rule. Instead, he wants to re-establish the Davidic line.

62. Perhaps Joash's name was prophetic. Joash received his name, "he despaired," because the people despaired of having a descendant of David to occupy the throne of David (Ginzberg, *LJ* 6:354).

63. Jewish lore confirms Joash's right to kingship, however, by recounting that David's large, heavy crown molded itself and miraculously fit the lad's head perfectly (ibid., 4:258). Another tradition that confirms Joash's legitimacy maintains the crown was so heavy that only its rightful wearer could support it (ibid., 4:354).

64. Ibid., 4:258.

65. Hobbs, *2 Kings*, 138.

66. However, in Jean Racine's play, Joash speaks. He confronts his grandmother, shows her the dagger marks she made on his chest, refutes her curse of David's line, and vows never to forget the God of David (Jean Racine, *Five Plays Translated into English Verse* [trans. K Muir; New York: Hill and Wang, 1960], act 5, V 6, V 7, 286–87).

67. Ginzberg, *LJ* 4:258–59, 355.

68. Hobbs, *2 Kings*, 138.

69. Camp, "1 and 2 Kings," 104. Kaufmann (*Religion of Israel*, 233) adds that the worship of Baal was seen as a foreign implant whose roots in Judah were less firm than in the northern kingdom of Israel.

70. Nelson, *First and Second Kings*, 209–10.

71. E. W. Nicholson, "The Meaning of the Expression *am haeretz* in The Old Testament," *JSS* 10 (1965): 59, 66, 61.

72. Ibid., 62. Dillard claims "the people of the land" are associated with the landed aristocracy (*2 Chronicles*, 173).

73. It is ironic that Jehoiada took great care in having Athaliah killed away from the temple; but years later when his son Zechariah rebuked the Israelites for transgressing the commandment of the Lord, he was stoned to death in the courtyard of the temple of the Lord (2 Chr 24:20–21; see Dillard, *2 Chronicles*, 183).

74. Nelson, *First and Second Kings*, 210.

75. In Israel, Zechariah reigned six months (2 Kgs 15:8), Shallum reigned one month (15:13), and Pekahiah reigned two years (15:23). In Judah, Amon reigned two years (21:19), Jehoahaz reigned three months (23:31), and Jehoichin reigned three months (24:8).

76. See Jer 38:1; 52:10–11.

77. Ironically, refuse as a theme figures in the deaths of Jehoram, Jezebel, and Athaliah. Jehoram dies of an incurable bowel disease; Jezebel's name car-

ries the connotation of excrement in translation; and Jezebel's flesh is eaten by dogs and her body becomes like refuse in Jezreel (2 Kgs 9:37).

78. Thiel, *ABD*, 3:814.

79. Brenner, *Israelite Woman*, 29–31.

80. Fewell and Gunn, *Gender, Power, and Promise*, 167.

81. Lockyer, *Women of the Bible*, 32,

82. The stories of Jephthah's daughter and the Levite's concubine (Judg 11 and 19) exhibit a similar lack of passion: no overt value judgments are made about the morality of the happenings.

83. Mary Evans, *Women in the Bible* (Exeter: Paternoster, 1983), 31.

84. Phyllis Trible, "Depatriarchalizing in Biblical Interpetation," *JAAR* 41 (1973): 31.

85. Chronicles shows that Athaliah, Ahab, Jehoram, and Ahaziah do not follow these commands. Therefore, they all fail. Jehoshaphat and Hezekiah do; therefore, they succeed.

86. Athaliah ranks among eight rulers in the Davidic dynasty who die violently, including Joram, Ahaziah, Jehoash, Amaziah, Amon, Josiah, and Jehoiakim.

87. See Walter Brueggemann, "Exodus," *NIB* 1:675–981, for a fine discussion of the Old Testament's existential approach to evil. The Old Testament expresses little interest in abstract issues such as how evil came into the word but is more concerned with faithful responses to evil from covenant people and effective coping by covenant people when faced with evil.

88. The book of Esther, the famine in Jacob's time (Gen 41), and the threat of Sennacherib against Jerusalem (Is. 36–37) are three such stories that can be read against a background of attempted extermination.

89. The theme of a remnant is picked up by the writing prophets in Ezek 9:8; Isa 11:11, Jer 23:3, and Zech 8:12.

NOTES TO CONCLUSION

1. Phyllis Trible has provided direction for my work in this area as in others. She acknowledges in her study of the Hebrew text that she finds a "theological vision for new occasions" (*God and the Rhetoric of Sexuality* [Philadelphia: Fortress, 1978], xvi). How refreshing! This insight gave me, as Trible says, a new theological vision.

2. Fretheim, *Exodus,* 36.

3. Brueggemann, "Exodus," 700.

4. Branch, "Women Who Win with Words," 316.

5. Brueggemann, "Exodus," 700.

6. Rizpah appears in two texts, 2 Sam 3 and 21; both are considered in this conclusion.

7. The stories of David's battle with Goliath (1 Sam 17), his winning of Michal by cutting off Philistine foreskins (1 Sam 18), and his politically advantageous marriage to Abigail (1 Sam 25) are three examples of his remarkable military, political, and social skills. Similarly, the rift between the Gibeonites and the house of Saul presents a political opportunity for David to rid himself of potential claimants to the throne.

8. Peterson, *First and Second Samuel,* 245.

9. See Prov 3:13, 19; 4:5–9.

10. Branch, "David and Joab," 20.

11. Lostracco and Wilkerson, *Analyzing Short Stories,* 11.

12. For example, consider the narrator's comment regarding David's actions of adultery with Bathsheba and arranging for the slaying of her husband, Uriah, which are recorded in 2 Saml 11. The chapter ends with this observation: "But the thing David had done displeased the Lord" (2 Sam 11:27b). Consider as well the narrator's comment on Jehoram's reign, "He passed away, *to no one's regret,* and was buried in the City of David, but not in the tombs of the kings" (2 Chr 21:20, italics added).

13. The books contain stories involving murder, fratricide, infanticide, disembowelment, lust for power, lust for another man's wife, a courageous battle with a giant, and formula lists of the reigns of kings.

14. Peterson, *First and Second Samuel,* 5.

15. An exception to this is the long prophetic word of Ahijah to the wife of Jeroboam (1 Kgs 14:7–14). Prophetic words also occur in 1 Kgs 17. God gives Elijah directions for his safety and sustenance, and Elijah tells the widow what God says. In the stories studied, oaths are made in God's name (2 Sam 3:9; 1 Kgs 17:1); a covenant is made again by the priest Jehoiada between the Lord and the king and the people (2 Kgs 11:17); and a previous action of the Lord is mentioned (2 Kgs 5:1).

16. Branch, "Genesis 20," 227.

17. I am grateful to Andrew Dearman for a discussion on this matter.

BIBLIOGRAPHY

Auerbach, M., and L. Smolar. "Aaron, Jeroboam, and the Golden Calves (Ex. 32; 1 Kings 12:28ff.)." *Journal of Biblical Literature* 86 (1967): 129–40.

———. "Jeroboam's Rise to Power (1 Kings 12)." *Journal of Biblical Literature* 88 (1969): 69–72.

Allen, Charles L. *When a Marriage Ends.* Old Tappan, N.J.: Fleming H. Revell, 1986.

Alsdurf, James, and Phyllis Alsdurf. *Battered into Submission: The Tragedy of Wife Abuse in the Christian Home.* Downers Grove, Ill.: InterVarsity, 1989.

Alter, Robert. *The Art of Biblical Narrative.* New York: Basic Books, 1981.

Anderson, A. A. *2 Samuel.* Word Biblical Commentary. Vol. 11. Waco, Tex.: Word, 1989.

Andreasen, N. E. A. "The Role of Queen Mother in Israelite Society." *Catholic Biblical Quarterly* 45 (1983): 1979–94.

Barker, Kenneth, ed. *New International Version Study Bible.* Grand Rapids: Zondervan, 1995.

Barmesh, Pamela. "The Narrative Quandary: Cases of Law in Literature." *Vetus Testamentum* 44 (2004):1–16.

Baumgarten, J. M. "Hanging and Treason in Qumran and Roman Law." *Eretz Israel* 16 (1982):7-16.

Ben-Barak, Z. "The Status and Right of the *Gebira.*" Pages 170–85 in *A Feminist Companion to Samuel and Kings.* Edited by A. Brenner. Sheffield: Sheffield Academic, 1994.

Ben-Yasher, M. "A Study of the Case of Rizpah Daughter of Aiah," *Beth Mikra* 27 [1966]: 34-41.

Bergen, R. D. *1, 2 Samuel*. New American Commentary. Nashville: Broadman and Holman, 1996.

Berlin, Adele. *Poetics of Biblical Interpretation of Biblical Narrative*. Sheffield: Almond, 1983.

Berman, Joshua A. *Narrative Analogy in the Hebrew Bible: Battle Stories and Their Equivalent Non-Battle Narratives*. Leiden: E. J. Brill, 2004.

Birch, B. B. "1 & 2 Samuel." Pages 947–1383 in vol. 2 of *The New Interpreter's Bible: A Commentary in Twelve Volumes*. Edited by L. E. Keck. 12 vols. Nashville: Abingdon, 1994.

Blenkinsopp, J. *Gibeon and Israel: The Role of Gibeon and the Gibeonites in the Political and Religious History of Early Israel*. New York: Cambridge University Press, 1972.

————. "Wisdom in the Chronicler's Work." Pages 19–30 in *In Search of Wisdom: Essays in Memory of John G. Gammie*. Edited by Leo G. Perdue, Bernard Brandon Scott, and William Johnston Wiseman. Louisville: Westminster/John Knox, 1993.

Branch, Robin Gallaher. "Athaliah, a Treacherous Queen: A Careful Analysis of Her Story in 2 Kings 11 and 2 Chronicles 22:10-23:21." *In die Skriflig* 38 no 4 (2004): 537-59.

————. "David and Joab: United by Ambition." *Bible Review* 19 (2003): 14–23, 62–63.

————. "Evangelism Via Power and Lifestyle: Elijah's Method in 1 Kings 17." *Missionalia* 31 (2003): 293–304.

————. "Genesis 20: A Literary Template for the Prophetic Tradition." *In die Skriflig* 38 (2004): 217–34.

————. "The Messianic Dimensions of Kingship in Deuteronomy 17:14–20 as Fulfilled by Jesus in Matthew." *Verbum et Ecclesia* 25 (2004): 378–401.

————. "The Wife of Jeroboam, 1 Kings 14:1-18: The Incredible, Riveting, History-Changing Significance of an Unnamed, Overlooked, Ignored, Obedient, Obscure Woman. *Old Testament Essays* 17:2 (2004): 157-67.

————. "Women Who Win with Words: Deliverance via Persuasive Communication." *In die Skriflig* 37 (2003): 289–318.

————. "'Your Humble Servant.' Well, Maybe. Overlooked Onlookers in Deuteronomistic History." *Old Testament Essays* 17 (2004): 168–89.

Brenner, Athalya, ed. *A Feminist Companion to the Bible.* Second Series, 8 vols. Sheffield: Sheffield Academic, 2000.

———, ed. *Exodus to Deuteronomy: The Feminist Companion to the Bible.* Second Series 5. Sheffield: Sheffield Academic, 2000.

———. *The Israelite Woman: Social Role and Literary Type in Biblical Narrative.* Sheffield: JSOT, 1985.

Bright, John. *A History of Israel.* Philadelphia: Westminster, 1981.

Bronner, Leila Leah. "Serah and the Exodus: A Midrashic Miracle." Pages 187-98 in *Exodus to Deuteronomy: A Feminist Companion to the Bible (Second Series).* Edited by Athalya Brenner. Sheffield: Sheffield Academic Press, 2000.

Brown, J. P. "The Role of Women and the Treaty in the Ancient World." *Biblische Zeitschrift* 25 (1981): 1–28.

Brown, Sally A. "Overturned: Jonah 3:1–4:3." *Princeton Seminary Bulletin* 24 (2003): 179–83.

Brueggemann, Walter. "Exodus." Pages 675–981 in vol. 1 of *The New Interpreter's Bible: A Commentary in Twelve Volumes.* Edited by L. E. Keck. 12 vols. Nashville: Abingdon, 1994.

———. *First and Second Samuel.* Louisville: Westminster/John Knox, 1990.

———. *Genesis.* Atlanta: John Knox, 1982.

Cahill, Jane. "Jerusalem in David and Solomon's Time: It Really Was a Major City in the Tenth Century B.C.E." *Biblical Archaeology Review,* 30 (2004): 20–31, 62–63.

Calvin, John. *Commentaries on the Four Last Books of Moses Arranged in the Form of a Harmony.* 4 vols. Edinburgh: Calvin Translation Society, 1852.

Camp, Claudia V. "1 and 2 Kings." Pages 96–109 in *The Women's Bible Commentary.* Edited by Carol A. Newsome and Sharon H. Ringe. Louisville: Westminster/John Knox, 1992.

Cazelles, H. "David's Monarchy and the Gibeonite Claim (II Sam XXI.1-14)." *Palestine Exploration Quarterly,* 87 (1955): 165-176.

Chadwick, G. A. *The Book of Exodus.* Vol. 2 of *The Expositor's Bible.* Edited by W. R. Nicoll. New York: George H. Doran, 1898.

Childs, Brevard S. *Old Testament Theology in a Canonical Context.* Philadelphia: Fortress, 1985.

———. *The Book of Exodus: A Critical, Theological Commentary.* Philadelphia: Westminster, 1974.

Cohn, Robert L. *Berit Olam: Studies in Hebrew Narration and Poetry: 2 Kings.* Collegeville, Minn.: Liturgical, 2000.

———. "Literary Technique in the Jeroboam Narrative." *Zeitschrift für die alttestamentliche Wissenschaft* 97 (1985): 23–35.

———. "The Literary Logic of 1 Kings 17–19." *Journal of Biblical Literature* 101 (1982): 333–50.

Cohn-Sherbok, Dan. "Theology in Praxis." Pages 1001–16 in *Companion Encyclopedia of Theology.* London & New York: Routledge, 1995.

Cornfeld, Gaalyahu, ed. *Pictorial Bible Encyclopaedia: A Visual Guide to the Old and New Testaments.* Tel Aviv: Hamikra Baolam, 1964.

Cryer, Frederick H. "David's Rise to Power and the Death of Abner: Analysis of 1 Sam 26:14–16 and Its Retaliation and Critical Implications." *Vetus Testamentum* 35 (1985): 385–94.

Davidson, JoAnn. "Genesis Matriarchs Engage Feminism." *Andrews University Seminary Studies* 40 (2002): 169–78.

Dean, Edith. *All the Women of the Bible.* Edison, N.J.: Castle Books, 1955.

DeMoss, Nancy Leigh. *Lies Women Believe and the Truth That Sets Them Free.* Chicago: Moody, 2001.

DeVries, Simon. *1 Kings.* Word Biblical Commentary. Vol. 12. Waco, Tex.: Word, 1985.

Dillard, Raymond B. *2 Chronicles.* Word Biblical Commentary. Vol. 15. Waco, Tex.: Word, 1987.

Drey, Philip R. "The Role of Hagar in Genesis 16." *Andrews University Seminary Studies* 40 (2002): 179–95.

Durham, J. I. *Exodus.* Word Biblical Commentary. Vol. 3. Waco, Tex.: Word, 1987.

Dutton, Donald G. *The Abusive Personality: Violence and Control in Intimate Relationships.* New York: Guilford, 1998.

Eales-White, R. *The Power of Persuasion: Improving Your Performance and Leadership Skills.* London: Kogan Page, 1997.

Eisenman, Tom L. *Temptations Men Face: Straightforward Talk on Power, Money, Affairs, Perfectionism, Insensitivity.* . . . Downers Grove, Ill.: InterVarsity, 1990.

Encyclopaedia Biblica: Thesaurus rerum Biblicarum. 9 vols. Jerusalem: Bialik Institute, 1950–1988.

Epstein, Isidore, ed. *Babylonian Talmud.* 18 vols. Part 2, vol.4: *Ta'anith. Shekalim. Megillah.* Part 4, vol. 3: *Baba Bathra.* Part 4, vol. 4: *Sanhedrin.* London: Soncino, 1961.

Evans, Mary. *Women in the Bible.* Exeter: Paternoster, 1983.

Exum, J. Cheryl. "The Mothers in Israel: The Patriarchal Narratives from a Feminist Perspective." *Bible Review* 2 (1986): 60–67.

Fagen, Jeffrey A., Douglas K. Steward, and Karen V. Hansen. "Violent Men or Violent Husbands?" Pages 49-68 in *The Dark Side of Families.* Edited by David Finkelhor, Richard Gelles, Gerald Hotaling, and Murray Straus. Beverly Hills, Calif.: Sage Publications, 2008.

Farmer, Kathleen Robertson. "Ruth." Pages 889–946 in vol. 1 of *The New Interpreter's Bible: A Commentary in Twelve Volumes.* Edited by L. E. Keck. 12 vols. Nashville: Abingdon, 1994.

Fee, Gordon, and Douglas Stuart. *How to Read the Bible for All Its Worth.* Grand Rapids: Zondervan, 1993.

Fensham, F. C. "Battle Between the Men of Joab and Abner as a Possible Ordeal by Battle? (2 Sam. 2:12ff.)." *Vetus Testamentum* 20 (1970): 356–57.

Fewell, D. N., and D. M. Gunn. *Gender, Power, and Promise: The Subject of the Bible's First Story.* Nashville: Abingdon, 1993.

Fischer, Kathleen. *Winter Grace: Spirituality and Aging.* Nashville: Upper Room Books, 1998.

Fokkelman, J. P. *Narrative Art in Genesis: Specimens of Stylistic and Structural Analysis.* Amsterdam: Van Gorcum, Assen, 1975.

Freedman, H., and Maurice Simon, eds. *Mishnah Rabbah.* 10 vols. Translated by H. Freedman. 3d ed. New York: Soncino, 1983.

Fretheim, Terence E. *Exodus.* Louisville: John Knox, 1991.

Frolov, S. "Days of Shiloh in the Kingdom of Israel." *Biblica* 76 (1995): 210–18.

Geyer, M. L. "Stopping the Juggernaut: A Close Reading of 2 Samuel 20:13–22." *Union Seminary Quarterly Review* 41 (1987): 33–42.

Gillespie, Thomas W. "A Question of Authority." *The Princeton Seminary Bulletin* 24 (2003):1–9.

Ginzberg, L. *Legends of the Jews.* 6 vols. Philadelphia: Jewish Publication Society, 1909–1938.

Goldfarb, S. D. "Sex and Violence in the Bible." *Dor le Dor* (1975): 125–30.

Gooding, D. W. "Septuagint's Rival Versions of Jeroboam's Rise to Power (1 Kings 11–12)." *Vetus Testamentum* 17 (1967): 173–89.

Gordon, Robert P. *I and II Samuel.* Grand Rapids: Zondervan, 1986.

Gray, John. *I and II Kings: A Commentary.* 2nd ed. Philadelphia: Westminster, 1970.

Halpern, B. "Levitic Participation in the Reform Cult of Jeroboam I." *Journal of Biblical Literature* 95 (1976): 31–42.

Hamilton, V. P. *Handbook on the Historical Books: Joshua, Judges, Ruth, Samuel, Kings, Chronicles.* Grand Rapids: Baker, 2001.

Hankins, Gary, with Carol Hankins. *Prescription for Anger: Coping with Angry Feelings and Angry People.* New York: Warner Books, 1993.

Harbin, M. A. *The Promises and the Blessing: A Historical Survey of the Old and New Testaments.* Grand Rapids: Zondervan, 2005.

Hemfelt, Robert, Frank Minirth, and Paul Meier. *Love is a Choice: Recovery for Codependent Relationships.* Nashville: Thomas Nelson, 1989.

Hertzberg, Hans Willem. *I and II Samuel: A Commentary.* Philadelphia: Westminster, 1964.

Heschel, A. J. *The Prophets.* New York: Harper & Row, 1955. Reprinted Peabody, Mass.: Hendrickson, 2007.

Hobbs, T. R. *2 Kings.* Word Biblical Commentary. Waco, Tex.: Word, 1985.

Hochman, B. *Character in Literature.* Ithaca, N.Y.: Cornell University Press, 1985.

Holder, J. "The Presuppositions, Accusations, and Threats of 1 Kings 14:1–18." *Journal of Biblical Literature* 107 (1988): 27–38.

House, P. R. *1, 2 Kings.* New American Commentary. Edited by E. R. Clendenen. Nashville: Broadman and Holman, 1995.

Huehnegard, John. "Nabi." *Eretz-Israel* 26 (1999): 88–93.

Hyatt, J. P. *Exodus.* London: Oliphants, 1971.

Instone-Brewer, David. "What God Has Joined." *Christianity Today.* October 2007, 26–29.

James, Fleming. *Personalities of the Old Testament.* New York: Charles Scribner's Sons, 1939.

Josephus, Flavius. *Complete Works.* Translated by W. Whiston. Grand Rapids: Kregel, 1981.

Kaiser, Walter C., and Moises Silva. *An Introduction to Biblical Hermeneutics: The Search for Meaning.* Grand Rapids: Zondervan, 1994.

Katzenstein, H. J. "Who Were the Parents of Athaliah?" *Israel Exploration Journal* 5 (1955): 194–97.

Kaufmann, Yehezkel. *The Religion of Israel: From Its Beginnings to the Babylonian Exile.* New York: Schocken Books, 1972.

Keil, C. F., and F. Delitzsch. *The Books of Samuel.* Edinburgh: T&T Clark, 1872.

Keinanen, Jyrki. *Traditions in Collision: A Literary and Redaction-Critical Study on the Elijah Narratives 1 Kings 17–19*. Gottingen: The Finnish Exegetical Society in Helsinki, 2001.

Kennedy, X. J., and Dana Gioia. *Literature: An Introduction to Fiction, Poetry, and Drama*. 6th ed. New York: HarperCollins, 1995.

Lasine, Stuart. "Matters of Life and Death: The Story of Elijah and the Widow's Son in Comparative Perspective." *Biblical Interpretation* 12 (2004): 117–44.

Leithart, Peter J. *Brazos Theological Commentary on the Bible: 1 & 2 Kings*. Grand Rapids: Brazos, 2006.

Levine, Baruch A. "Vows, Oaths, and Binding Agreements: The Section on Vows in Light of Aramaic Inscriptions." *Eretz Israel* 26 (1999): 84–90.

Lockyer, Herbert. *All the Miracles of the Bible*. Grand Rapids: Zondervan, 1965.

———. *All the Women of the Bible*. Grand Rapids: Zondervan, 1967.

Lostracco, Joe, and George Wilkerson. *Analyzing Short Stories*. Dubuque, Ia.: Kendall/Hunt, 1998.

Malamat, A. "Doctrines of Causality in Hittite and Biblical Historiography: A Parallel." *Vetus Testamentum* 5 (1955): 1-12.

McCarter, P. K., Jr. *I and II Samuel: A New Translation with Introduction, Notes, and Commentary*. Garden City, N.Y.: Doubleday, 1984.

McConville, J. Gordon. *I and II Chronicles*. Philadelphia: Westminster, 1984.

McCue, Margi Laird. *Domestic Violence: A Reference Book*. Santa Barbara, Calif.: ABC-CLIO, Inc., 1995.

McDonald, Patricia M. *God and Violence: Biblical Resources for Living in a Small World*. Scottdale, Penn.: Herald, 2004.

Miller, Donald G. *Luke*. Richmond: John Knox, 1966.

Moore, Rick Dale. *God Saves: Lessons from the Elisha Stories*. Sheffield: JSOT, 1990.

Mulzac, Ken. "Hannah, the Giver and Receiver of a Great Gift." *Andrews University Seminary Studies* 40 (2002): 207–17.

Nelson, Richard D. *First and Second Kings*. Atlanta: John Knox, 1987.

Nicholson, E. W. "The Meaning of the Expression *am haeretz* in the Old Testament." *Journal of Semitic Studies* 10 (1965): 59–66.

Olson, Dennis T. "'Oh Lord God, How Am I to Know?' The Pentateuch and Contemporary Understanding of Truth." *Princeton Seminary Bulletin* 22 (2002): 86–99.

Overholt, Thomas W. "Feeding the Widow, Raising the Dead. What Counts as Cultural Exegesis?" Pages 104–21 in *Text and Experience: Towards a Cultural Exegesis of the Bible*. Edited by David Smith-Christopher. Sheffield: Sheffield Academic, 1995.

Park, J. E. "Exodus." Pages 831–1097 in vol. 1 of *The Interpreter's Bible*. Edited by G. A. Buttrick. 13 vols. New York: Abingdon, 1951–1957. Repr. Nashville: Abingdon, 1998.

Peterson, Eugene H. *First and Second Samuel*. Louisville: Westminster John Knox, 1999.

Pfeiffer, R. H. *Introduction to the Old Testament*. New York: Harper & Brothers, 1948.

Post, Elizabeth L. *Emily Post's Etiquette*. 15th ed. New York: HarperCollins, 1992.

Pritchard, J. B., ed. *The Ancient Near East, Volume 2. An Anthology of Texts and Pictures*. 2 vols. Princeton: Princeton University Press, 1975.

Provan, Iain W. *1 and 2 Kings*. New International Biblical Commentary on the Old Testament. Vol. 7. Peabody, Mass.: Hendrickson, 1995.

Rabin, C. "Origin of the Hebrew Word *Pileges*." *Journal of Jewish Studies* 25 (1974): 353–64.

Racine, Jean. *Five Plays Translated into English Verse*. Translated by K. Muir. New York: Hill and Wang, 1960.

Rappoport, Angelo S. *Ancient Israel: Myths and Legends*. 3 vols. London: Senate, 1995.

Rawlinson, George. *The Kings of Israel and Judah*. New York: Fleming H. Revell, 1889.

Reinhartz, A. "Anonymous Women and the Collapse of the Monarchy: A Study in the Narrative Technique." Pages 43–65 in *A Feminist Companion to Samuel and Kings*. Second Series 7 of *A Feminist Companion to the Bible*. Edited by A. Brenner. Sheffield: Sheffield Academic, 2000.

Robinson, J. *The Second Book of Kings*. Cambridge: Cambridge University Press, 1976.

Rofé, Alexander. "Classes in the Prophetical Stories: Didactic Legend and Parable." Pages 143–64 in *Studies in Prophecy: A Collection of Twelve Papers*. Edited by G. W. Anderson. VT Supplement 26. Leiden: E. J. Brill, 1974.

Roop, Eugene F. *Ruth, Jonah, Esther*. Vol. 4 of *Believers Church Bible Commentary*. Edited by Elmer A. Martens and Willard M. Swartley. 20 vols. Scottdale, Pa.: Herald, 2002.

Roth, Cecil, ed. *Encyclopedia Judaica*. 16 vols. Jerusalem: Keter, 1972.

Russell, Letty M. "Practicing Hospitality in a World of Difference and Danger." *Princeton Seminary Bulletin* 24 (2003): 207–15.

Sakenfeld, Katharine Doob. *The Meaning of Hesed*. Missoula, Mont.: Scholars, 1978.

Sangster, Margaret. *The Women of the Bible: A Portrait Gallery*. New York: Christian Herald, 1911.

Schulte, H. "The End of the Omride Dynasty: Social-Ethical Observations on the Subject of Power and Violence." *Semeia* 66 (1994): 133–48.

Seow, Choon Leong. "The First and Second Books of Kings: Introduction, Commentary, and Reflections." Pages 1–295 in vol. 3 of *The New Interpreter's Bible: A Commentary in Twelve Volumes*. Edited by L. E. Keck. 12 vols. Nashville: Abingdon, 1994.

Siebert-Hommes, Jopie. "The Widow of Zarephath and the Great Woman of Shunem: A Comparative Analysis of Two Stories." Pages 231–50 in *On Reading Prophetic Texts: Gender Specific and Related Studies of Fokkelien Van Dijk-Hemmes*. Edited by Bob Beeking and Meindert Dijkstra. Leiden: E. J. Brill, 1996.

Simon, Uriel. *Reading Prophetic Narratives*. Translated by Lenn J. Shramm. Bloomington: Indiana University Press, 1997.

Slotki, I. W. *Kings: Hebrew Text & English Translation with an Introduction and Commentary*. London: Soncino, 1950.

Sorenson, S. *How to Write Short Stories*. New York: Macmillan. 1994.

Stone, K. *Sex, Honor and Power in the Deuteronomistic History*. JSOT Supplement Series 234. Sheffield: Sheffield Academic, 1996.

Toews, W. I. *Monarchy and Religious Institution in Israel under Jeroboam I*. Atlanta: Scholars, 1993.

Trible, Phyllis. "Departriarchalizing in Biblical Interpretation." *Journal of the American Academy of Religion* 41 (1973): 30–48.

———. *God and the Rhetoric of Sexuality*. Philadelphia: Fortress, 1978.

————. *Texts of Terror: Literary-Feminist Readings of Biblical Narratives.* Philadelphia: Fortress, 1984.

Tsevat, M. "Marriage and Monarchical Legitimacy in Ugarit and Israel." *Journal of Semitic Studies* 3 (1958): 237–43.

Ussishkin, David. "The Fortified Enclosure of the Kings of the House of Omri at Jezreel." *Eretz-Israel* 25 (1996): 1–14.

Vanderkam, J. C. "Davidic Complicity in the Deaths of Abner and Eshbaal: A Historical and Redactional Study." *Journal of Biblical Literature* 99 (1980): 521–39.

Van Winkle, D. W. "1 Kings xii 25–xiii 34: Jeroboam's Cultic Innovations and the Man of God from Judah." *Vetus Testamentum* 46 (1996): 101–14.

Voinov, V. "Old Testament Kinship Relations and Terminology." *The Bible Translator* 55 (2004): 108–18.

Von Rad, Gerhard. "The Levitical Sermon in I and II Chronicles." Pages 267–80 in *The Problem of the Hexateuch and Other Essays.* Edited by Gerhard von Rad. New York: McGraw-Hill, 1966.

Walker, Lenore. *The Battered Woman.* New York: Harper & Row, 1979.

Wallace, H. N. "Oracles Against the Israelite Dynasties in 1 and 2 Kings." *Biblica* 67 (1986): 21–40.

Walsh, Jerome T. *1 Kings.* Collegeville, Minn.: Liturgical, 1996.

Wexler, Barbara. *Violent Relationships: Battering and Abuse Among Adults.* Information Plus Reference Series. Detroit: Thomson Gale, 2003.

Williams, Michael E., ed. *The Storyteller's Companion to the Bible.* Vol. 3: *Judges–Kings.* Nashville: Abingdon, 1992.

Williamson, G. I. *Westminster Confession of Faith for Study Classes.* Philadelphia: Presbyterian and Reformed Publishing Co., 1964.

Wiseman, Donald J. *1 and 2 Kings: An Introduction and Commentary.* Tyndale Old Testament Commentaries. Downers Grove, Ill.: InterVarsity, 1993.

INDEX OF MODERN AUTHORS

INDEX OF NAMES AND SUBJECTS

Index of Ancient Sources